BACK FROM THE BRINK

BACK FROM THE BRINK

PAUL McGRATH

WITH VINCENT HOGAN

C

CENTURY · LONDON

Published by Century 2006

2 4 6 8 10 9 7 5 3 1

First published in Great Britain in 2006 by
Century
Random House, 20 Vauxhall Bridge Road,
London SW1V 2SA

www.randomhouse.co.uk

Addresses for companies within The Random House Group Limited can be found at:
www.randomhouse.co.uk

The Random House Group Limited Reg. No. 954009

A CIP catalogue record for this book
is available from the British Library

ISBN 13 9781846050763
ISBN 1846050766

The Random House Group Limited makes every effort to ensure that the papers used in its
books are made from trees that have been legally sourced from well-managed and credibly
certified forests. Our paper procurement policy can be found at:
www.randomhouse.co.uk/paper.htm
Printed and bound in Great Britain by
Clays Ltd, St Ives plc

To all of my children and to the late Dr Patrick Nugent.

CONTENTS

ACKNOWLEDGEMENTS

A special thanks to all who contributed to the compilation of this book, particularly to Vincent Hogan who I believe has managed to bring wonderful shape and clarity to a story that has, up to now, been largely muddied.

Thanks to Juanita for putting in place the structures that made the book possible in the first place, to my editor, Tim Andrews, and to all at Random House for their efforts in making it such a professional production.

And thanks especially to the many people who co-operated with Vincent in uncovering the true story of Paul McGrath, a story that could not possibly have been told without their assistance. They are in alphabetical order: Ron Atkinson, Victor Boyhan, Mick Byrne, Jack Charlton, Gordon Cowans, Fr Aidan Crawley, Sir Alex Ferguson, Kiernan Forsyth, Fran Gavin, John Givens, Eoin Hand, Ray Houghton, Kevin Moran, Frank Mullen, Mick McCarthy, Dr Barrie Smith, Frank Stapleton, Graham Taylor, Shaun Teale, Charlie Walker, Jim Walker and Norman Whiteside.

Thanks, too, to my mother, Betty, to Claire and to the boys, Christopher, Mitchell and Jordan.

And, finally, sincere thanks to the supporters out there, be they of Manchester United, Aston Villa or Republic of Ireland persuasion who stood by me through good and bad. I will never forget that.

Paul McGrath.

INTRODUCTION

On Saturday, 17 December, 2005, I flew to Birmingham to meet Jim Walker.

We took in that afternoon's Premiership game between Aston Villa and Manchester United at Villa Park. It was an abject game, won 2-0 by a United team never required to leave second gear.

Afterwards, in a directors' lounge, Jim introduced me to Dr Barrie Smith, the former Villa team doctor. Both men had been left deeply unimpressed by Villa's performance. 'Compare that to what we were used to when big Paul was playing' sighed Walker.

There was a distinct air of melancholy to the conversation between a man who had been the club's senior physio for seventeen years and one who had been team-doctor for twenty-four.

For the benefit of this book, they swapped anecdotes about McGrath and the remarkable seven years he spent as an Aston Villa player. Both men clearly retained a deep affection for Paul.

That night I flew home and, two rows in front of me on the Aer Lingus flight, sat a guy in a Villa shirt. He was 15 at most, yet – on the back of his shirt – was the number five and the surname McGRATH.

Nine years after he left the club, Paul's legend was still vibrant enough for that kind of tribute. He had been due to travel with me that day, but cancelled because of feeling 'unwell'. I felt a pang of regret that he wasn't with me to see that kid.

On touchdown, I texted Paul to tell him the day had gone well. And I mentioned the guy in the McGRATH shirt. Paul immediately texted back. It read 'Glad all went well. Talk soon.'

And it struck me that seeing his name on a kid's jersey wouldn't have offered the buzz to Paul McGrath that it might have offered most other ex-professional footballers. It never could. Because, throughout his life, Paul hated few things more than he hated the limelight.

He is, undeniably, Ireland's best loved sportsman. But he is also painfully shy and, worse, guilt-ridden over a life spent visiting the edge of chaos. Large chunks of that life are a blur to Paul and, for that reason, this book is threaded with other voices. Voices from inside and outside the game. Voices belonging to people who have had a bird's eye of his remarkable story unfold.

With their help, Paul invites us into the heart of a life less ordinary. I trust you enjoy the read as much as I did the journey.

Vincent Hogan, 11 August, 2006

Prologue

GOOD TIMES

18 June 1994. Down to the last, stubborn seconds in New Jersey and it sounded as if the earth itself had begun to whistle. I couldn't hear myself breathe. Ireland were within seconds of beating the mighty Italians at the World Cup.

All around, people were jumpy, eyes now burning a path towards the Dutch referee. I could see Big Jack flapping on the touchline. 'Fook's sake!' he was mouthing, angrily tapping the watch on his wrist.

An Italian player, Daniele Massaro, came surging through. I tracked the run, forcing him wide and – just as he spun to cross – launched myself to make the block. Bullseye. The crowd convulsed. Ninety-three Fahrenheit in the evening sun and time for just one last Italian corner.

So I chugged back in to take up my station. Massaro played the ball short to his full-back. And that was when it happened. That was the moment somebody turned down the sound and everything slowed. The moment I felt unbreakable.

As the full-back prepared to cross, I knew it no longer mattered where I stood. The ball would find me. He was a fish in a barrel.

It came to me as if radar-guided and I cleared, an Italian player lunging into my back, knocking me to the ground. I heard the whistle. An Irish free. Roy Keane pulled me to my feet again and grabbed me in a headlock. The stands trembled like a green bouncy castle.

And I could feel the tingle of goosebumps.

On the really good days, football could be like that. Child's play. The effort wasn't conscious. I could play at an independent pace, bossing the striker with my ability to read things, to anticipate. On the really good days, you see, football was never physical. It was a mind game.

I reckon I was maybe sixty per cent fit for US '94 and playing largely on instinct. My left arm was useless because of a virus in my shoulder and I needed about five paces simply to find my stride.

Against the likes of Guiseppe Signori and Roberto Baggio, that made for a pretty nerve-wracking ordeal. If you look at photographs of that game, my arm might as well be in a sling. It's hanging limp down by my side, like a snapped branch on a tree. Yet the longer the game went on, the more confident I became.

There's a chemistry that kicks in between defender and striker. One eventually knows that he is being manipulated by the other. That day, Baggio was no longer inclined to move in my direction. Signori had been substituted. It was over.

The final whistle triggered an extraordinary outburst of emotion, and a cavalry change from the Irish dugout.

I stayed sober from start to finish of Ireland's involvement in that World Cup, and being dry allowed me to absorb that victory over Italy fully. I remember the Italians being quite gracious afterwards. Paolo Maldini, Baggio . . . just hugs and respect. No hard feelings. Franco Baresi? Maybe less so.

I remember the feeling of having achieved something pretty monumental here.

After that game, the Irish players moved literally next door, to a party at the Meadowlands racetrack. I stayed on the bus. The windows were blacked out, so no one could see me sitting there. It was heaven. I didn't feel remotely envious of the other lads and the ease with which they could mingle with our supporters and down a few beers in celebration.

What did I feel? Euphoria? Not really. My abiding feeling was simply that I was sober and in a good place. I was safe.

1

BORSTAL BOY

I am sitting in a cubicle, the width of a Portaloo, handcuffed to the side.

A fist keeps thumping the panel by my head. A voice keeps searching. 'Who's in that one? Who's in there? Cat got your fucking tongue, mate?' Doors are banging. The fumes of the prison van carry up through the floor. Someone screams that we're going to suffocate in here. I am headed for Manchester Crown Court. Humiliated and trembling.

There's an ugly, weeping scab on my forehead. I keep fingering it, as if hoping it'll disappear and I'll wake up in a familiar bed. But the doors keep banging and the voices keep on tearing at me.

'Guggi, that you Guggi?'

'Yeah.'

'What's the story?'

'I'm goin' down!'

'Nah.'

'Definitely, I'm goin' down . . .'

I catch a glimpse of the lad in the cubicle opposite. He's a Pakistani and he winks. I nod back, warming to his sense of calm.

Then the door slams shut again and the van lurches away from Stretford Station. And I sit there thinking that I'm now at the bottom of the barrel. Nowhere left to sink.

It doesn't feel like it yet, but I'm here for my own good now. The angles have been getting narrower. I'm running out of places to go, people to ring. My bolt-holes have begun to dry up. I am now, officially, of 'no fixed abode'. I hate the man I have become, but I'm angry too. For twelve hours, I've been asking the same questions. What am I being charged with? What have I done? Who am I supposed to have hurt?

Maybe I am in denial over that last one. I'm not a violent man, but I've still spent much of my life hurting the ones I love. The policemen are kind, but evasive. 'Settle down Paul, don't worry, you'll be in and out in no time . . .'

They had picked me up the night before after a call from Claire. She had had enough of the drunkenness and the bullshit. Claire is my first wife and mother of my three eldest boys. With my second marriage now in meltdown, she had taken pity and allowed me to crash under her roof. Actually, she had done much more than that. She had weaned me back off the alcohol with painstaking patience, only for me, typically, to abuse her kindness.

At the time, I was in free fall, drinking everything I could get my hands on, popping tranquilisers. My relationship with Caroline had completely broken down. I was barred from the house. I was free, essentially, to drink myself into an early grave and I felt trapped. Trapped by that very isolation.

Phoning Claire was the final, pathetic gesture. We'd been through a painful divorce ten years earlier, spending three days in court under the full glare of media scrutiny. Yet, the recriminations had never dipped towards hatred. Already, our three boys – Christopher, Mitchell and Jordan – were back living with her after moving out of a house in which their barred father had become an object of disgust.

Now I was begging to follow suit. Claire had moved on. She was in another relationship, pursuing a profession and, generally, living a life free of angst and dysfunction. Yet, she took pity.

I still retain this awful image of my slow rehabilitation in a spare room of her home in Northenden. It is of Jordan, our youngest boy, bringing me up a mug of wine. That was the weaning process. Smaller quantities of alcohol every day until, eventually, you can get through twenty-four hours without a drink. It was difficult and fraught, but Claire's compassion had brought us all through. Habitually, she would explain to the boys that their father's addictions didn't make him a bad man. She was a mother, friend and counsellor rolled into one. And, remarkably, in a matter of weeks she had me healthy.

Yet, that image of Jordan – who would have been fourteen at the time – coming to the door with a mug of wine is one that doesn't leave me. When you live the kind of life that I've lived, there are certain snapshots that tend to reef at your senses. And that one still lingers and troubles.

To rehabilitate an alcoholic, you first need to understand their capacity for deceit. To tap into their deviousness. To recognise the mind games that become instinctive. Without even realising I was doing it, one of the first things I would have done on arrival in Claire's would have been to stake out the nearest pub. Not because I had a specific plan to go there. Just subconscious strategy. Getting my bearings.

Claire knew what she was dealing with. She'd been through it with me before. She recognised the signals, knew the angles. We've spoken many times about this illness. She makes no bones about the fact that she hates the person I become with alcohol. She knows it's slowly killing me. It's ruining the relationships I have with my children. She sees them go into themselves when I'm drinking. Suddenly, they've got a father who makes an exhibition of himself in public. Who can't socialise properly. Who just becomes a drunk with no interest in anything beyond sourcing his next bottle.

Yet, she sees the positives of when I'm well too. The palpable change in the kids. The confidence they take from having someone resembling a decent human being for a father. The inexplicable love they still show me. That would have been her motivation in taking me in. I don't remember the actual moment that I threw it all back in her face. By and large, I never do. Remember, that is.

All I know is I started drinking again. Heavily. All told, I had been under her roof for about a year – lapsing occasionally – when I returned to an old trick of hiding bottles in the house. Vodka. Brandy. Southern Comfort. Under the bed. In wardrobes Claire would search the house as thoroughly as she could, locking anything she found in the boot of the car, then taking the car keys with her to work.

She understood the futility of this, of course. She couldn't lock me in the house and I was now a glassy-eyed regular in the pubs of the area. I was routinely picked up by the local police and ferried home for my own safety. They were always sensitive. 'This is going to have to stop Paul . . .' One night, I slept rough outside the house, slumped face down on a little grass area maybe fifty yards away, unable to find my way home. I woke up freezing, aching for the warmth of a strong drink.

It had to come to a head and it did soon after. This night, I returned to the house, extremely drunk. I had fallen and cut my forehead. The boys wouldn't let me in and I walked around banging on doors and windows. It must have been scary for the children and I particularly remember Christopher and his girlfriend, Lucy, the expressions on their faces as I yelled at them to, at least, throw me out my car keys.

Thankfully, they didn't. Next thing I knew, I was in handcuffs.

The police station cell was small and claustrophobic. A heavy mattress on the floor, one flimsy yellow blanket. No pillow. They had taken my shoelaces and belt away, apparently for my own safety. Every half-hour, the little viewing latch on the door clicked open and abruptly shut again. The noise was unrelenting, doors being kicked, people screaming obscenities at their jailers. A girl's voice in the midst of it.

Sleep was impossible. I just lay there, feeling a conflict of terror and anger, one voice wrestling with another. 'You've brought this on yourself you know,' then 'Fuck it, I didn't assault anyone, I wasn't driving a car . . .'

Next morning, one of the police officers dipped his head into my cell. He was going off duty. 'Look,' he said, 'I just wanted to say that I used to stand on the Stretford End when you played for United. You were a hero of mine. I hope you get yourself well.' The door closed again and I felt like weeping. His kindness filled me with shame. I looked down at my shoeless feet. I peered over at the empty bowl I had just emptied of cornflakes, like a man who hadn't eaten for a week. I listened to the noise of prison life. This was my domain now.

I had been charged with threatening behaviour. To me, it was a trumped-up charge. I hadn't threatened anyone. But I knew people were losing patience. Claire. The boys. The police I had come to use as an almost nightly taxi service.

Poor Claire was inconsolable. I spoke to her by phone from the police station. She was crying. 'I didn't want to, but I had to do something,' she said. I knew she was right. That this had been the only kindness left to her. 'Jesus, do you know something?' I said, suddenly guilt-ridden at her distress. 'You may have done me the biggest favour. Because I don't ever want to come back to this place.'

So, the morning after, I am given back my shoelaces, but not my belt. I am handcuffed again and led out to that prison van. Uncuffed, then recuffed again to the cubicle. Recuffed again on arrival. Led into the courthouse. Silent. Humiliated.

'Paul, do you want a cell on your own?'

'Would you mind?'

'No problem mate.'

'Could I go to the toilet?'

'Course you can.'

They undo the handcuffs. In the toilet, I find the furthest cubicle and vomit loudly. Wheeling around, I look in the mirror. The reflection is of an animal. Bleeding, trapped, defenceless. A police officer reads my panic.

'Paul,' he says, 'I'm sorry, but I'll have to put the cuffs back on you again to bring you into court. Look, I'm going to get you out of here as quickly as possible. Don't worry, don't be panicking. When it's over, we'll bring you out the back way.'

Everyone knows me now. The whole world is nudging, pointing at me, squinting. I'm brought into this little dock, handcuffed to a policeman. It strikes me that I must be perceived as a threat to someone. All this security. All these chains. There are maybe seventy people in the court and most of them look like students. Rows of them, gathered maybe out of nothing more than idle curiosity.

I can feel their eyes burn through me. I know I'm being recognised. And oh sweet Jesus, the shakes have set in. My body is screaming for alcohol. I'm still coming down. And I can hear a chorus of voices in my head, reciting the same thing over and over: 'God, isn't it sad to see him like that . . .'

I have been provided with a solicitor. A total stranger, thank the Lord. My own solicitors are based in an office block directly across the road from the courthouse. Can't bear the thought of them happening upon this scene. Want them still to think of me as an upstanding member of society. That is assuming they already do.

Three men face me with expressions I read immediately as hostile. The one in the middle is telling me to speak up. I want everyone to whisper. Then the anger begins to kick in again. Someone is asking me how I plead. *How do I plead? I'm not guilty, for God's sake. I haven't actually done anything. Maybe I haven't been whiter than white in the past, but I've done nothing here.*

The word 'affray' is used. I am unequivocal. I might have 'knocked loudly' on the window, I say. I might have 'shouted something in at my son'. But I didn't threaten anyone. Hear that? *I did not threaten anyone.* I am advised to plead not guilty and am remanded to appear at a later date.

The nightmare is just beginning.

It is just after eleven in the morning as I walk out of a back door of Manchester Crown Court. Without the belt, my jeans keep slipping down. Of late, I have been drinking too much and eating too little. A court official informs me that my belt and mobile phone will be available from the police station in a couple of days.

So I am a free man in the centre of Manchester with nowhere to go and no money to get there. What do I do now?

I roll my jeans up to stop them dragging on the pavement and decide to get out of the city as quickly as I can. The journey will take me through Moss Side. Now Moss Side can be a hard and dangerous place to walk through, but right now I see it as the quickest route to becoming invisible. Paranoia grows with every step. Walking past bus stops I feel more conspicuous than I've ever done in front of a packed football stadium. I know people are whispering.

Once in Moss Side, I decide to buy some time. I need the cover of darkness. I can't bear being seen like this. So I start walking circuits. Through the park, around the back of the office buildings, their windows always staring. Painfully slow, tentative circles. Maybe an hour, each time. If someone is walking my way, I double back. I am like an animal in the bushes.

The jeans are almost around my ankles now. I am losing all

self-respect. Losing my mind, it feels. I hear voices. I feel I am hallucinating. Mentally and physically I am slipping under.

This black man walks past me in the park. Black as the ace of spades. He looks at me and spits out the word 'Nigger'. I smile back weakly. I feel like I'm going to get a good kicking here. It's just minutes away. Someone's going to descend upon me any moment and beat me to a pulp.

I turn after the black man and mouth the words 'Fuck you, you twat' making sure it's not loud enough for him to hear me. I keep walking.

There's a warm voice in my head, telling me to go to a pub. To say to the barman 'I'm Paul McGrath' and I'll drop the money in later if he'll just let me have the comfort of a few pints.

I had walked past a hotel, advertising rooms for £44. All I wanted was a pillow, somewhere to lie down, to become invisible.

Another voice has been gnawing away ever since leaving the court building in Deansgate, telling me I should be headed for Old Trafford. Just tell the receptionist that you're terribly sorry, but could anyone please lend you £100 and you'll promise to drop it back to them. Pride is the only barrier. The stadium was no more than a mile away when I walked out that back door. Someone was bound to take pity. 'Come in big man, let's get you sorted . . .' But I knew how I looked. I knew I couldn't let them see me.

So it's coming up to six in the evening. Seven hours since I was set 'free'. I've sat down just once since leaving court. I walk into this building and ask a girl at reception if she knows the name of a priest or a social worker who might help. I tell her I have nowhere to go and she can see that I'm not bluffing.

She gives me a can of Coke, the number of a hostel and 40p to make the call. 'Tell them your situation and they'll take you in,' she says. I feel I've met an angel. The Coke is magically soothing on my throat. I go to a phone box and dial the number. A voice at the other end is giving me directions. He's telling me what time

I need to be there. The beeps go off. He is in mid sentence when the line goes dead. I am alone.

I haven't the nerve to ask the girl for more money. I am walking again. Up past the stadium now, its back turned towards me as if I never existed. It feels surreal. Straight up towards Stretford in the direction of Sale.

Just short of Stretford, I stop at a dental clinic and ask the receptionist for a glass of water. I am desperately dehydrated. My next port of call is the house of an old friend, but she is out. Her son, who looks about sixteen, answers the door. He doesn't know me and, from his expression, isn't inclined to change that. Can't blame him as I probably look menacing. After another glass of water, I leave the poor lad in peace.

The darkness is a comfort now. I'm becoming invisible. Yet, a group of black kids recognise me and shout across the street, 'Hey, how's it goin' Paul?' They're being nice and I just give a breezy wave. I know what they're thinking though. 'Fucking hell . . .'

Now, I am outside a development on the edge of Altrincham where my old mate Norman Whiteside lives. I stand at the private gates, peering in like a hungry man looking through the window of a busy restaurant. I know Norman will help me if I can just reach him. Two ladies approach from inside and, with a buzz, the gates swing open. I want to charge straight through, but choose the diplomatic route instead.

'How ya doin', would it be alright if I just go in, I'm a friend of Norman's and . . .' One of them brusquely pulls the gate closed after her, mumbling something about not knowing Norman's number. She doesn't like what she sees.

It's at that point I see Steve. I know this bloke. He's standing across the street, looking towards me. Maybe forty yards between me and him. I shout towards him. He pretends that he can't hear me. There was a time when Steve was all over Paul McGrath. When I was a player, he used to come at me with a blur of business proposals. But I'm not a player now.

I can hear what he's saying. 'It *is* him, holy shit . . .' Steve walks briskly off in the opposite direction. I know that he's seen me. Silently, I curse. I keep walking.

Three more miles. I think about sleeping on a park bench. Just one thing stops me. I am scared of rats and I recall someone once telling me about how accomplished rats are at climbing. The thought of me lying asleep on that bench, with a rat tiptoeing across me is terrifying. I only sleep rough when I'm too drunk to care. Now I'm excruciatingly sober.

My tongue is sandpaper. There's a deafening hum in my head. The wound on my forehead keeps weeping. I feel as if death would be a release now.

Bill Woofe is my last hope. Bill and Lorilea. He's a corporate lawyer who's always been a good friend. Lorilea's a music teacher who taught Christopher and Mitchell the piano. I'm too drained now to care about the humiliation of turning up on their doorstep, so filthy and disheveled. It's almost midnight and, deep down, I know I've been walking towards this house all night.

So here I am, maybe thirteen hours after walking out of that courtroom, standing on an Altrincham doorstep, praying that there's someone home. Through those thirteen hours, I reckon I've been on my feet for all but ten minutes. My mind was in too much of a frenzy to let me sit down. Constant overload. Where should I go? Who do I need to avoid? How do I get through this unseen?

A light comes on in the porch when I press the doorbell. I pray Bill comes to the door. 'Please God, let him be home. Please God . . .'

Bill opens the door. 'Jesus Paul, what's happened?'

Hot tea has never tasted better, kindness has never been more welcome. Bill listens to my story. He listens without giving an impression that he's judging me. He just shrugs, shakes his head and gives little words of reassurance. A bed is made up for me in the guest room above the garage. Bill assures me that everything will be sorted out tomorrow.

I can't explain the relief I feel at walking into that guest room and seeing that bed. I feel more shattered than I ever thought possible this side of death. I feel like crying again. I shower and shave, then fall into bed like a man without the remotest intention of ever getting up again. I am asleep before my breathing settles.

The next morning, this beautiful Swedish au pair greets me in the kitchen, as if I'm a member of the family. The kids dip in and out, tossing light hellos my way. I'm being made incredibly welcome, though everyone must know that only something bad has brought me here. Bill cancels all meetings for the day. He's already been to the police station and retrieved my belt and phone. He's been on the phone to Frank Mullen in Dublin. They're getting me help again.

We drive over to Claire's house so that I can get a suitcase. I am barred from entering now, so Bill goes in. He explains to the kids that their dad is going back to Ireland to 'get some treatment'.

It is then that Christopher comes out of the house with Lucy. He leans into the car and gives me a big hug. I am shivering and ashamed. I have worn out my kids again, worn out Claire, worn out anyone who wants to help me. No one knows what to do anymore.

I glance into Christopher's eyes and I see that familiar look of emotional ruin. That's what I've done to him again. I see the enormity of it, but I've seen it before and still reached out to a glass for comfort. I can't trust myself to be a decent father. A decent man.

Driving away from the house, Bill senses what I'm thinking. There is nothing to say now. We travel in silence, headed for the Priory again. Arrangements are being put in place to establish my next port of call. Frank is coming over on the ferry to take me back to Dublin. I am booked into the Rutland Centre.

My last visit there precipitated sixteen months of sobriety and peace. I may be back at the foot of the mountain right now, but I know I have the strength to climb it.

2

END GAME

Ipswich. November grey. Handshakes. Back slaps. 'Well played big man . . .' Lies.

I had always lived in fear of the end, and now I wasn't exactly bowing out on Broadway. The next day's papers recorded that there were 9,695 people at Portman Road for the home side's 2-2 draw with Sheffield United. Mostly, I was spared the embarrassment of detail. Mid-table obscurity brings its blessings.

Walking off the pitch, I sensed Caroline's embarrassment. She was shaking her head, almost avoiding eye contact. This performance had been coming for a while, but it still shocked her. I wanted to sprint for the tunnel and hide. My right knee ached, but it wasn't much compared to the sting of humiliation ringing between my ears. A familiar voice was goading me: 'So what the hell was that then?'

I've played games in my time that stank the house down. I've been half drunk on a pitch. I've had days where I've tried to hold my breath so the centre-forward wouldn't keel over from the fumes (Alan Shearer, for one, would probably vouch for the fact). But I had never felt like an extra in some Monty Python sketch. Not sober at least.

This time, all contact between brain and legs had been severed. I'd tripped, stumbled and lunged my way through a farcical ninety minutes in East Anglia. I'd fluffed ten-yard passes. I'd mistimed tackles. I'd tried jumping for balls and failed to get lift-off. I'd become an accident waiting to happen.

A few weeks earlier, I'd also had a bit of a mare against QPR at Bramall Lane. Something was beginning to give. I could sense a loss of trust around me in the dressing room. People were squinting. Wondering.

I didn't know it, but coming off that Portman Road pitch on 9 November 1997, I had played my last game as a professional footballer.

When I got to the dressing room, the reflection in the mirror was jarring. There were great bags under my eyes. I looked old. Some of the kids gelling their hair next to me were literally half my age. Energy came off them in waves. They were headed out on the town now. I felt envious.

This had been building. I was making inexplicable mistakes: trying to deliver a fifty-yard pass and just under-hitting; an intended ball over the top dropping on the chest of a startled midfielder. My legs were getting weaker and weaker. I was a liability.

Ipswich had been just my twelfth game in a Sheffield United jersey. I liked playing in the First Division. The grounds were decent and full of atmosphere, yet there wasn't the same draining pressure I had begun to feel in the Premiership. The scrutiny was gentler. Maybe, I was just more comfortable at that level now.

There was a sense of denial too. As the knees ached and the off-days accumulated, I reasoned that – if need be – I could just drop down another division and keep playing. Retirement was still a long way down the road. I wouldn't countenance it. After all, here I was still playing almost eight years after Manchester United reckoned my career was over. Proving people wrong was my thing.

Not sure who I thought I was kidding.

My right knee just wasn't functioning properly. A week after Portman Road, I had it washed out by a specialist in Sheffield and set myself a strict training regime for recovery. But I could never get back. It never felt right again. I found I couldn't kick the ball any distance. Training with the youths, I had regular moments of embarrassment.

'Paul, give it, give it . . . FUCKING HELL PAUL!'

This is how bad it had become. I would stand thirty yards out from goal and try to chip the ball into an empty net, only to watch it barely trickle across the line. The pain was constant. I was thirty-seven and finally busted. So I made the call before it was made for me. No histrionics, no melodrama. 'Gaffer, I think I'm going to have to quit.'

I never said anything about being petrified.

Nigel Spackman was the United player-manager and, in playing terms, a contemporary of mine. He understood the way an old pro's legs could begin to betray him. 'Paul, you've got to do what is best for you,' he told me. I could detect a small strain of relief in his voice.

More than my knees had begun to slow me. I was a barely functioning alcoholic now addicted to tranquilisers. It had always been assumed that my drinking and my knees were parallel stories. To some extent they were. I had eight knee operations during my time with Manchester United, and often chose to dull the loneliness of rehabilitation with serious binges.

But even playing the best football of my life at Aston Villa, I was still drawn towards the pursuit of oblivion. I didn't drink rationally. I drank to blackout. There was no pleasure in the social pint for me. Players would have seen the madness at close quarters. Sometimes, I needed a drink just to go training. I'd stop off at an off-licence the way others might dip into a newsagent's.

Pre-season was the worst. After maybe six weeks out of the dressing-room loop, I dreaded meeting up again. I remember at one point commuting to Villa pre-season with Michael Oakes and

Alan Wright. Two kids. We'd take it in turns to drive and I'd routinely suggest stopping off somewhere en route for 'a couple of cans'.

Always the same dialogue. 'No Paul, we can't, we can't . . .'

'Please lads, you have to do this for me . . .'

I was a veteran of the first team, someone they were supposed to be looking up to and here I was, pleading with them to help me get tanked up on the way to training. I could see their turmoil. I was manipulating them. They knew what I was doing was wrong, but out of loyalty (or fear?) they wouldn't break the confidence.

It didn't even have to be pre-season for me to do this. Habitually, throughout the season, I'd have a few cans in the car on the way to training. I might be fighting the shakes and feeling the need to settle myself before arrival at Bodymoor Heath. Then I'd miscalculate the amount I required to function properly and arrive the worse for wear.

It's a horrible feeling when you know you've lost control. You're craving a heavy hit of something just to bring you back to what you perceive to be normality. And that's the weird thing. Sometimes you manage to function. Sometimes you get through it in a relatively inconspicuous way and find yourself thinking, 'That was fine today.'

Then you try to do the same with tranquilisers . . .

It was quite late in my Villa career that I discovered the miracle of Zimovane. Just a late-night card game and the customary eve-of-game sleeping tablet. 'Last hand' had been called. I swallowed the tablet, expecting to be in bed within ten minutes. Half an hour later, I was still at the table. Floating.

I felt warm and invincible. Betting without fear. 'Hold on a minute,' I remember thinking, 'this might just be the answer . . .'

The idea that I had found a substitute for alcohol seemed, to begin with, a seismic discovery. It made such perfect sense. Take a tablet for confidence. Two, if you're feeling really fragile. And it wasn't difficult to get a prescription.

'Struggling to sleep Doc, lot of pressure at the club.'

'No problem Paul, just take one at night if you feel you really need one.'

Hallelujah!

Of course, two soon became four. Four became six. I was running out of tablets within days of getting the prescription. 'Sorry Doc, can't find where I put that last batch. Would you mind . . . ?'

I soon realised that I needed a more prolific and less scrupulous supplier. In a footballer's life you come across all sorts. I knew I had friends in low places. It just took a phone call to some toerags in Manchester and soon I was on the vicious merry-go-round. I'd tank myself up with alcohol just for the trip to Moss Side, and go down there with loads of cash, trying to look savvy and hard and unafraid.

Once, I got mugged, this group of kids surrounding me, prodding, pushing, taunting. It wasn't even scary. I was so drunk I remember thinking 'I can't fight. If I try to throw a punch, I'm just going to keel over . . .' They took my Cartier watch, but spared me the humiliation of a kicking.

Everything I did now was strictly covert. I had one particular supplier who I knew was overcharging me extravagantly. It didn't matter. I needed those tablets and I had money. In one deal, I might take anything between six to eight hundred tablets off him, hand over a couple of grand, hide them in the car, then wait for an opportune time to unbox the bounty.

Deceit became an impulse. A great deal of thinking went into the procedure. I was like a low-life dealer myself, biding my time for the right opportunity to organise the stash. The trick was to put them into sealed plastic bags, maybe fifty at a time, and plant them all over the house. It might take two to three days to do it. The only hiccups came with carelessness.

If I took too many, I'd lose the subtlety needed for the crime. Caroline might find a bag. We'd row and, unconvincingly, I'd promise that that was the extent of my stash. I had, of course, now chosen to ignore the fact that I was still drinking. My original motivation for taking them had long since burned away.

The problem was I was turning my brain to mush. I was lying habitually. Drunks don't make smart con men. I might just walk over to a cupboard, pull the bag from behind some jars, turn around . . . 'What's that in your hand Paul?'

Oh shit!

You lose your inhibitions, but you lose the ability to be smart too. Your brain power goes. Often I would even forget where some of the tablets were stashed. They might turn up months later when I was well again. I'd put my hand into the pocket of a bag or jacket and eureka, fifty Zimovane. What to do?

That's when the voices would start going off in the head again. Good angel, bad angel. Like the crisp ad with Bobby Robson and Terry Venables. Bad angel always wins. 'Jesus, must be my birthday. Cheers Terry.' The one thing I always knew was that I'd never flush tablets down the toilet. Precious bullion.

By the time I moved to Derby County in 1996, I was hooked. Hooked with a modicum of control, mind. By and large, I wouldn't take them the day of a game. It never seemed a big deal. The football never frightened me. Life beyond was the problem.

Jim Smith was Derby's manager and he treated me like an adult. 'Just be right for Saturday' was his attitude. He signed me, essentially, to keep the club in the Premiership. My wages were performance related. If Derby stayed up, I'd benefit through my bank account. Even through my most chaotic lows, money had a way of concentrating my mind. On Saturdays, wearing the white of Derby, I'd go to war.

Jim just wanted me to report Thursday, train (kind of) Friday, play Saturday. He was brilliant to deal with. Real old school. Human. My debut was an October home game against Newcastle that went absolutely brilliantly until the last minute when Alan Shearer scored the only goal.

Trouble was, I had only known my teammates for two days. In the dying seconds, this ball comes in. All day, Shearer's been in my pocket. I'm presuming the left-back has tucked in behind me, like he would have done at Villa. I go for the ball and quickly realise I'm not going to get it. Turn for the full-back. Shit, he's gone to a post.

Two touches and Shearer kills us. Bang. Ninety-three minutes. Nightmare.

It seemed an ominous portent, but the season went remarkably well. I played twenty-four games for Derby and we stayed up with a little to spare. Better still, our run included Premiership wins over both my former clubs and only a late Patrick Vieira thunderbolt prevented us from beating Arsenal. Maybe, most stirringly, we beat Villa in the fifth round of the FA Cup.

Knocking Villa out of the Cup left me with very mixed emotions. I still felt a huge affection for the club, if not the manager – Brian Little. His decision to let me leave still stung. In both games against them, I marked Dwight Yorke, who had been like a little brother to me from the moment he arrived at Villa Park in 1990 as a seventeen-year-old from Trinidad and Tobago.

I loved Dwight. He was so happy-go-lucky, trusting and devoid of any agendas, I actually felt protective towards him. I even loved Doug Ellis, the chairman, who – contrary to caricature – had been kind and thoughtful towards me during my seven years with the club.

Coming off the pitch after that Cup game, I remember going up to maybe the best friend I've ever had in football, Villa physio Jim Walker, and saying, 'They shouldn't have sold me Jim!' I had been so wound up before the game, determined to prove a point to Little. To this day, I believe that if he had put me in the Villa team for that 1996–7 season, I would have more than repaid his faith.

But, not unreasonably, he wanted to go with younger blood. In the end, it was Walker – himself a former Derby player – who alerted Jim Smith to my desire for a move.

> Jim Walker: 'I knew he could do a huge job for them. I just said to Jim Smith, Look, he might not train from one end of the week to the other but, come Saturday, he'll be your best player. You won't go wrong with him, I guarantee that. He'll be immense for you."'

Villa still meant more to me, though, than was probably healthy. I felt a real conflict after that Cup game. A sense of disloyalty, almost. It was one of the most confused feelings I've had in football. Not that I showed it, naturally. I remember, before the game, joking with Yorkie that he wasn't to dare trying to run me.

I don't think I actually tackled him once in the ninety minutes. I didn't have to – I just kept nipping in in front of him, reading things, guessing his runs. Afterwards, people were asking me how it felt to 'get one over on Villa', expecting me to be triumphal. I couldn't say as much, but I actually felt sick that they were out of FA Cup.

At Derby, you see, I still felt a bit of a stranger. There were a lot of young lads in the dressing room, cocky kids who weren't exactly gentle when spotting weakness. Some of the more surreal memories are of how utterly dismissive a few of them were of Smith's assistant, Steve McClaren.

They wouldn't have known, of course, that they were dealing with a future England manager. It showed. McClaren was a nice guy and an innovative coach, but he never quite seemed comfortable with the industrial banter of the changing room. Some of them devoured him.

I couldn't believe the attitude towards him. You could see he had a huge interest in the game and that he cared about methods of preparation, but maybe he was just a little too technical for some of the bigger shots in that dressing room. Some footballers just respond better to noise than information.

Steve, sensibly, left most of the group stuff to Smith. He focused on communicating one-to-one with selected players. I was invariably one of them. I liked him. He was pleasant and supportive.

I'll always remember my first day at Derby. A little heading exercise. I was paired off with a kid and − staying true to my Villa training routines − I effectively disengaged. I wouldn't even jump for the ball. The kid won everything. I remember Jim and Steve standing, watching, arms folded, faces frozen.

I knew what they were thinking. 'What the fuck have we bought here?'

The following day we played Newcastle and, though we lost, my performance against Shearer at least reassured them that I had some kind of role to play. I loved playing for Smith. He encouraged the team to go for the jugular. To be bold. The squad included a lot of talented individuals, especially two really good Croatian internationals, Igor Stimac and Aljosa Asanovic. The things they could do on the training ground would almost leave you dizzy. So it just wasn't in the psyche of the team to try and grind out boring draws.

One memorable day we went to Old Trafford and stunned the Premiership by winning 3-2.

Sir Alex Ferguson: 'Derby were playing with three at the back at the time. But they changed for that game. I remember they were staying up in Mottram Hall. I used give my team to the television people on a Friday night to help them with their preparation and I decided I'd play just one up, to make it difficult for them. Next thing word came back that they were going to play 4-4-2 against us.

'When I saw their team, I said, "They're playing 4-4-2 with McGrath?" I mean, at that stage, he's in his late thirties. So I changed my team. I played two up and kept saying to them, "Pull McGrath into the corners, pull him wide."

'Did he go to the corners? Would he come out of the centre-half's pitch? No chance. He was man-of-the-match, absolutely brilliant. On the Monday after the game, I remember sitting in my office with Brian Kidd and we were talking about him. "I tell you one thing," I said "you have to wonder what a player Paul McGrath should have been . . ."'

Derby stayed in the Premiership with something to spare, but Jim decided to let me go. There were no hard feelings. He admitted I had more than delivered on the job he brought me in to do. I knew I had played one or two ropey games for him, maybe an inevitability given my off-field difficulties. There were a few days I particularly remember feeling the pace. My knees weren't great.

I especially recall an incident at Wimbledon on the second week in January 1997. We were desperate for a result. The score was tied at 1-1 when I mishit a pass inside my own half and the ball was intercepted by Efan Ekoko. Now the Wimbledon striker had the build and pace of an Olympic sprinter. He was straight in on goal. It looked game over.

I chased frantically and, at the last second, lunged, just about toe-poking the ball back to our keeper. I got to it through sheer terror. Some people lauded it afterwards as 'classic' defending. It wasn't. My mistake had created the problem. It was firefighting. Something I was having to do a little too often for comfort.

But, mostly, I played well for Derby. In one game, I even drew a loud '*Ole*' from the crowd. It was a Midlands derby against Coventry. Dion Dublin came charging towards our box like a runaway train. I remember his face especially. It was so contorted with effort, it could have been pressed against a windowpane.

I didn't even attempt to tackle, I just read the spin of the ball and, as it arrived, back-heeled it to a teammate, leaving Dion chasing thin air. Armchair defending, I suppose. It looked so nonchalant, the crowd went into convulsions. I loved it. The footballer loses many things over the years, but rarely his vanity.

By season's end, though, Jim just reasoned that he wouldn't get another year like that out of me. And time would prove him right.

The only row I ever had with Jim Smith was over a Cup game against Middlesbrough. He had told me I'd be playing, then changed his mind. I might not have shown it very often, but deep down I had a process of psyching myself up for a game. Having been told I would be playing against Middlesbrough, I was now immersed in that process. And, suddenly, Jim announced that some young fella would be taking my place.

Maybe I just sensed what was coming down the line, the slow demise of an old footballer. I was too angry to speak when I heard it. It's one of the few times I've completely lost my temper in foot-ball. I just walked out of the room, got in my car and drove back to Manchester, seething.

The following day I'm in training and Jim calls me into his office. He was straight up. 'Look, I'm sorry', he said. 'I had made a decision, then changed it. I shouldn't have told you that you were playing.' His straightness defused the situation. We shook hands and I binned my anger. I liked him because he was honest. He didn't spin bullshit.

Signing for Sheffield United effectively confirmed the end of my Premiership career. I didn't care. The wages that were now routine in English football meant I was still earning far more from the game than at any time in my career with Manchester United and through a large chunk of my stint with Villa.

Nigel Spackman had recently graduated to the position of player-manager after Howard Kendall's decision to return to Everton. I knew Nigel from old battles against Liverpool and Chelsea. He was a manager who liked to delegate. He wasn't one for emotional dressing-room orations. Just a simple 'C'mon lads, we're going to do it . . .'

We started the season well, but the club's financial predicament soon began to interfere. They had accumulated serious losses in a vain bid for promotion the previous season, and now the board felt compelled to trim the wage bill. In time, some of United's better players like Brian Deane, Jan Aage Fjortoft and Don Hutchison were sacrificed at the altar of expediency.

The sales torpedoed the season. By March, an exasperated Spackman had resigned, his cause not exactly helped by the permanent departure of his Irish centre-half: I was three months retired by the time Nigel waved the white flag.

On the surface, I was coping. Actually, to begin with, retirement was almost enjoyable. I had more time with the kids. The largely unseen pressure of having to perform was gone from my life. I told anyone who asked that my days were now filled with a magical serenity. But deep down, I was lying. Deep down, I was terrified.

My international testimonial had been penciled in for 17 May in Dublin and, while outwardly it was a project to keep me focused, my instinct was to run away. The very idea of being an 'ex-footballer' just hit all the wrong nerve ends with me. For fifteen years, the game gave me an outlet for whatever tensions, stresses or worries might threaten to come crowding in. It wasn't coincidence that some of my worst drinking sprees tended to dovetail injuries.

Now everything was stored. Coming towards the big day, I was back seeking refuge in the booze and the tranquilisers. It wasn't overt. Just the same old secretive stockpiling.

The day went brilliantly, Lansdowne Road being packed to capacity. I loved having the kids on the pitch with me. I loved the warmth of the crowd. But I hated every second of the game.

The plan had been that I might come on for the last ten minutes. Physically, I wasn't too sure I'd even manage that. But the crowd was impatient. They were chanting my name. Forty-odd thousand of them, looking to see me back in the green of Ireland. It was decided I'd best go on earlier.

So I go in with the plan of tiptoeing through the remainder. Roll a pass here and there. Feign the odd challenge. And the crowd greets every touch like I'm a matador with the bull at my mercy.

Then Dean Saunders comes on for the international selection. Dean's a good friend. The score is 1-1 and everyone seems happy to see out time. Next thing, Dean scores. You can hear a pin drop. 2-1 to the supporting cast. Minutes later, someone rolls the ball towards me and, as it arrives, Dean comes clattering in. The tackle forces me over awkwardly on my ankle and I see out the last few minutes of my testimonial limping and wincing. Cheers mate!

In the end, only a late goal from my old Villa colleague, Gareth Farrelly, rescues Irish pride and the game finishes 2-2.

Jim Walker: 'Paul's come into the changing room after and his ankle's swollen to almost twice its normal size. So Dean's effectively upset the day. He's a good lad, so enthusiastic, but he doesn't seem to see what he's after doing. So I say to him, "I can't believe you!" And he says, "What's up now?"

'"Everybody's happy at 1-1 and you come on and score."

'"I know, it's habit!"

'"Then you kicked Paul."

'"I'm telling you, if he ain't fit, he shouldn't be playing Jim."

'It was so funny. Dean used to look out for Paul. They were real mates. The day before the testimonial, he came to me and told me Paul wasn't in the best shape. He'd picked him up that morning and Paul was complaining of a headache. He asked Dean to stop so he might get some paracetemol, but Paul's come back with two bottles of vodka and stuffed them in his bag. Needless to say, I've gone and taken them out of the bag.'

I knew I was heading to a bad place again. After maybe a week of tying up loose ends – some of which I didn't quite tie – I settled back in Manchester, ready to begin the rest of my life.

That was when it finally hit. I'd wake up each morning and it was like a bolt of electricity through my ribcage. 'Oh my God, it's over.' The testimonial had left me financially secure, assuming I didn't blow it, of course. But that was a hefty assumption to make.

By July, with pre-season starting, I was yearning to be part of it again. Missing the banter. Pining for the five-a-sides, the pain even. Finishing felt like a bereavement. Suddenly, the biggest physical challenge of the day was just to get out of bed. I felt cut adrift.

The game was up, though. I needed to start making plans outside the comfort blanket of football. So I took a deep breath and poured myself a stiff drink.

3

BETTY'S STORY

My name is Betty McGrath. You don't know me and, in many ways, I don't want you to.

Paul was ten weeks old when I handed him over and – though we are extremely close today – I have, I suppose, spent the past four and a half decades trying to get him back. For years, journalists found their way to the front gate of my home in Crumlin, doorstepping me for a reaction to his latest fall from grace. For years, they were wasting their time.

I don't like the attention. I don't trust it. I am an elderly woman now, praying every day for my son's health and happiness. Sometimes, when he is missing, I wish for selfish things. I wish he was sitting before me in the front room, drinking even. Better he'd drink in the security of home than find himself cut adrift among strangers who probably only care for his celebrity value.

Does that sound callous?

Above all, I want Paul to be safe. The world I see frightens me. I never venture out after dark. I hate being away from home. I read the newspapers, I watch the television news. It seems to me there are so many damaged people making headlines. I wonder, sometimes, how Paul is still alive. I wonder how he comes through so many scrapes still sane and relatively healthy.

Maybe, deep down, I know. It must be his guardian angel.

But, this is my story. Why tell it? Because Paul has asked me. There are parts of it that he won't have heard before. Maybe parts of it I'd even prefer he didn't. I love him with every ounce of my being but, sometimes, I feel I'm still trying to get to know my son. I still ask myself if he fully understands why, in the early days of 1960, I gave him into foster care. Does he truly forgive me?

Words couldn't ever capture the pain of that ordeal. But, maybe, circumstance will explain why it came to pass.

I was brought up on the Crumlin Road, one of four girls living directly opposite Loreto College. My father was Patrick P. McGrath (the middle P was very important to him, it stood for Paul), a hard-working, hard-drinking builder who didn't brook argument on any subject. My mother was Elizabeth O'Connor from Arklow Town, a kind, easy-going woman.

Routinely, my father's temper invaded the house and we'd retreat from it, listening to him roar at Mammy, worrying that he might take offence at the slightest move or sound. He wasn't a bad man. Just hard and old-fashioned and prone to picking arguments out of nothing.

Dublin was a tough city at the beginning of the sixties. Mammy worked just as hard as my father, making cakes in DBC Bakeries on Stephen Street. We were happy children, Mary (the eldest), me, Patsy and Claire. Certainly, we never felt any more deprived than the kids we played with.

I met Paul's father — a Nigerian medical student — at a students' dance in the Four Province club on Harcourt Street. His name was Festis. We went out for about a month and, to my horror, I fell pregnant. When I went up to the student quarters to tell him, Festis slammed the door in my face.

I knew, instantly, I'd have to leave home. Daddy would have

been absolutely enraged if he knew. So I looked up the *Evening Press*, searching for any live-in work available in England and found the number of a Jewish couple in Cricklewood. Within weeks, I was on my way to London, effectively as their housekeeper.

It was all a little terrifying. Just the sight of the red buses and phone boxes would make me feel homesick, reminding me that I was now a long, long way from home.

The couple had two children and were kind people who knew more than they let on. As my 'bump' got bigger, I never imagined they had long since put two and two together.

But, with my weight climbing, I slipped a disc in my back. Now, I could barely walk. Actually, I became useless to them. The woman gave me a walking stick and, for a few weeks, I just hobbled around their home. It was getting embarrassing.

Eventually, it became clear that I was in need of formal help. Contact was made with a nuns' home in Acton, where I could see out the last weeks of my pregnancy. So I was put on a bus and told which stop to use. I asked the conductor to let me know when we got there. He agreed, then dropped me off at the wrong one.

It was getting dark as I hobbled the rest of the journey, lumbered with a bag and heavily pregnant. I was terrified. Sometimes, I think my fear of the dark may actually have taken root that evening in Acton.

Very late, I finally arrived at these big iron gates and rang the bell. This nun came down. She was purple with rage, shouting at me. 'You're late!' she screamed. I tried to explain about the bus conductor and the long walk, but she wasn't listening. I wanted to turn and run.

She brought me into this office and started gesticulating, a fountain pen in her hand. In her rage, she brushed against a bottle of ink which spilled all over the desk and across the page she was about to write on. 'Look what you're after making me do!' she raged. It was, in many ways, a telltale welcome.

Most of the other girls in the home were just like me: Irish and pregnant. The nuns treated us like dirt. They were always hostile. Everyone had their jobs to do and mine was preparing the vegetables for dinner. A ritual of washing, chopping, scraping. And eavesdropping.

Sometimes, one of the girls would get stomach pains and presume she was going into labour. An ambulance would be called. If the same girl came back that evening after a false alarm, the nuns went apoplectic. It was unbelievable. We all started living in more fear of that rage than the actual pains of childbirth.

The day I started getting my pains, I waited. And waited. I couldn't bear the idea of facing that onslaught if the ambulance had been called for nothing. In the end, I barely made it to the hospital in Ealing on time. Paul was born in ten minutes flat. I remember it vividly. Lying there in the ward, looking at the clock. It read ten minutes to ten. When I looked again, Paul's cries filling the air, it was ten o'clock exactly.

In my confusion, I thought maybe it was already ten at night. But it wasn't. Paul McGrath had come into the world at exactly ten a.m. on 4 December 1959. Just me and him. And not a friendly face in sight.

The nuns were unequivocal. He had to be put up for adoption. They were desperately aggressive. In the first weeks of Paul's life, they regularly beat me, forcing a pen into my hand, clasping it shut like you do with a baby as if you're teaching them to write, while trying to get me to sign adoption papers.

I wouldn't. I knew if I signed, I'd never see him again. I cried with exasperation. 'No, no, some day I will get him.'

Eventually, agreement was reached that I'd hand him into foster care. Contact was made with the Catholic Crusade on Anne Street in Dublin. I would get the boat home and be met at the pier. The instructions were simple. Wait until everyone else was off the boat. Then they would take my child.

So that's how I spent my last hours with my infant boy. Hauling him about the boat in a carrycot, both of us crying. I remember at one point standing on deck, staring at the churning water below, momentarily contemplating jumping with my baby. I felt incredibly alone.

But I did meet this lovely old man on the boat who, for some reason, reminded me of my father. We got talking. I think he was a builder too, just coming home for the weekend. He'd sit with Paul when I was going to get a bottle heated. He was the first kind face I had seen in what felt like an eternity. I often thought in later years how I'd love that man to have known who the baby turned out to be.

The nuns had warned me not to take pictures of Paul, but I couldn't help myself. Watching me with the camera, the old man seemed to know instinctively what I was facing. 'If I was you, I'd take your baby home,' he said.

'Oh no, I couldn't,' I said. 'My father will kill me if he knows I got pregnant.'

'He won't. Believe me. If I was you, I'd go home.'

'No, I can't.'

'Well, what are you going to do?'

'I'm coming back to England on this boat tonight.'

'This boat doesn't come back tonight.'

I almost fainted. The nuns had told me I'd be coming straight back. Now, suddenly, I had visions of having to sleep in some doorway for the night. He saw my panic and gave me some money. I don't know how much. Two shillings maybe. Soon enough, we were docking. He shook my hand and wished me well. Terrified, I watched him leave.

I did as they had told me, waiting until everyone was off the boat. Then these two women appeared, and literally yanked Paul from my grasp. The women weren't even dressed as nuns. I was hysterical. I screamed at nobody in particular. I wailed for my lost baby. The handover had been quite brutal. Now I was very much alone.

In a daze, I got off the boat and started wandering. I remember walking past all these little huckster cafes, thinking I had enough for a cup of tea. But I couldn't bring myself to go in. People were staring. At least, that was how it felt to me. It was as if they knew who I was and what I'd just done.

Eventually, I came upon a telephone kiosk and decided to phone my friend, Bernie. I was crying hysterically on the phone, telling her that I was going straight back the following day, that no one was to know. She talked me into meeting up with her and her sister. So we met in the Palm Grove on O'Connell Street and sat, discussing my future, over an ice cream.

To this day, I don't know how she did it. But Bernie talked me into going home.

I must have looked a total mess. It seemed to me that my parents would see through me, that they'd instantly guess my secret. But there was something else tugging at me. I missed them. I missed home. I missed my friends. Before I knew it, I was standing at the front door (the key was always left in the latch), Bernie striding in ahead of me. I can still see my mother standing at the sink.

'Someone here to see you Mrs McGrath' said Bernie. My mother's eyes met mine and we rushed to each other in tears. It was lovely to feel her arms around me.

I stayed for about a week, telling them of an imagined life in England. My baby? That had to stay a secret, even to my mother who, deep down, I knew would be kind about it. I just couldn't risk telling my father. Because to do that would be to risk being banished for good.

Back in England, I got a job in Rye Bakeries. I used to send money to the Catholic Crusade to help pay for Paul's foster care. Then I fell pregnant again. The father of my second child was another Nigerian, an education officer called Pius Egbi. Unlike Paul's dad, Pius wanted us to be a family.

When I gave birth to a beautiful daughter, Okune, on 25 September 1961, the plan was that we would go to live in Nigeria. Pius wanted Paul to be with us too. Actually, it was him who finally persuaded me to tell Mammy about Paul. 'If you don't, I'm writing to her,' he warned. Pius was an intelligent, thoughtful man who was adamant that we all could live happily in Nigeria. And I believed him.

He left England to go home and the plan was that, in time, we would follow. But, first, I brought Okune back to Dublin. She wasn't a strong child. We discovered she had a blood disorder that would make large parts of her life a virtual hell. It led to these great, raw veins opening on her skin, starting on her neck, then running down her back, ultimately invading most of her body. They looked like little clusters of blackberries.

When she was a baby, I used to have to cut her vests off. The general consensus was that she would not live beyond the age of eight. The poor thing went through hell, often bleeding heavily from her wounds.

But she was blessed with her father's brains. Though Okune could never enjoy the simple freedoms of a healthy childhood, she would prove wonderfully intelligent and artistic. She also defied all medical prognoses, living to the age of thirty-two and even making her own wedding dress at a time when she could barely move her right arm.

Despite my fears about his reaction to Paul, my father grew to adore Okune. She was a gorgeous-looking child and her cute-ness just won him over. I still intended moving to Nigeria and actually got the necessary injections against yellow fever. But my mother was appalled by the thought. A cousin of mine, Frances, had spent some time in Africa. She wrote my mother a letter saying that a girl would be 'treated like dirt' in Nigeria, if she didn't have any 'letters behind her name'. Mammy didn't tell me about the letter.

We had another relative, Father Pat, who had been to Lagos. According to my mother, she asked him, 'Father, what do you think of the white girls with the black men?' He knew my story. 'Put it this way,' he told her, 'if I had a sister going, I'd put a gun to her head to stop her.'

One night, she asked him to speak to me. Father Pat was emphatic. Nigeria was no place for a young, unqualified Irish girl.

I didn't go in the end. It wasn't that I had been persuaded out of it by family. There were practical issues. In hindsight, I think my decision to stay had more to do with a lack of the airfare than anything Father Pat had said. And anyway, Okune was struggling.

She would be in and out of hospital right through her childhood. By the time she was fourteen, her right arm was in serious jeopardy. I remember one day being told in the Richmond Hospital that they would have to amputate. I was heartbroken, though I tried not to let her see me. Every bit of news we were getting was negative.

One of the most harrowing images I have is of them pulling the curtains around the hospital bed and announcing they had some 'bad news' about her arm. But Okune was incredible. She just took it in her stride. 'Suppose that means I'll be a bit like the bionic woman,' she said.

I took her once to a specialist just off Dawson Street. His words cut through me. 'Look,' he said firmly, 'we can't work miracles.' Another in Fitzwilliam Square took a completely different slant.

'Does she drink milk?' he asked me.

'Yes.'

'Then she'll be OK.'

The thought of Okune losing her arm, though, was just beyond my comprehension. Worse, it was even suggested that parts of her back and chest would have to follow. In desperation, I went to Dr John O'Connell's clinic on the Crumlin Road, just looking for advice.

I remember there was a queue outside. I talked to a few people in the queue and, to me, it seemed their problems were incredibly trivial. One of them had had their bike stolen.

Eventually, our turn came and Dr O'Connell asked me curtly what the problem was. I explained about Okune and the plans to amputate her arm. I asked him if I brought her to Great Ormond Street Hospital in London would they be able to save it. I told him I'd do anything in the hospital to pay. Empty bedpans, anything.

'Where do you work?' he asked me.

'I'm a confectioner in Harcourt Bakery.'

'How much a week are you on?'

'Eleven pound.'

'What does your husband work at?'

'I don't have a husband.'

'Meaning?'

'He went back to Nigeria.'

Dr O'Connell shrugged and started asking me about social welfare. I was incredibly ill-informed. If anything, I was virtually begging. Eventually he said, 'Leave it with me.' The words went through my heart like a nail. I presumed I'd never hear from him again.

But he did write to Great Ormond Street and they took an active interest in Okune. Her condition was so rare, it intrigued them. At first, they thought she might have been a thalidomide child. They took pictures of her, and a Mr Matthews kept corresponding.

He sent some of the photographs to Our Lady's Hospital in Crumlin where one particular doctor took grave umbrage at what he saw as outside interference. He absolutely lambasted me when I called up. 'The cheek of you telling us we don't know how to do our job here . . .' was the gist of what he said to me.

But there were no miracle answers. Okune had an enlarged heart. It would beat four times faster than normal. Eventually, a decision was taken to do an operation in the Richmond. It was explained to me that Okune had only a fifty-fifty chance of survival. That was on a Wednesday. The operation was due to happen on the Friday.

I was panic-stricken. It was the week before her fourteenth birthday. I had always been telling her that we would go to Lourdes one day. She was a deeply religious child. Now I felt that that day had come. I ran up to the credit union and withdrew the money immediately. When they heard what it was for, they just handed it to me.

So we went to Lourdes and, when we got home, I was supposed to bring her straight to the hospital from the airport. But I couldn't do it. Actually, I never brought her back. She never did have that amputation.

We just went home and every two or three months, the bleeding would come in cycles. I had a basin for her feet and big pads for her back and chest. In some respects, Lourdes sustained her. After that trip, her heart beat perfectly for about a month before regressing again. It was enough to convince her that Lourdes had special qualities and she would travel there twice more in the coming years.

During that time, Okune grew into the most remarkable woman you could hope to meet. Because she bled from her hands and feet, people used come to the door asking her to pray for their 'special intentions'. Routinely, they'd come back some time later saying, 'Tell Okune I got my request.'

Everywhere we went, we'd bring pads, scissors, plasters. You couldn't have known her suffering to look at her, though. Okune was beautiful and utterly immune to self-pity. This thing was growing inside her, yet she was full of life and fun. Actually, she went on to do just about every single thing she wanted. She went to the Grafton Academy of Design. She married John O'Reilly. She had a beautiful daughter, Maiwa.

39

She even became especially close to the brother who, to begin with, she didn't know existed.

My abiding memory of Paul and Okune together is taken from much later. Okune had to be careful because she got out of breath so easily. When Paul would come home from England, he could make her laugh at anything. He'd walk in the door, just make a face and she'd wheel away, wheezing hysterically. I'd have to take her out the back to catch her breath. They came to adore one another.

How did Paul come back into my life? We had absolutely no contact for the first five and a half years of his existence. I just spent the time imagining his face, wondering what food he liked, what games he played. Then, out of the blue, I took a phone call. Paul had been fostered by a Mrs Donnelly out in Whitehall. Her daughters were on the line. They weren't able to handle him anymore. He'd have to go to an orphanage.

Everything happened very quickly and in a panic. Suddenly, I was going to see my little boy again, knowing that I couldn't possibly look after him. I had Okune now, yet I was still an unmarried mother. Paul was still a secret being kept from my own father.

So my mother and I went in to the Catholic Crusade to collect him. Everyone was crying. Me, my mother, the Donnellys. The scene was just horrific. Paul didn't really know me. He must have been totally bemused. We brought him out and bought him chips. I had to find a home for him and I had to find it fast.

The options weren't exactly vast, so we contacted the Protestant-run Smyly Trust Homes and it was agreed that I could bring Paul to their Bird's Nest orphanage on York Street in Dun Laoghaire. This would be his home for the next five years.

It was harrowing having to let him go again. That little time we had together, we spent at a friend's flat on the South Circular Road. I couldn't possibly explain to Paul that I was handing him over again so we said something about going to visit a little boy

he knew. It was heartbreaking to have to leave him in those circumstances.

I needed a father's signature on the application form for the
orphanage, and so my friend signed 'G Nwobilo'. Paul thus became
known from then on as Paul Nwobilo.

All of his school reports over the next six years were under that
name, even though on his birth certificate he was still Paul McGrath.
It was messy and sad and more than a little confusing.

From that point on, I started visiting. By now, I was working
in the Penny Farthing cafe on Exchequer Street and I would take
a half day on occasional Wednesdays, go down to Trinity College
and get the 46A (sometimes having to jump off early if I didn't
have the full fare) out to Dun Laoghaire. Bernie used to come
with me. Sometimes Mary, my sister.

There was a little shop beside the orphanage and I used to buy
these penny fizz bags for all the boys. Paul would tell me they'd
be watching out the window, hoping to see me coming. It was
lovely seeing him, always heartbreaking to walk away again.

In some ways, I suppose I tried to compensate. I bought him the
Chelsea kit once. Some time later, I bought him a bike. It wasn't
ideal. There was a lot of guilt involved. In years to come, I often
wondered how much I might have been to blame for Paul's troubles.

I used to visit him with Okune and it was obvious this made
him uneasy. 'Who is she?' he'd ask me.

'She's your sister, love,' I'd say.

Paul was confused. Okune was confused. I was walking on
eggshells.

When he became ill in his late teens, I actually thought we
were going to lose him. A phone call came through to the Penny
Farthing and my boss, Mrs Morton, just told me, 'Quick, go in a
taxi.' He was in Elm Park Hospital and they wouldn't let me go
near him. He didn't seem to know anybody. I just have this vivid
image of him lying on a stretcher, the Afro hair sticking out.

While he was there, he had to be restrained. They were feeding him through a drip because he wouldn't eat. He kept tearing the tubes out. The doctors took a view that he was rebelling. They said that they couldn't be sure he'd ever walk again, let alone play football.

It was an horrendous time, because no one seemed to know quite what was happening. He was just left lying, developing horrendous bed sores. To this day, he is still marked on both knees where the limbs literally fused together because of his immobility.

One day, two lads came in, helped lift him off the bed and the sheet was completely covered in blood.

I remember visiting him once. By now he was heavily sedated. The doctor wanted to see me before I went in. Paul was sitting on the floor in the ward, his back to his bed. 'Just sit down beside him,' said the doctor. 'Act as if it's normal.' So I went in and did as I was told. I felt self-conscious. It was a big ward with seven or eight beds and there were other visitors.

There was a plate of spaghetti on a tray beside Paul. He wasn't talking. He didn't know me. 'Would you eat a little bit of your dinner Paul?' I said. 'One spoon even?' Suddenly, he leaned over. I thought he was going to pick up the fork, but he just lifted up the plate and turned it upside down on his head. The spaghetti came spilling down his face. It was a nightmare.

For a time, we just weren't sure he'd ever function as a normal human being again. He was just slipping deeper and deeper into whatever trance had got him. The conditions he was being kept in were appalling.

Then one night I went in to visit, only to be told he had been moved to St John of God's on the Stillorgan Road. No one had seen fit to even keep me informed. Okune and I would visit, with my husband-to-be, Noel Lowth. But Paul didn't know us. He just stared into the distance.

Eventually, he ended up in St Brendan's, Grangegorman. Once

I brought him a dressing gown, pyjamas, shaving gear and a big radio. The next day I visited, the radio was beside someone else's bed and another patient was wearing the dressing gown. I almost wondered if it was his way of getting back at me.

It was a harrowing time and, in many ways, it's miraculous that he came through. But St Brendan's cured him. It took months, but gradually they nursed him back to life.

One funny thing. Many, many years later, when Paul was a star with Manchester United, my father was dying from his angina. He was a patient in St James's Hospital. One night he said to my mam and me, 'Know who was here last night?'

'Who?'

'Paul.'

'Are you sure Da?'

'Yeah, Paul was in here to see me.'

He was raving. I suppose the medication was taking its toll. Paul was in Manchester now, a full-time professional footballer. And I thought it ironic that the boy I was once so afraid to tell my own father about was now, clearly, a source of such pride to him.

Okune's remarkable life came to a sudden end in March 1994. She had outlived the most hopeful medical prognosis by twenty-four years. Paul was at the bedside for his sister's final hours in St James's Hospital. We wept uncontrollably when she passed. To this day, I believe Okune was a saint sent down to bless us.

I suppose I live a lot on my nerves now. I worry endlessly about Paul. I worry about someone taking advantage. I worry about him being hurt physically. When he doesn't ring me, I always fear the worst. But I believe Okune is on his shoulder. And I pray to her. I say, 'Okune, whatever you do, don't leave him. Stay with him all the time.' And she will, I know. She'll stay with him.

Because she's his guardian angel.

4

THE NEST

The biggest and, maybe, worst deception was in the name.

'Bird's Nest' evokes a kind of gentle, protective picture of the big, narrow house on York Road in Dun Laoghaire. Actually, it was a dark, forbidding, barrack-like place with granite walls clad in ivy and ugly, brick window surrounds. A horrible, frightening building when seen through the eyes of a child.

There were two big doors at the front, one with a sign for 'GIRLS' above it and – fifty yards down the road – another for 'BOYS'. Just inside the doors, there was a massive piece of scripture on the wall. Although children of all denominations were being brought in, there was a powerful Church of Ireland ethos in the orphanage. From the first day of arriving there, it was drummed into you that although you may have been a minority in the Dublin of the mid-sixties, you were a pretty superior minority being brought up in the Protestant tradition.

The board of trustees was made up of stockbrokers, solicitors, that type of professional person. Even the deputy governor of the Central Bank lent his name to the charity.

The Smyly Trust Homes orphanages did not have a policy of

reintegrating families. In fact, they discouraged contact. Some felt that this might have been because they were funded – per head – by the Health Board. Others just took is as a firm belief that they could do without any outside interference in their mission to polish up these children they had, effectively, taken off the streets.

Whatever the truth, my first day there was just about the most traumatic of my life.

I had felt safe and loved under Mrs Donnelly's roof in Whitehall. She was a warm, jolly woman who treated us all as her own. And, of course, I had the extra protection of Denis. For the first five years of my life, I firmly believed that Denis was my brother. He was maybe seven years older than me and undeniably Caucasian.

But a child of three or four doesn't tend to make distinctions on skin colour.

All I understood about Denis was that he'd fight my corner at the first sign of trouble. I had a way of irritating the bigger kids by joining in the games of street football long before I could kick a ball properly. I kept getting in the way, like an excited terrier under busy feet.

Denis would round on anyone who took umbrage. He was my one-man security team, my first role model in a way – a tough kid quite happy to clip someone around the ear if they decided to pick on the little black boy.

Where he is today, I have no idea. The last I heard, his life had taken a bit of a turn for the worse. I did go back to meet Mrs Donnelly many years later – when I was playing with Manchester United – and we had a lovely reunion.

It turned out that her house was only a couple of hundred yards up the road from where my old St Patrick's Athletic teammate, Joey Malone, lived. He had bumped into her a few times and then rang me one day to say, 'She'd love to see you again Paul ...' I was so glad I got to be reunited with her because she was, effectively, my mother for the first five years of my life. I knew I had a real mother somewhere else in Dublin. Betty wasn't allowed to visit but I knew that she existed out there.

You might imagine that this had a traumatic impact on me. It didn't. If anything, I felt blessed to have two mothers when most kids had one. Mrs Donnelly died many years later and I was so relieved I had taken up Joey's suggestion of paying her a visit.

Amazing though it seems in hindsight, I don't remember being that panicked when the time came for me to leave Mrs Donnelly's. Maybe it's because of the hidden bond a child has with its natural mother. I remember a priest being present and a row of people on one side of the room. I remember a lot of people crying. I'm sure I was crying too, but it was as if I knew instinctively that the woman coming to collect me felt something deep towards me.

What immediately followed though, blew a great, gaping hole in my little world.

I thought I was going to live with my mother for good. Those first days out of Mrs Donnelly's were perfect. Once, Mam brought a little kid roughly the same age as me over to visit. His name was Ernest Dureke, and Mam, me, Ernest and a woman I presumed to be Ernest's mum went out for chips. It was a real treat and, I imagined, a signal of the life ahead of me.

But I do vividly recall the man in my mother's life at the time. He was black and I didn't like him. He cooked African food, this kind of potato mix that you dipped in different sauces. I thought the food was absolutely disgusting. He also insisted on cutting my hair – thick Afro at the time – into a style that irritated me.

There was, though, one redeeming moment. He bought me a football and we went up to the Phoenix Park where I showed off what I imagined to be exotic skills learnt on the streets of Whitehall.

To me, my days in care were now over. Betty had come to find me. We were clearly mother and son. And, if I wasn't quite warming to the man in her life, I did feel a genuine liberation at being part of a relatively conventional family structure at last. In other words, I felt 'normal'.

Then, one Sunday, they told me that we were going to visit Ernest. I was delighted. I remember feeling quite excited on the drive to Dun Laoghaire. There were sweets and crisps in the car. I could see little snatches of the sea as we swept out towards York Road. I felt the sun would stay shining in my world for ever.

To begin with, there was no reason for suspicion. Though the building frightened me a little in the way of an old, unfriendly schoolhouse, Ernest was there to meet me. So I wandered around from room to room, only vaguely inquisitive of the kids' faces staring coldly back at me.

I remember the point of separation vividly. We were in a room on the top floor when some kind of sixth sense overtook me. I turned to say something to my mother and found myself talking to an empty space. Something exploded inside me. I knew, instinctively, what had happened. I panicked.

There was a bath in the room and I lashed out at this other kid, knocking him into the bath. I screamed and flailed and cried out for my mother. I knew, though, I was crying into a void. She was gone again.

My next memory is of sitting on a girl's knee in that room as she tried to cuddle and reassure me. By now, I had cried myself weary. I had no more anger left within me to express. I was just sullen and empty and more than a little terrified.

I'm sure my mother thought it was done in the best way possible but I've lived with the memory since. In a sense, it haunts me. I sometimes think that that one day instilled an anger in me that has never convincingly dissipated.

Betty left it a while before she came to visit. I suppose she wanted me to settle in, to find a routine. And I came to love her visits. All the kids did. She would arrive with bundles of sweets, fizz bags and penny bars, the bigger girls taking them to the tuck shop, from where we could reclaim them later on. As much as possible, I would devour what I could before the sweets would be taken off for 'safe keeping', because often those sweets would never be seen again.

Women dominated the Bird's Nest. It was a strange, regimented place. Routine became gospel. Individualism was discouraged.

Every morning at 7.30, we rose and stood beside our beds for inspection. We didn't wear pyjamas, just these awful nightshirts with leather buttons covered in some odd material. That morning inspection became a harrowing personal ordeal. I was a bed-wetter, you see. I wet my bed until I was nearly sixteen.

The punishment for staining the sheets was vicious. You had to hold up your nightshirt, prostrate yourself over the bed and get lashed across the bare arse by a big, wooden brush. There was no such thing as extenuating circumstance. If you wet the bed, you were beaten.

Sometimes people wouldn't prostrate themselves, taking a chance that their bed wouldn't be checked. Given there were maybe seventy boys and forty girls in the house, it was worth a try. But, if you gambled and got caught out, the beating would be twice as brutal.

My own recollection is that I was beaten just about every morning. The other boys made fun of my predicament. There'd be jokes in the schoolyard that I had wet the bed again. When they'd see me, they'd shout, 'Piss the bed, piss the bed . . .' I'd fly off the handle when they did that, routinely getting into fights over an argument I couldn't win.

The evidence was there every single morning. It glowed, red raw in welts across my backside.

I tried everything to solve it. I would try staying awake for as long as I could. I would try not drinking anything after six p.m. Often, this left me absolutely gasping with thirst through the night, and in desperation I'd drink water from the toilet on the landing, scooping it as it flushed down, believing this to be hygienic.

Some nights I'd try to dry the sheets myself, creeping along the dormitory and hanging the sheet from a window. There was also an electric heater with a pull switch, but I was afraid to hang the sheet across it, for fear I might start a fire. Other times I'd try swapping my sheet with another bed while someone was actually sleeping in it. Little ever worked, though. Always, it seemed, I'd wake to that horrible wetness, a voice in my head wondering, 'Why is this happening to me?'

When your bed was wet, the same ritual always followed: strip the bed down, stand the mattress on its side. There was almost an element of putting the bed-wetters on public show. You were disgraced by the image. Then you brought your sheets to the laundry room, collected a clean supply, marched back up to the dormitory and made up the bed again.

The element of disgrace led, inevitably, to bullying from bigger boys. Some staff were sympathetic but, by and large, there seemed an unspoken belief that bed-wetting was caused by laziness. And that maybe the attendant bullying might discourage you from 're-offending'.

Even some of the bed-wetting beatings from staff were accompanied by little, racist comments. 'Dirty little nigger boy', that type of thing. The implicit message was that I could stop this if I wanted. That I was, essentially, misbehaving.

There was no internal toilet in the dormitories. We slept on metal beds, placed end to end, with thin mattresses, a pillow, a sheet and this old-fashioned, brown, woollen blanket. The dormitories were graded on the basis of age: babies, middle infants, juniors and so on.

You also had a senior kid matched up with a junior, to take you on long walks, and thereby tire you out. This was meant to nurture a kind of friendship between the two, but it often developed into a mildly abusive relationship, the bigger child bullying the smaller one.

In some respects, I became a bully myself. The orphanage wasn't brutal maybe, but it was hard. It was dog eat dog. A pack mentality prevailed. If you didn't stand up for yourself, you'd be devoured. So I pretty much attached myself to the tougher kids. One of them, Klaas Lee, I especially looked up to.

Klaas was also black, and a little nerveless. He just waded through the world, challenging anyone who cared to try and stop him. I looked up to him because he was manipulative and very, very cool. A lot of the other kids were in awe of Klaas. He had a sharp tongue, was a tough little fighter and almost wore his colour as a badge of defiance. There were maybe twenty to twenty-five boys in each dormitory, with different bedtime slots, depending on the age group in that dormitory. The youngest kids would go to bed about 5.30. I don't think anyone was still up later than eight. We were like a closed order, existing in this mysterious world behind big, high walls. Walls that few outsiders ever got to peer behind.

We had no garden, just the yard. A plain vista of tarmacadam and concrete. The yard was enclosed by three monstrously high walls and the orphanage itself. We didn't have a blade of grass. We didn't have a tree. As far as you could look up, there were just these walls stretching towards the sky. Escape was impossible.

If a fight went off in the yard, there was nowhere to hide. The only thing to do was run. And, if you weren't a good runner . . . It was, for want of a better description, like a juvenile prison. There was a television set, locked into a cabinet so that you couldn't change stations. We had access to RTE and HTV (Harlech), but little else.

The punishment for getting into fights would be a few lashes of a belt, administered either across the arse or the back of your legs in an office opposite the main dining room downstairs.

There were always chores to be done. It could be emptying the piss bucket in the morning (a bucket, sadly, I rarely contributed to). That bucket would have to be brought down and emptied in a wash house across the yard.

Generally, you were made to feel odd and unloved. There was a routine comment made in moments of temper that you were 'Only here because nobody else wants you'.

We were a uniform to school. Brown jumper, tan, check trousers, blue blazers with 'BN' on the lapel. We were going to Monkstown Primary, a school that didn't have a uniform, so we stood out when that was exactly what we didn't want to do. In summer, we wore yellow and white check shirts, like something cut out of a table-cloth. We wore green jumpers and shorts. We wore sandals.

There was regular hair-combing for lice which, for someone with an Afro, would be routinely painful. There was also a regular dosage of milk of magnesia given out, in the apparent belief that it offered some kind of magical protection from illness.

At school, the other kids had lunch; we just brought jam sand-wiches from the orphanage. We kicked a ball while they ate. We were not individuals. That was the inherent message. It's not that we were immune to mischief. Sometimes we'd empty the piss bucket out the window. A few lads would keep guard on the top of the stairs. You could see right down through the timber rails at every single floor, so it was easy to tell if the coast was clear.

Other nights, the more timid kids kept guard while those of us inclined to be unruly hammered each other with pillows. A burst pillow was virtually a recipe for a tribunal. There'd be hell to pay.

I remember one night, someone swung from a curtain rail and it came crashing down. I can still see it to this day. A primitive thing with big, clumsy hooks. No one owned up to breaking it, so everyone took the rap with some kind of communal punish-ment. In matters of civil disobedience, there was always an inherent fear there. People were being pitched against each other.

You tended to get worn down. There was this state of constant anxiety. High alertness, if you like. We were constantly being told we would be moved to other institutions. People were violated and abused mentally, sometimes physically. In later years, even evidence of some sexual abuse came to the surface.

I made some really good friends in the Bird's Nest, but it took me a long time. In many ways, I was too full of anger and suspicion. Fist fights were regular. Bullies are invariably cowards too but, in a system like that, most kids acquired a distinct toughness. It became the done thing that you bullied if you were able.

I settled relatively comfortably into that mindset. Even walking to school, if you didn't like someone, you'd trip them up. You'd make them cry. Looking back, I feel a little sickened at how I picked on some kids. I knew myself that it wasn't nice when someone bigger than you gave you a kick up the arse or a dead arm without the slightest provocation.

You had to stand up for yourself. Sometimes that drew you into an uneven fight and you ended up taking a hiding. That was the way of the world in there. Eat or be eaten.

Some of the girls were even harder than the boys. They'd take no shit. I remember especially this girl called Lily. She was a hard, hard girl. Once she beat up a guy who had been fighting me. She made mincemeat of him with a succession of accurate punches that wouldn't have been out of place in an Olympic boxing ring.

There was another guy called John whose younger brother, Nigel, I bullied. So John bullied me. That was how the food chain worked.

Through all of this, football was the one thing that gave me confidence. Even at that young age, it brought out something in me. It overrode the awful insecurity, the low self-esteem. I mean I could be boisterous in class as part of the group but, individually, I had no confidence. I could never speak up when asked a question. Football, alone, gave me the opportunity for expression. It was the one thing that gave me wings.

Apart from Betty's visits – which weren't yet all that regular – there were no sweets, no affection, no outside contact. Our only toys were a batch of used tyres in the yard, supplied by a nearby garage, Archers. We would roll the tyres or beat them with sticks for entertainment.

Christmas was different. At Christmas, we would pick our way through a bag of second-hand toys delivered to the orphanage as an act of charity. On Christmas morning, luxury of luxuries, we'd even get an egg with our toast. By and large, though, our childhoods were stark and eternally anxious.

School would finish at two and we'd march back up in pairs, holding hands, put our uniforms away, place our shoes in bags and hang them on hooks by the beds. We'd play with the tyres for maybe an hour, then be locked into the 'study room' from three to five to do our homework. No one could leave their table for those two hours. If caught talking, you might not get fed that evening.

Then teatime arrived and you'd march into the dining room and stand behind your chair. Anyone who sat down before being told got clouted across the head. There'd be a scripture reading and then one of the kids would be asked to say grace.

'Thank you God that the world is so sweet; thank you for the food we eat; thank you for the birds that sing, thank you Lord for everything.'

The food was never good. Maybe a sausage on a slice of bread, the bread always smeared with margarine. Perhaps a cup of cocoa, the skin thick across the top. We were in a state of perpetual hunger. There was no picking, no choosing. You ate what you were given. It was never enough. You were thankful.

The meat invariably had a lot of gristle. I have a distinct memory of trying to hide it in my mouth because you had to eat what was put on your plate. Sometimes the meat would be unchewable, so you'd hold it in the back of your mouth while eating pudding, a bit like someone trying to conceal drugs at a security check.

Only when you left the dining room could you spit it out discreetly.

If, through disciplining, you missed tea, the hunger would just consume you. Whenever the opportunity arose to sneak into the kitchen, I would take it and try to make myself a sandwich of sugar and dripping. Sometimes one of the kinder members of staff might give you something extra. Food was always in the subconscious.

Of the meals, breakfast was the one I hated most. Always porridge. Always this strange, grey gruel filled with mysterious lumps. Just the texture of it would have me retching. To this day, I can't even look at porridge without feeling nauseous.

For me, though, the strangest thing was my name. I was now Paul Nwobilo (pronounced Wobilo, ignore the N). The name meant nothing to me. But, when my mother called to see me, that was the name reverberating off the wooden floors and up through the open landings.

'Paul Nooooobilooo, your mother's here to see you.'

There's a pretty blunt message printed on the application form for getting me into the Smyly Trust Homes on 17 September 1965. It reads: 'The child cannot live with his mother, her people don't want him and his father is in a flat and is at present resident in a hospital. There is no one to care for him. It is both parents' wish that he is brought up Protestant as his father and his people are Protestant and he will eventually return to Nigeria, taking the boy.'

The application form also suggested that my parents intended to marry.

I knew nothing at the time of Okune, my sister. In time, Betty would start bringing her on visits to the orphanage and I found this extremely difficult. On the one hand, I was slightly embarrassed by Okune's physical disability. At that age, I suppose a kid just doesn't want to be associated with any kind of abnormality.

On the other hand, I think Okune's visits stirred a resentment within me that my sister could live at home but I had to stay in an orphanage. The question 'Why me?' kept rolling through my head.

It's a little odd, in hindsight, to see 'Paul Nwobilo' as the name on all my school reports from that period. Those reports reflect a general decline in my academic performance and behaviour.

In December 1965, my senior-infants report observed: 'Paul is making very good progress and is most attentive and polite in class.'

By June 1966, the observation ran: 'Paul could do much better if he tried. Written work is quite good.'

December 1967: 'Spelling weak and needs attention.'

December 1968: 'Capable of doing much better work.'

June 1969: 'He is intelligent, but lazy and needs to work harder.'

December 1969: 'Paul is still weak in all subjects except arithmetic.'

June 1970: 'Inclined to inconsistency occasionally; on the whole a good boy.'

December 1970: 'Capable of better results.'

The more streetwise I became, the less inclined I was to co-operate. I remember a particular day when I had to polish a wooden floor upstairs with one of my closest friends, Michael McCrossan. Michael and I were thick as thieves. I think we shared the same, mischievous streak, a streak that sometimes threatened to get us flattened by bigger kids.

This time, though, pure innocence got us in trouble. There was a tub of Vaseline beside the floor polish and we discovered that the Vaseline brought up a fantastic shine on the floor. So Michael and I piled on the Vaseline, not realising that we were turning the floor into a skating rink. It was absolutely lethal.

Soon after, another good friend, Victor Boyhan, came charging into the room, lost his footing and went crashing to the floor, breaking his leg in the process. Despite this, Victor remains a good friend to this day, and we laugh about the incident now. He is a successful politician, a TD representing the Progressive Democrats in Dun Laoghaire.

In fact, he became one of the most outspoken voices in ensuring that Smyly Trust Homes would be covered under the State Redress Scheme, investigating the abuse of children.

Victor grew up with me right through the system – through the Bird's Nest, Glen Silva and – eventually – Racefield. He actually had brothers in the orphanages too, though for a long time he didn't even know they were his brothers.

I don't mean to depict our lives in bleaker terms than is justified. There were kind people. Some of the women working in the Bird's Nest – mostly former residents themselves – were lovely. It was the system that abused us. Not the individuals.

We grew to crave the presence of people from outside. Sometimes, when we were a little older, a Miss Rafter would come in the evenings from the Irish Church Missions. We'd have scripture readings and talk about God, Moses or whoever. That may sound boring in the context of a normal childhood, but to us it was enjoyable. It broke the cycle.

Yet it felt as if there was an inherent threat hanging over us all the time. Once a year, we were brought into another Smyly orphanage on Grand Canal Street. There were older boys there, harder types. The house was an old Odlums Mills wheat bakery building like something out of Victorian London. We were terrified of the place, and the people.

The message was that this could become our next home when, at the age of eleven, we had to leave the Bird's Nest. The prospect of that was suffocating. This place belonged to another world. We were mannerly and, maybe, a little withdrawn compared to these other boys. We were timid by their standards.

Those visits followed a bizarre ritual of always watching the same film in which Ingrid Bergman is trying to lead all these Chinese children to safety.

I have since identified the film as an innocuous production called *The Inn of the Sixth Happiness*, based on a true story in which Bergman plays a British maid who became a missionary in China during the years leading up to World War Two. The Japanese are beginning to invade China and, as the town of Yeng Chang comes under attack, she finds herself leading almost a hundred orphans to safety across the countryside.

Eventually they reach safety, marching into town, singing 'This old man . . .' We came to know every single syllable of that film.

Saturday was our favourite day. We were given a half-hour lie-in before having breakfast (porridge or toast, tea or cocoa) and locked out into the yard until the bell for dinner rang at 12.30. Some Saturdays, 'nice people' would come to visit.

This was, hindsight would reveal, a bit of a game of Russian roulette. The 'nice people' essentially came to select children they would like to take out on weekend breaks or – in some instances – summer holidays. We'd be spanking clean for their visits, always dressing in our best clothes and lining up across the yard in readiness for inspection.

We'd be told the people coming might be looking to adopt a child even though, back then, you couldn't adopt beyond the age of seven. There was a sense of excitement, of being on trial. A lot of the kids wouldn't have known their individual circumstance in that the natural parents, though often completely absent from their lives, had to give legal consent for adoption.

Most of the people who came were genuine and caring in their motives. They simply wanted to give us poor orphans a day at the seaside maybe or, on occasion, a decent summer holiday. So, they would sign a form, taking responsibility for our welfare, outlining the time they would return us safe and sound to the orphanage door.

I was lucky enough to come in contact with Sam and Phyllis Morton from Clontarf. They were a lovely couple who had no children of their own. Sam was a real outdoors person, heavily involved in the Scout movement and a member of the St John's Ambulance Brigade. The Mortons would regularly take myself and another friend, John Bateman, off camping for weekends. I also fondly remember summer holidays spent with them in chalets near Newry.

There was always a sense of real adventure on those breaks. Sam ensured we were involved in everything, putting up the tents, fetching water, setting the campfire. Some of the happiest memories of my childhood come from days spent with the Mortons.

Another family I have only fond memories of was the Richardsons from Blackrock. As a teenager, I spent one Christmas with them along with another orphan, another black kid called Danny McGuire. It was a revelation to me to see the dynamic of a proper family at work.

They had a hardware store in the village and we were encouraged to help out, lifting bales of peat briquettes out to cars, that sort of thing. We loved it. Their children just accepted us as part of the extended family and, that Christmas, every single one of them presented Danny and me with some kind of present. Better still, all the kids were into sport so we seemed to play football from one end of a day to the other. Danny and I were in our element.

Some kids, sadly, were less fortunate. Stories emerged many years later of how a few were abused. It was a strange environment. I mean there was a constant turnover of kids. You would suddenly realise that someone was gone. It might draw a fleeting comment. Then you moved on.

This may sound a contradiction but, over time, we came to feel safe inside those walls. I mean there was terrible cruelty. Not simply physical, but mental. You were constantly being put down, kept in your place as they saw it. You were made to feel small.

But, after a time, you almost find comfort in that. You become institutionalised. You don't want to leave.

We used to go out for walks, holding hands, all wearing the same coats, same scarves, same gloves. One long line of us, girls and boys, walking around Dun Laoghaire. Everyone knew we were the orphans. You could sense them looking.

It almost gave you the feeling of being a little star. You could all but hear the people go 'Aaaah . . .' There was a guy with a little sweet shop down by the train station. He'd see us coming and be out to meet us with a bag of sweets. Everyone got something. A toffee, piece of liquorice, gobstopper, whatever.

You could sense people's sympathy. A 'poor little things' kind of vibe. And that pity made us feel special, in an odd way. At that moment, seeing that man coming out with his bag of sweets, we thought we were almost a cut above other kids.

You know it's actually the same kind of feeling I used to get later in life, stepping off a team bus, everybody staring. This curiosity that attaches itself to people considered different. To celebrities. I'd be a liar if I said I didn't like it.

For most of my life, I wanted nothing more than to be ordinary, just one of the crowd. But I suppose those little walks around Dun Laoghaire nurtured a private vanity. Paul Nwobilo, the little star.

Then my name and residence changed again.

5

GLEN SILVA

The threat of Grand Canal Street hung over me until my last days in the Bird's Nest.

The alternative destination was Glen Silva, a lovely, red-bricked house, maybe a mile away in Monkstown. It was like waiting to be told whether you were headed for a palace or penitentiary. When the moment came, there was no grand announcement, no preparation.

One morning towards the end of June 1971, I was just about to walk down to my last day of primary school when I was handed a box tied with a string (containing all my worldly possessions) and told to present myself, that evening, at the door of Glen Silva. It was like winning the lottery. There would be maybe three of us moving at the same time, so we wouldn't even be alone.

It was in Glen Silva that I eventually ceased to be known as Paul Nwobilo. In fact, from day one, I acquired the somewhat starker identity of 'number three'. That sounds more sinister than it was. Everyone had a number which was stitched to your clothes, towel and washbag, and scribbled in marker on your possessions. It was their way of keeping order.

You used the cubbyhole bearing your number, hung your shirts on the appropriate hook, slept in the appropriate bed. Numbers were called out for different duty rosters and that's what you fell in with. 'Number three, toilets.' And toilets it would be.

The house was big and stately, sitting on maybe three acres in the heart of upmarket Monkstown. The dormitories were smaller than in the Bird's Nest, with maybe eight boys in each, some rooms less. There were no girls. The Master of the house, Mr Croxon, lived in with his wife, effectively as house parents.

The day you were brought in, it almost felt as if they were de-licing you. You were unclean and had to be bathed. You got a bar of carbolic soap and virtually had to wear it out before you got a fresh one. You got one pair of shoes a year and had to make do with them.

It was a strict regime, with everyone having jobs to do, be it brushing the floor, washing up, helping with the laundry. It worked well as a kind of co-operative.

There were two gardens at the side of the house in pretty bad decay and, over time, we levelled them both, turning the combined stretch into a football pitch. After the suffocating concrete of the Bird's Nest, to have grass was a revelation. This would be where I'd start living the dream. But it took time and, maybe, a little humility for me to find my feet in Glen Silva.

To begin with, I withdrew into myself. And with good reason. Having seen myself as a top dog (and bully) in the Bird's Nest, I was now bottom of the rung again. And I had arrived with a few bills to pay. Some of the kids I had pushed around in my previous abode now had older brothers sitting in wait for the new arrival. My reputation had travelled before me and it exposed me to some pretty painful retribution.

One or two bigger lads gave me an awful time. They were nasty pieces of work who had it in for me. No question, I paid for some previous sins. During my first few months in Glen Silva, I took a number of serious beatings. I became expert at avoiding certain people.

The early weeks amounted to a kind of softening-up process that just had to be endured. On one occasion, I remember climbing out onto an upstairs window ledge and threatening to jump if one particular individual didn't leave me alone.

Bed-wetting was still a major problem for me too. In Glen Silva, there would be no physical chastisement for it, but there was still this sense of putting you on parade for the 'crime'. I remember, once, my mattress being thrown out the window. You were expected to wash the sheets yourself, then hang them out to dry.

The food was better, though. For a start, the porridge was edible. We even had the occasional option of cornflakes. Dinner would be meat and vegetables. Tea might be sausages with beans. Sometimes, we were even treated to apple tart for afters. On special occasions like birthdays, a cake or barn brack arrived onto the tea table. Mrs Rice ran the kitchen and she was a lovely woman, always trying to look after us.

To miss a meal through disciplining was devastating, and hard though I tried to avoid that fate, it now happened to me routinely. Often, I felt I was being reported for the most minor of mis-demeanors. I was being picked on.

There was a kind of hierarchy at play and you had to work your way up the ladder. That took time. There was also another, even more worrying, thread to my change of circumstance. It was called secondary school.

Again we were only too aware of the possibilities. The jackpot would be Newpark Comprehensive. The short straw? Sallynoggin Vocational School. The 'Noggin' as we called it. This time, our luck was out.

The Noggin was notoriously hard. Victor Boyhan left after a year because he just couldn't hack it. We were seen as posh kids you see. We came to school from Monkstown on bicycles. We spoke differently. We were Church of Ireland and that made us very different.

Every Monday morning, we'd sit in the assembly hall for the usual pep talk about behaviour for the upcoming week. Then the Protestant people, or 'Smyly People' as we were known, would have to leave as the local priest arrived to say a Catholic prayer.

That meant we stood up in front of everyone and slipped out for our own Protestant tuition, usually from the rector of Glenageary. We'd be mortified, the other kids sneering and smirking at our discomfort. If we were hoping to be inconspicuous, Monday mornings effectively blew our cover.

Away from the schoolyard, there was a lot of intimidation, a lot of bullying.

Sallynoggin in the seventies was one of the biggest social housing schemes on the southside of Dublin. The people were tough. They all belonged to the same social strata, wrestled with the same problems. Most of us Smyly boys were frightened out of our wits going there. We felt that we were sitting ducks.

Klaas had gone the year before me, but it didn't soften my own landing. From day one, my colour made me a target. I got it from all angles. 'Nigger, you fucking nigger . . .'

For me, it felt like an enormous backward step. I hated it. I felt I had to redefine everything again. I had to act hard, almost to confront people physically. I wanted these lads to know they couldn't take liberties with me. It wasn't unknown for them to pull some of us off our bicycles and my attitude was that, if it happened to me, they wouldn't do it a second time.

All of this happened outside the school gate. The principal was a lovely man. He couldn't have known what we were being subjected to. We never said anything. You never did.

Victor Boyhan: 'As a group, we were instinctively very protective of each other. Whatever we might say about each other, we would stick together. Paul was very much one of our front men. He started there the year before me. He could look after himself.

'I remember one day we took this fella down a lane – now I would be very meek and mild, maybe a bit of a mouth – but we kicked this fella into pulp.

'He had attacked one of our lads, Jackie. A very delicate little chap. Stuck nails in the tyres of his bicycle. So we took our revenge. That was the pack. We were closer than family. Now we would kill each other back in the house. But, by God, no outsider was going to kill us. Instinctively, we were very loyal to one another.

'We were basically a pack of hounds. You didn't divide us.'

There was a certain stigma attached to us. We carried a lot of baggage, a lot of guilt. As much as possible, we wouldn't walk around together because we didn't want to be identified as 'the orphans'. Going home from Sallynoggin, it became a routine to get off the bus one stop early so it wouldn't be obvious we were going to Glen Silva. It was a bit of a contradiction in that we craved individuality, yet – deep down – clung to the collective.

I wasn't a conversationalist. I didn't comfortably engage in any dialogue. I hated being asked a question in class. I was an outsider, nursing a siege mentality. I played the tough guy, almost challenging someone to confront me. But then something pulled me into the mix.

At break time, they'd get this tennis ball out in the yard and play soccer. It was like a bolt of lightning going off in my head. I remember thinking, 'That's your way in . . .' I could play soccer. I could stand my ground against anyone in that yard and not feel remotely vulnerable.

Within a few days, the change was unbelievable. I was no longer 'Nigger', I was Paul. It was the old cliché about football being the international language. Suddenly, I was accepted. An ability to play amounted to a badge of respect.

The soccer games didn't make me like the Noggin any better, but they made it bearable. They broke down barriers. Maybe for the first time, I had friends who weren't fellow orphans. There might be fifty lads playing that match at break time, killing each other. They were real rough and ready games. Survival of the fittest.

It was through them that I got to know 'Gramps', real name Kiernan Forsyth, John Young, Colin 'Gilly' Bartley, Marti Finn and – by extension – Kevin 'Keano' Keenan, who couldn't actually kick a ball out of his way, but became one of the clan.

Once we got the pitch built, they started coming up to Glen Silva after school. There was a pavilion around the side of the house, in which we played table tennis. As non-residents, the lads weren't allowed in the house itself, but they became regulars for the games.

There was a group of us that started to barrel around together, climb a few walls, rob a few orchards, the usual stuff kids do.

Most of the lads played for a junior team, Pearse Rovers, in the Dublin and District Schoolboys League. They'd come to school every Monday morning with stories of their weekend games against the likes of Cherry Orchard, Lourdes Celtic, Crumlin United or despised local rivals, St Josephs. The big thing was to buy Tuesday's *Evening Herald* to find out who they'd be playing at the weekend.

'Joeys' were the dominant force. A lot of their players at the time – Anto Whelan, Chippy Devlin, Mick Shelly – went on to have decent careers in the League of Ireland. Anto would actually be on trial with Manchester United around the time that I arrived there.

Anto's father, Jimmy, was head man with Joey's. They were brilliantly organised and won everything. Pearse Rovers had a more off-the-cuff approach, by comparison. In many ways, that comparison lingers to this day.

Joeys have a fantastic clubhouse and, last I heard, run something like thirty-three schoolboy teams. Pearse still play out of what amounts to a little shack on the side of a pitch just down the road from the National Rehabilitation Centre on Rochestown Avenue. But Pearse became my team because Pearse was where my friends played.

On the evidence of the schoolyard games Gramps and the boys alerted their manager, Tommy Heffernan, to the fact that there was this young black kid in the Noggin who was pretty handy with a ball. Tommy came down to the yard one day and liked what he saw.

But, to begin with, he had trouble persuading Mr Croxon that it would be good for me to play competitive soccer. Actually, to begin with, Mr Croxon flatly refused. I think he saw it as potentially unsettling on the other boys in Glen Silva to see me sauntering off to training and to matches.

Yet, football was all that interested me now. I was fixated. I remember doing push-ups and sit-ups from about the age of twelve, convinced that a strong physique would improve my game. This was even before I got to play with Pearse Rovers.

Victor Boyhan: 'He'd be doing these push-ups in the dormitory. Lying underneath a bed, lifting it up and down. Just doing it off his own bat, without any tuition or coaching. Physically, Paul wasn't that big at the time. He was a stocky, little fella. But he was a kid on a mission.

'I would have to say that, even then, we were all conscious that he was something unique. You could just sense it in him. He was fiercely determined. I always reckoned he'd have made a wonderful businessman, because he loved money and was very good at sums. And there was this competitiveness in him.

'I mean he'd race you up to the shop and, literally, throw himself into that race. He'd keep changing the goalposts for himself. Setting the challenge higher and higher. Sometimes, he'd set up a game in this timber pavilion we used to call "the gym". We weren't supposed to play soccer in there, just table tennis.

'But Paul would set up these little five-a-sides. He'd put someone standing on these timber panels, keeping lookout. The teams would be loaded to make it harder for him. He was strategic in everything. And there always had to be a bet, even if it was only tuppence.

'So he'd organise these teams and he'd just want to do everything. He'd set up this little league. If someone decided maybe after twenty minutes that they'd had enough, he'd go ballistic. I remember my brother, Cyril, got this big, clumsy old tape recorder and used to do pretend commentaries – "McGrath on the ball", all this stuff.

'It was quite amazing. In some ways I think Paul used to imagine there were thousands of people watching him in those games.'

It was brilliant. Cyril Boyhan was actually a very funny, entertaining guy. He'd be doing these commentaries and I'd be trying to emulate anything I had seen the previous Saturday on TV, bicycle kicks whatever. Half the time, I'd be doing a commentary myself.

My path into competitive football was eventually smoothed by a man called Severin Kennedy. Severin would have an extraordinarily positive influence on my life. He was a member of the Glen Silva staff, still in his twenties and a young man who took a genuine interest in us as people rather than residents.

He came from the North, a teacher with the gift of listening. Severin was always probing, motivating, encouraging. He was unflappably positive. If someone showed the remotest interest in any subject, Severin was immediately looking to nurture that interest. Maybe for the first time in the system, we came across someone who saw the individual as paramount.

I suspect he read the danger signals of keeping kids in such a regimented environment, then effectively releasing them into the outside world the moment they become young adults. He made a huge difference to a lot of people in Smyly Trust Homes. I think maybe he sensed a need to dilute the overemphasis on academic achievement and work more towards developing us as rounded people. Just as well in my case too. Because, academically, I was losing ground.

Soccer was my world now, Chelsea my team. We had access to ITV and I watched them win the 1970 FA Cup replay against Leeds, feeling haplessly smitten with the glamour of it all. Robert Taggart, a fellow orphan, adored Chelsea and I followed suit.

Every day I stepped into the the Noggin yard or out on the Glen Silva pitch, I was some kind of amalgam of Osgood, Cooke, Webb and Co.

Severin recognised the obsession and encouraged Mr Croxon to let me play with Pearse. A compromise was eventually reached. I could play the games, but I wouldn't be allowed down to train with the club.

This was liberation for me. Now I had an outlet. Tommy Heffernan started me as a centre-forward and, at the time, I presumed that that would be my future in the game. We didn't go on to win very much at Pearse Rovers, though. Joey's mopped up just about every cup and league from under-12s to under-18s.

At one point, Jimmy Whelan tried to get me to make the move across, but it would have felt like a betrayal. I was playing football with my mates. That's all I wanted.

By now, I was seeing a lot more of Betty too. Despite persistent discouragement from Mr Croxon – who seemingly thought it unfair that one boy received regular visits from a parent while others virtually never got to see theirs – she was unperturbed. We were definitely building a relationship, but I was still a little unhinged by the presence of Okune on some visits.

It has to be said that we weren't the most attentive students in the Noggin. Over time, we acquired slightly rebellious routines. Every Wednesday afternoon, we were due four periods of Mechanical Drawing. This we took as an invitation to go 'on the hop'.

There might be five of us: Gramps, Gilly, Keano, John Young and me. We'd walk to Bray one day, maybe up Killiney Hill the next. Just messing around, dossing in amusement arcades, hanging around by the 'metals' (train tracks). Sometimes the lads would bring a golf club and wander down to Dun Laoghaire Golf Course, pick out a few holes at the top of the course (furthest from the clubhouse) and play them.

I'd tag along, but golf didn't interest me. If we saw anyone coming, we'd just scoot into the trees and wait for them to pass. It was normal kids' stuff really. Anything was better than Mechanical Drawing.

Gramps: 'I suppose it got to the stage where we were just never expected in that class. I had a good scam. I was really tiny. I had a growth deficiency so I had to get growth hormone injections, two of them every week for about three or four years. T'was a gift. If there were ever any questions asked, it was always a case of "Listen, I've to go for my injection."'

I suspect some teachers might have been relieved to see a few of us on the hop. I wasn't the most compliant of students. I wouldn't be openly disruptive, but I could certainly be surly and disinterested. During class, I would wander off into a private world, not a single word of the lesson registering.

This got me into trouble once. The teacher in question wasn't particularly popular and one of the lads threw something at the board while he was writing on it. It wasn't me. Hand on heart, I can say I was actually a million miles away in thought.

Anyway, this teacher walked up behind me and smacked me across the back of the head. I was absolutely furious. He had hit me for no reason, so I just jumped straight up and went for him, hell for leather. A few of the lads, rushing to my support, jumped on top of him too. There was absolute pandemonium and I think a few of us came close to being expelled.

A story started doing the rounds later that I began jabbing the teacher, whilst reciting Muhammad Ali's mantra of 'Floats like a butterfly, stings like a bee', but I can honestly say that that story was down to embellishment.

Given the effort (or lack of it) I was putting in, I suppose it was inevitable that my days in the Noggin would end with expulsion. Yet, I wasn't at odds with everyone. We had an English Literature teacher, Jon Douglas, who played hockey for Ireland. He was a real cool dude, maybe only about seven years older than his students and – from what I can remember – nobody messed in his class. He just had a way of keeping you interested.

One thing that really galled us in the Smyly contingent was a stipulation that, once a week, we had to stay back after school for religious instruction from the vicar. This was tantamount to punishment.

All I wanted to do was play football. Every evening, with company or without, I would spend hours out on the pitch in Glen Silva. People could probably see me from a distance, because the house was on a hill. I was a complete obsessive, all the time convinced that every minute spent practising was another step towards fame and fortune.

Yet, as ever, there was a big, black cloud beginning to loom on my horizon.

6

RACEFIELD

In September 1975, I was on the move again.

Smyly Trust Homes were opening a new residential unit for teenage boys within walking distance of Glen Silva. The home, to be known as Racefield House, offered a level of freedom virtually beyond our imaginations.

It was, essentially, an open house. A beautiful old Georgian, rectory-style building. Gramps and all my friends from 'the outside' were free to come and go as they pleased. There were no restrictions, no suffocating rules. I had my own room, which immediately became a joint shrine to Chelsea Football Club and Farrah Fawcett Majors.

We could cook our own food, we had our own TV room, even a snooker room. We could go to the cinema in town. There were no set bedtimes, no hint of any curfews. In time, I would even get my own dog, a lovely German Shepherd called 'Mac'. It was what they called a 'transitional house'. Traditionally, boys would leave the orphanage for army service, girls would end up housekeeping. Now a little enlightenment was kicking in.

On the surface, this was a cause for great celebration. But, deep down, I was apprehensive too.

This, I knew, was my last stop before the moment of truth arrived. After Racefield, I had nowhere left to go. I would be released into the 'real' world to fend for myself. This was, effectively, the beginning of the countdown to my eviction from the orphanage system. Flawed though that system was, it was the only world I knew. And I didn't want to leave.

Much was now changing in my existence. At some point, the young man known as Paul Nwobilo had ceased to exist and I returned to being known by the name on my birth certificate. Even more significantly, I got to meet the man I had been called after.

I had grown up with a pretty terrifying image of my grandfather, the fearsome Patrick P. McGrath. By now, Betty's visits to me were more frequent, and she would often come accompanied by my granny, a hilarious woman with a gift for storytelling. It seemed they were always recounting yet another tale of my grandad's notorious volatility. 'That man is driving me insane,' Betty would say, Granny nodding in agreement.

Then in December 1974 it was agreed that the time had finally come for me to spend a Christmas with my family. I remember feeling hugely apprehensive. And, yet, I was comforted by an odd logic too. At fifteen, I felt big enough and bold enough to fight my corner, no matter who the opponent. After all, what could he do to me? How bad could he be?

I'm not sure how or when Betty had broken the news of my existence, but that Christmas Patrick P. McGrath didn't prove quite the ogre I had imagined. The overwhelming memory I have of him is his booming voice. He didn't ask for things, he demanded them. He routinely found fault.

The dinner was never quite to his liking, something was always out of place in the house. He existed in a state of permanent vexation. Every day he'd go to the pub at the bottom of the road, and often needed to be helped home by friends that evening. If, in later years, I was looking for clues to the cause of my drinking problems, some of the answers were undoubtedly to be found back then in the life of Patrick P. McGrath.

There was a surreal dimension to that first Christmas with family. Bear in mind that, from the age of five, I had been reared in a staunchly Church of Ireland environment. Whatever Betty might have revealed about my circumstance, she could never have admitted to that at home.

So I had to play the dutiful Catholic. I was sleeping in a bed literally at the foot of my grandparents' bed, and in the evening had to be seen to kneel at the end of it and 'do the blessing'. Looking back, it's no wonder my religious beliefs ended up a little skewed.

It's not that this ritual particularly bothered me at the time. I would have gone through any charade just to ensure my grandfather's temper stayed under wraps. I even quite liked him in a way. He had such a grip on the atmosphere in the house, it was almost comical. Just the rustle of his newspaper tended to have people jumping to attention.

My mother bought me a really nice bike that Christmas and, in many ways, the visit served to demystify the image I had of home and the childhood I presumed I had been deprived of. My grandfather wasn't the monster I imagined, just an old man with a leaking temper and, I suppose, an overcompliant family.

I wasn't especially depressed returning to Glen Silva where, it seemed to me, the life I was now leading had more than a little to recommend it. It suited me to keep the visits 'home' sporadic.

Racefield, then, brought further liberation. Having my own room gave me a wonderful sense of independence. I was at an age where I was acquiring heroes. I loved Phil Lynott and Thin Lizzy, for example. The fact that he was originally from Crumlin was a factor. The fact that he was black and successful even more so.

My colour was always an issue in the subconscious. I latched onto black heroes, black teams. Even going back as far as 1970, seeing a predominantly black Brazilian team win the World Cup exhilarated me. I hooked onto the sheer style of heroes like Pele and Muhammad Ali.

In a sense, I suppose I was trying to build up my own self-esteem through their achievements. The better they were doing, the better I felt in myself.

Beyond the football, though, my application to work in the Noggin showed little sign of improvement. You see, at Racefield, I started to abuse my freedom. I 'mitched' from school all the time now. Academically, I was stuck in neutral. The report cards offered a kind of social commentary on the art of dossing. A selection from December 1975 reads:

English – Grade E. Extremely lazy pupil. Not working at all.
   Very unsatisfactory.
Mathematics – Grade E. Absent-minded and lazy.
Woodwork – Grade C. Not improving, giddy, time-waster.
Science – Grade F. Does very little work.

The following summer, I got five passes and three fails in an unin-spired Inter Cert. By now, Severin Kennedy had moved up to work in Racefield and he could see where I was headed. I was in constant trouble at the Noggin, suspended on a routine basis.

Severin contacted Newpark Comprehensive to see if they might accommodate me in Transition Year. But they had no places. So, reluctantly, Sallynoggin Tech accepted me back into Fifth Year and Severin set about trying to rehabilitate me.

He had his work cut out. I was now suiting myself. I was a free agent, mitching from school, following an independent timetable. There was a cleaning lady in Racefield who I would play cards with during the day. Study was out of the question. To some extent, I was keeping the outside world at arm's length.

But life was good.

Gramps: 'The lads in the orphanage had things that we didn't have. We used to be thinking "Jesus, these orphanages are great spots!" I mean we were never out of Racefield. They had a three-quarter size snooker table. They had table tennis. You could go in and have a cigarette.

'Sev [Severin Kennedy] would be there and it was very easy-going. There was a lot of freedom. We were always watching sport on the telly up there. Everything from tennis at Wimbledon to the show jumping from the RDS.

'It's only when you got older that you realised they didn't have what the rest of us just took for granted. I remember one particular day at school, in the woodwork shop, someone called this young fella from the orphanage a bastard. Just a throwaway line. "Go away you bastard!" And I remember this lad getting so upset.

'I couldn't understand it. Someone could have called me a bastard all day and it wouldn't have upset me. But it had a different meaning to him than it did to me. It was the first time I really thought about the difference.

'I had me Ma and Da, seven brothers, three sisters. I had a family to go home to. When I went into a room at night, I wasn't sitting there, wondering "Why am I here?" I look back now and think it must have been rough enough for Paul and the others, this feeling of not being wanted or whatever.

'And yet Paul was a little different to most of the others. He'd say to me, "I won't be around this weekend, I'm going over to see my mother." And I'm thinking "But I thought you were an orphan . . ."

'At the time, though, all I could see was the material things. The snooker, the table tennis. I mean we'd be out until all hours at night on bicycles, flying around Dalkey. My mother used to come out looking for me. We thought it was a grand oul spot.'

Gramps and I were on the hop a lot of the time now. There's a famous photograph taken of us strolling down O'Connell Street after one of our regular trips to the Ambassador cinema. This old man was well known for stepping out in front of people on the street, taking their photograph and handing them his card.

In this instance, I think Gramps and myself had just been to see *The Godfather*. 'Gilly' Bartley had recommended it to us as a brilliant film. But that would have been one of our more respectable choices. We were both into our movies but, being honest, we weren't particularly discerning or self-conscious about our choice of entertainment.

I do remember *The Exorcist* being out around that time too, but quite often Gramps and I would settle for some awful, soft-porn rubbish, *Night Nurse*, *Rosie Dixon*, that type of thing to wile away the afternoons. The cinema would be virtually empty. They'd be happy to take our money.

I used do a pretty decent Jimmy Stewart stutter at the time. And I had few equals as Henry Fonda in *The Grapes of Wrath*: 'Whenever there's a cop beatin' on a kid, I'll be there . . .' That'd be Gramps and me. The two of us cackling and sniggering in the back seats while some genuinely awful soft-porn movie crawled to a close.

Maybe it was inevitable that I'd never quite get around to doing my Leaving Cert. I had been expelled from the Noggin before the opportunity arose. There was no specific crime involved. I was a recidivist offender. There were incidents with a couple of teachers, but none of them – apart from the one already recounted – actually extended to physical assault.

In one, naively, I thought I was just having banter with this teacher but it turned out he didn't appreciate my humour.

Expulsion, though, didn't mean a complete break from the Noggin. I was, by now, one of the key players on the school soccer team and, though I wasn't actually allowed to step foot inside the school any longer, the teacher running the team decided I could still do a job for him.

Severin tried, in vain, to get me focusing on the future, but to me the only future was devilment.

With school no longer on the agenda, efforts began to find me a job. My schoolboy football career with Pearse Rovers had run its course too, and now, along with most of the guys – John Young, Gramps, Marti, Gilly – I moved to Dalkey United. In many ways, this move kept me safe.

It was at Dalkey that I would come under the influence of men like Frank Mullen, Johnny Dunne, Tommy Cullen and the legendary Manchester United scout, Billy Behan.

Billy was a lovely man, vice-chairman of the club, and his son, Terry, played on the team with us. Now this was a convenient arrangement for someone like me, determined to get noticed. I would switch between right-back and centre-back during that first season in Dalkey. The football was a lot more physical, a lot more competitive than I had been accustomed to with Pearse Rovers. But I relished that physicality.

My very first match for the club was actually against a German side, Wattenscheid, up in Hyde Road. Dalkey had built up a relationship with the Germans and the clubs tended to visit one another on alternate summers. I loved the idea of playing a German team. It felt as if I was now an international footballer.

Frank Mullen: 'I was standing beside Billy Behan at that game and Paul was absolutely brilliant. The match was only about ten or fifteen minutes on, but everyone realised they were just watching someone a class apart for his age. We knew virtually nothing about him, but he was awesome. It was breathtaking to look at him.

'And Billy said to me, "Look, whatever else happens, this kid is going to Old Trafford . . ."'

Gramps: 'From day one, Paul just ran the back four. He was that good. I mean a lot of the lads were decent players, but Paul was head and shoulders above everyone. He was the talk of the town straight away.

'Now he wasn't one for tricks. He wasn't one to juggle a ball on the back of his neck. But he never seemed to be stretching himself. I've always said that if Paul was marking a guy who was running at 10mph, Paul would run at 11mph. If the next guy was moving at 15mph, Paul would up it to 16mph. He always did enough to control the game. He could just step up a gear. Paul would play at the back with this older guy from Sallynoggin, Eddie Brien. Now Eddie was a little overweight, but he was a handy player. And tough.

'He'd play sweeper beside Paul. Eddie used to say if anyone got by Paul, he'd have to kick them. Because if someone was good enough to get by Paul, he knew he was in trouble.'

This was the summer of 1978. I remember it especially fondly for the nights we spent watching the World Cup finals in Argentina. The 'ticker tape' finals as I remember them. There might be maybe twenty of us piled into the TV room, watching the likes of Kempes, Ardiles and Luque win the tournament for their own people.

I specifically remember the night they played Peru, needing to win by four goals to progress. Brian Clough came on the TV and confidently predicted that they'd make it. They won by six. The banter afterwards:

'Something dodgy there . . .'

'Yeah, defo . . .'

'Nah, I think it was straight . . .'

'Did Peru look like they were trying to you?'

'Actually I thought they were . . .'

'Nah, Cloughie knew what was coming . . .'

Nothing was ever said to me about Billy Behan's interest at the time, but I knew who he was and the status he held in the game. I was now on a mission. Every time I played for Dalkey, I would check the sidelines for Terry's dad. Long term, I felt my life would resolve itself through football.

Short term? It was definitely time to panic.

Having had a premature end drawn to my schooling days, I was now faced with the challenge of fending for myself in the workplace. Worse, the time had come to slowly, initiate my departure from Racefield. Severin was especially sensitive to the latter. He knew how much I wanted to stay.

In April, I had got a job as a warehouseman in The Great Outdoors on Chatham Street. I was punctual and relatively industrious, but the job bored me. Within four months I decided to leave.

Again, Severin tried to pick up the pieces. He'd arrive every morning, stressing the need to be up and about, checking the papers for vacancies. A job was eventually found for me in Crumlin with the suggestion that I might go to live with my mother. I didn't want to. My friends were in Dalkey.

Through the football club, I got a job in November that allowed me stay put in the area. It was as a slater and tiler with Jimmy Hammond, whose family had been involved with Dalkey since the club's inception in 1953. Jimmy was a lovely man and the whole family would take me under their wing just as the chains tying me to Racefield began to snap.

Needless to say, I had no experience of roofing. But the Hammonds were good people, content to apprentice me gently into the job.

My relationship with Severin was certainly under strain now. A flat had been located for me on Northumberland Avenue. I remember it vividly. Number 28. Yellow door. The idea was that, to begin with, I would stay there on individual nights, just to become acclimatised. Maybe bring some clothes down. But I didn't want to know.

At this stage, Severin was effectively the Master of Racefield. He was treating me with kid gloves. We all feared leaving and he knew it. We were terrified of the transition. I had huge respect for him, but now I railed furiously against everything he said.

My abiding memory of that flat is the cold. And all I ever ate there was beans on toast. I hated it. I felt isolated and vulnerable there. I did have a flatmate but, to this day, I don't remember a solitary thing about him. Not even his name.

It was a very, very scary time for me.

Victor Boyhan: 'We just weren't prepared for life, you see. We had never been treated as anything other than boys. I remember one of the lads saying to me a few years later that he looked in the mirror one morning in the orphanage, saw whiskers on his face and had no idea what to do. He didn't know how to shave.

'As kids, we were just terribly insecure. So Paul wasn't ready to leave. None of us were.'

To be fair to Severin, he always encouraged contact. It was never a case that once you left Racefield, you would never be allowed return. On the contrary, the door was always open. And, gradually, I came to terms with the fact that I couldn't stay in care indefinitely. Sporadically, I'd stay overnight with the Hammonds. I also began flitting in and out of a flat on Mellifont Avenue in Dun Laoghaire.

I felt part of the family now with Dalkey United. By spring 1979, the return trip to Germany was on the horizon. Except for the first six weeks of my existence, I had never been outside the country before. The prospect of travelling on a plane absolutely thrilled me.

There were a few complications involved in organising my passport as my father was now, officially, 'unknown'. But those complications were overcome with the help of a local politician, David Andrews. So, at last, I was headed for Germany. And a week that would turn my life on its head.

7

THE CRASH

It started with Pernod and sherry.

Bottles of duty-free in the room I was sharing with John Young. 'Don't overdo it now Paul . . .' Don't overdo it? I was eighteen-years-old and on my first trip abroad. The warmth of the first swig got me interested. There was talk of heading for a disco. I needed something, anything, to subdue that voice in my head: '*Hey, don't bother trying to look cool. You know they're going to see through you, don't you?*'

I needed Dutch courage.

Most of the lads were older than me and infinitely more street-wise. They could see trouble in the way I was swallowing. They kept warning me about walking into the fresh air, about the kick I was facing. 'Don't overdo it Paul . . .'

I overdid it.

I had never drunk before, so this was quite a discovery. I felt something profound happen. 'Jesus, this is magnificent,' I thought. I sat there in the room experiencing this sense of calm flood through me. I began to feel invincible. I was in Germany about to check out the local Fräulein. Get them in boys!

Then it was time to leave the room and the warm sensation gave way to a tugging nausea. I remember losing it very quickly. The next day, the lads filled me in on my performance. 'Fucking hell, what were you like last night?'

It didn't stop me. I was hooked on that feeling of liberation now. I wanted more. Every night in Germany I drank. Every night, I got drunk. The drink helped me shed all feelings of self-consciousness. That voice in my head was silent. True, the mornings became a ritual of being told how much of 'a pain' I had been. But the nights? They were about feeling indestructible.

The lads in charge of the team never got to know, basically because my older teammates covered over the cracks. John and myself were still teenagers. Jimmy Pluck too. But the rest of the lads were grown men. They weren't going to be told what they could or couldn't do.

So, I was protected out there. And I discovered that, even with a few on board, I could still play decent football. A discovery, in hindsight, that I could probably have done without.

I remember playing well in Germany, scoring a couple of goals in one game. But I did take a knock. A bang on the head that – coupled with my alcohol consumption – left me feeling uncomfortably woozy.

I came home, played a game against Dunleary Celtic in Sallynoggin on the Wednesday, took another bang on the head that night, but – again – just put it down to experience.

One thing I did on arriving home was stop drinking. Why? I'm not so sure. Maybe deep down I could sense that alcohol would be a passport to trouble. Just something about the way it made me feel in Germany – both good and bad – sowed little seeds of anxiety.

I'm not sure exactly how long I was back from Germany when the crash came. But this is how I saw it.

It's around midnight and I am walking on Dun Laoghaire pier. Just walking and walking and walking. I can't get to the end. No matter how hard I walk, it's still the same distance away. I'm getting frustrated. I'm

*getting angry. Why the hell aren't I getting anywhere? There is no one about.
I turn around and mentally mark a spot. And I walk. Maybe for five
minutes. Then I turn and there it is. The same spot. Right beside me.
Something's happening and I don't like it. I go back to the flat. My flatmate's staring at me. He's seen a ghost. I'm talking at him in riddles, asking
him why all the furniture in our flat is so tiny, why it was made for a doll's
house. He's phoning Severin. I'm watching him do it. I'm floating above
him, flying. I'm a great bird, yet I'm in my flat. Trapped. There are people
talking now. 'C'mon Paul, you'll be fine . . .' Then I'm being eased into
the back of an ambulance. I'm strapped tight to a stretcher. I'm not a bird
anymore. I'm not anything.*

The next twelve months or so of my life, I can only recount
through the voices of others. For most of it, I was trapped in my
body. Physically I went into meltdown. Mentally, I became stuck in
neutral. I was taken to St Vincent's Hospital where I began a voyage
of unimaginable strangeness.

It seemed as if all light inside me had now dimmed. Was any of
it related to what had happened in Germany? The bang on the head?
The introduction to alcohol? The first, unequivocal break from the
orphanage system? I can't honestly say. Certainly, the trip to Germany
coincided with my final break from Racefield and that was a cause
of serious anxiety.

In St Vincent's, the medical staff formed an early opinion that I
was just rebelling.

I have garbled memories of bed sores, cold baths, people talking
at me. It was like an out-of-body experience. I was there for a month
and there would be recriminations over how I was treated.

Victor Boyhan: 'When I saw him in Vincent's, he was totally
naked. I was appalled that they would allow somebody to be
in the state he was in. There was a sheet over him. They told
us that he was incontinent. He didn't know me, definitely not.

He'd gone very thin and he was angry. If someone said to me that here was a guy who had come out of electric shock treatment, I'd nearly have believed it. The sweat was pouring out of him, his hair had been cut really tight.

'This was what you could best describe as just some sort of animal. I mean, this wasn't a case of being able to say, "Paul, cop onto yourself, this is Victor. Sit up there. What's wrong with you?" There wasn't that level of communication. It was as if he had just totally tripped it. There was no connectivity there.'

I was lost. Watching the world from a mysterious perch. Every sound muffled, every picture blurred. Cast adrift in a place where I couldn't be reached. Floating.

It felt like I was being badly treated but I couldn't articulate a complaint. My voice had left me. I was lying in one position for so long my knees actually stuck together. They had to be prised apart. I remember that moment vividly, having one knee pulled from the other. My legs are still scarred to this day.

I knew I was poorly, but that was the extent of my knowledge. I had no explanation for it. Something had broken inside me. They were giving me a lot of medication. I presume the cold baths were intended to stimulate me, to get some reaction, but they stimulated nothing. I was basically just shutting down, drifting further and further into myself. I was becoming a zombie.

The days passed and no one grew the wiser. I remember my mother talking to me. But I wouldn't verbalise anything. I wouldn't communicate. I was grunting occasionally. I was an animal.

A kind of consensus seemed to be arrived at by the medical staff that I was being willfully uncommunicative. I was being fed through a drip but, in my agitation, I kept tearing the tube from my arm. I ended up being restrained to the bed.

And, maybe, a degree of neglect set in. It seemed that I was left, largely, to fester in my own body fluids. The condition I ended up in would generate a fairly heavy traffic of communication between the Health Board and Derek Stewart, a solicitor working on behalf of Smyly Trust Homes.

I actually have copies of a number of those letters, reflecting Derek's manful efforts to have someone take responsibility for the decline in my condition while in St Vincent's. In the end, I think he just hit a brick wall.

Eventually, I was moved on to St Brendan's in Grangegorman, from there to the Vergemount Hospital in Clonskeagh and then St John of God's in Stillorgan. There was evidently a gradual improvement in my condition, and in time it was decided that the best place for me was my mother's house in Crumlin.

Betty McGrath: 'When the breakdown happened, I went straight to the hospital but they wouldn't let me go near him. The nurse wouldn't let me touch him. He was just lying on this stretcher. He didn't know anybody. Over time there, he'd wet the bed and they'd just leave him lying in it. My sister, Mary, and I would bring up sheets, pillows and bath towels. I'll never forget it as long as I live.

'When he eventually came home, he was fine for a while. I'd bring him to the Penny Farthing to dry the knives and forks. The girls were delighted. They used go mad because there were no fellas working there.'

There was no question of me playing football. But Johnny Dunne, the Dalkey secretary, used to call to the house and bring me to their matches. Just to have a cup of tea, mix with the lads. They kind of drip-fed me football again. 'Here, have a kick Paul . . .' 'Look, why not try ten minutes of training Paul . . .' 'Aaah, you haven't lost any of the old magic son . . .'

Slowly a certain normality returned to my life. And I resumed playing. I wasn't exactly fighting fit again, but I was on the mend – superficially, at least.

The relapse came absolutely without warning. By all accounts, my mother brought me breakfast in bed one morning and everything seemed fine. When she returned to the room maybe half an hour later, I was grinding the bacon and egg into my hair. Laughing insanely. Lost again.

This time, they brought me straight to St Brendan's.

From what I can gather, all my faculties were now in meltdown. At one point, there was even a suggestion that I might never walk again. In Brendan's, I was placed in a large room with just one bed in it. I think my mother was a little mortified to see me end up there. A lot of people probably were. The stigma of ending up in a mental hospital was a little too much for some to swallow.

Gramps: 'A few of us had gone to see him in Elm Park [St Vincent's], but we didn't realise just how serious it was. Then, when he went to Brendan's, the penny kind of dropped. We used to play Leinster Senior League games against Brendan's out in Grangegorman. Still do. You'd be playing out there and you'd see all these patients wandering around in their nightgowns. Now, suddenly, Paul was one of them.

'I remember the first time I saw him there, he was just lying on his side. There were sores on the side of his face. His eyes were all glazed. He looked awful. Like something out of *One Flew Over The Cuckoo's Nest*. That's what it reminded you of. It was a big movie around that time.

'Paul wouldn't even look at you, he wouldn't open his mouth. It was unbelievable. For us, Brendan's – being on the Northside – was an awkward place to get to. None of us had cars. So we'd have to get a bus into town and walk all the way up to Phibsboro, right up by Dalymount Park.

'John Young was driving a delivery truck at the time, so he

got in to see him more than the rest of us. He'd keep us up to speed on Paul's condition. When we did go up, we'd bring a ball. Eventually, we'd have him walking out in the grounds, out into this little landscaped garden. He'd be in slippers. We'd push the ball towards him and he'd kind of throw his leg at it. It was horrible. Scary.

'He'd be just like a zombie.'

I do have a memory of people talking to me. My ma. Okune. Aunt Mary. Frank Mullen. John Young. Gramps. Some of the boys from the orphanage. Victor. Mark Hadnett, who'd take me out for walks. I would recognise them. But I didn't seem to be able to speak to them. Although they came for months, I never talked. I thought I was communicating in a way, but it wasn't happening.

It was frightening and confusing. I kept wondering why they were throwing footballs at me. It was surreal. It was as if someone had me on a spinning board. They'd throw the ball, but I wouldn't move my hands. It either dropped into my open palms, or fell to the ground.

Even other patients were doing this, trying to stimulate me. That's how far I had fallen.

I do have little snapshots of happiness. There was one beautiful nurse working in St Brendan's who, deep down, I think I fell in love with. I remember one day, my mother saying to her proudly, 'Oh he's a footballer. He's going to play at Wembley some day.'

Daft as it seems, I remember wanting to confirm that view, to tell this girl that yes, as a matter of fact I would indeed be playing in an FA Cup final at my earliest convenience. At the time, I was barely able to stand up, let alone kick a ball.

I have another memory of my mother and the man she would eventually marry, Noel Lowth, coming up to visit. Now Noel was a lovely guy and a decent footballer himself who actually played with Shamrock Rovers. Much later, I would like nothing better than coming home from Manchester, popping up to his local and spending the whole night arguing with Noel. Let's just say he loved fencing with people.

But, on this occasion, Noel and Betty were doing what everyone else did at the time: trying to reunite me with a football. My mother was wearing sandals and kicking the ball as hard as she possibly could. I knew it was hurting her. I'm standing there, thinking 'She's kicking it the wrong way, it must be hurting her toes . . .'

But all of this was internal. I wasn't saying anything, just watching my poor mother put herself through agony in an effort to prise me from my shell.

It was a weird, weird time.

Ultimately, it took months of painstaking effort to rebuild me as a person. I was utterly oblivious to much of the effort, cocooned from reality by a mixture of heavy sedation and some strange power failure deep within. I have to give the people from Dalkey enormous credit – Frank, Johnny, Tommy Cullen. They were unrelenting. Most of them lived on the Southside, so Brendan's wasn't exactly a convenient port of call.

But they kept coming, kept trying to coax some reaction from me. You have to remember that we're talking about Dublin at the end of the seventies now. It wasn't an especially enlightened time for dealing with mental illness. The 'sick' were largely forgotten, kept out of general view and heavily sedated.

I could easily have been abandoned. But neither the staff in St Brendan's nor that tight circle of family or friends were inclined to take the easy option. They kept prodding.

Football had ceased to exist for me. This thing of having a ball kicked towards me became utterly futile. I wasn't interested. I would just blank the people. It felt as if I was staring out at them from inside someone else's body. Worse, I was settling again into that mindset of wanting to be institutionalised. St Brendan's felt safe. Having been removed from the orphanage system, I was back under someone else's control again. That was how I wanted it.

My nerves were gone. Football? For a time, I recoiled from the very idea of it. You see, to some degree, I had come to associate it with pressure. Not the pressure of playing, but the pressure of people speculating about me. Of people predicting a move to England. If I couldn't cope beyond the walls of the orphanage, how the hell would I ever cope with a move across the channel?

Victor Boyhan: 'He'd have slippers on. He looked pathetic. He sort of knew us, but the medication had him zonked out of his head. There might be dribble coming from his mouth. He was not the Paul McGrath we knew. He'd just follow you from one room to the other, shuffling. His mother would sit with him for hours.

'I remember looking at him one day and saying to somebody, "This lad will never kick a football again." What was even sadder, I felt, was that he wouldn't *want* to kick a ball again. My fear was that everything he was good at he would reject.

'I thought we were looking at someone who would be constantly in and out of psychiatric places. Doing tablets and bombed out of his head. Just basically finished. Now I would be a very optimistic person for most people in bad situations, but I thought "This guy's gone!" Have you ever looked at someone who the stuffing has just been ripped out of? This was not the same fella at all. Not inside, not in the guts. This looked like a fella who could never be anything again.

'He was wasted down to the bone. His physical structure had collapsed. I mean, in Vincent's, it had been like looking at a raving, sweating, hot, angry dog. It was amazing to think that someone could regress to that extent and still come out of it.

'There was something vaguely psychotic about it all.'

I don't recall any definitive moment of clarity on the road to recovery. There was just a slow, painfully gradual thaw in my condition. Eventually, the ball that was thrown at me did get kicked back. I started to communicate in language again. I began to eat.

It took roughly six months but, in time, I was released back to Betty's care and the whole process of rehabilitating me as a footballer recommenced. Again it was Johnny Dunne who took up the role of chauffeur and, in part, master of deception. 'Just come up Paul, you won't have to do anything, honest . . .'; 'Em, why not bring your boots this time Paul . . . ?'; 'Ten minutes Paul, just try ten minutes . . .'

Dalkey were brilliant. They got me to slip back into things as if nothing had changed. No one spoke about the missing days. It was as if some of the lads didn't even know what I had been through. Normality just slipped down again. There were no grandiose announcements. No special attention.

Frank Mullen: 'When he was released from Brendan's, the view had been that he would be back. It wasn't a very optimistic prognosis. Actually, it was dreadful. But things turned out differently. He recovered very quickly when you consider the very serious condition that he was in. I know that time can cloud your memory, but his recovery was amazing.'

Back on a football pitch I was back at ease with myself. I resumed playing Leinster Senior League with Dalkey and, by the summer of 1980, I was back in demand again. Living in Crumlin now, I started playing the summer five-a-side circuit with a strong Fatima team, powered by the Reids, Victor, Billy and Co. Billy Reid is the father of current Irish international, Andy.

They'd call for me on Keeper Road in this little pickup truck and we'd nip around to all these inner-city venues, playing five-a-side for a cash prize. It was great fun. I really admired the Reids because they were cracking little footballers and we were rarely, if ever, beaten on that circuit.

But Fatima were among Dalkey's fiercest Dublin rivals at the time and, as a new season dawned, they tried to convince me to sign for the club proper. The offer was tempting, especially as I was now living right beside them in Crumlin. I though about it, but Frank Mullen and Tommy Cullen persuaded me not to. In a sense, I suspect, that Billy Behan's continuing presence at Dalkey may have been the decisive factor.

Billy was still monitoring my progress in a gentle, understated way. I was aware, too, of scouts from other clubs showing an interest. There was talk of Tottenham making regular checks. It came to the point where I found myself eyeing the sideline before games for anyone who looked like they might be there on business.

It wasn't just me they'd have been coming to see, mind. John Young was a fabulous footballer too, a lovely, off the cuff, Glen Hoddle-type player who was commanding his own share of cross-channel attention.

As luck would have it, Dalkey's first game of the new season pitched them against Fatima. It would prove a full-blooded, hot-tempered affair with a number of dismissals. Because of the approach to yours truly, there was now even more baggage to the fixture. I was subsequently sent off myself in a later game against Fatima, jumping to the bait of a familiar comment about my colour.

I remember kicking out at the culprit in the stomach, then walking off before the referee could even send me. A Leinster League disciplinary hearing ordered Dalkey to pay a fine of £3, but the club refused on principle. Correspondence continued for weeks but, to this day, the £3 remains outstanding.

That was the kind of unbending support the people at Dalkey were inclined to give me.

I had given up the job with the Hammonds and now took on a new career in security! A chap called Mick Fenton owned CP Security and he gave me a break, essentially working as nightwatchman at a number of different premises around the city. They moved me around.

One of my 'jobs' was at a library right beside Ballymun flats where, every now and then, a few scallies would climb onto the roof, trying to get in. They'd give me dogs' abuse when they'd see me. The usual stuff. 'Go back to the fucking jungle black man . . .' But there was always at least one decent voice in the din, protesting, 'Aah Jaysus, give it a rest lads.'

The nights would be long and lonely on that beat. Sometimes, I'd be starving and just lock up the place, slipping away to get a Mars Bar. To be honest, I never felt particularly threatened there. The people were, generally, good people.

Another night, I'd do security at the James Connolly Memorial Hospital in Blanchardstown, 'minding the hospital' as I called it. After that, I might be guarding a warehouse in Coolock. That was my favourite gig. We had a football team in CP, and often all the boys would arrive up to the warehouse and we'd play seven-a-side or, sometimes, just have a training session.

I made a lot of good friends with CP Security, none more so than Aidan Crawley, who went on to become a priest and one of my most loyal and treasured friends. Fr Aidan is now based in Cork but we still see each other regularly.

Fr Aidan Crawley: 'The soccer team in CP Security was made up mostly of culchies [country people] who'd go home for the weekend. I remember we had this game coming up against Maynooth College, who had recently won the Collingwood Cup. We were down on numbers.

'I knew nothing about Paul as a footballer. So I asked Paul if he was able to play. He just said "Yeah." I reasoned we might put him in goals if need be. We just wanted him to make up the numbers. I remember thinking "I hope to God he's able to kick a ball."

'So we're out this Sunday afternoon in Maynooth. "Just do

your best," I told him. What happens? We win five or six nil. Paul scores four or five goals. Little did we know . . .'

With regular money (£90 a week) in my pocket, I now acquired a social life. I also discovered slot machines. There was an amusements arcade just off O'Connell Bridge called the Fun Palace and, routinely, I'd head straight there with my wage packet on a Friday. To this day, slot machines hold a strange and worrying attraction for me.

Gramps had a car now, a Datsun Cherry, and we'd take it up to the Phoenix Park where he'd let me behind the wheel and we'd go bombing around the place, imagining we were first on the road in the Circuit of Ireland rally.

Girls started coming into the picture too. We got to know a few nurses out in Blanchardstown. One, in particular, I fell head over heels in love with. She was from Scariff in County Clare, and one weekend, Gramps and myself drove down there in his Datsun on what I imagined would be a romantic voyage.

It didn't quite come to pass, though. Her father ran us from their house and we ended up sleeping in the car, almost blue with cold. It was the middle of winter and we were virtually camped there for two days. This girl and her mate would come up to a local pub where we were playing cards with the locals. We'd see them for a few minutes, then they'd be gone again.

It never quite developed into Bogart and Bacall.

But, around this time, I did get involved in my first serious relationship. Jacinta lived on the same road in Crumlin. She was a beautiful girl in every way. Very reserved. Very calm. Exactly the type of person I needed in my life.

And that life was undeniably good now. All the terror and chaos of the crash seemed to have drifted away. I was working. I was playing football. I was in a relationship with a special girl.

I also made what was, in hindsight, a bizarre trip back to Germany with Gramps, just the two of us. He hadn't been on the previous tour and I suppose I had begun to portray this rather exotic image of Bochum, the dull, humdrum city in the Ruhr area of Germany where Wattenscheid were based.

Gramps: 'It was off the cuff. We didn't even have a hotel to stay in. We just found this place, a kind of a hostel, and ended up booking back in every evening. To be honest, I thought the place was a bit of a kip.

'I remember my brother, Donal, brought us to the airport. We were picking Paul up at Liberty Hall, right in the centre of Dublin. Donal was getting a bit agitated because it was around five in the evening. The traffic was chock-a-block, the footpaths were crammed. "How the fuck are we supposed to spot this fella?" he says to me. Donal hadn't a clue that Paul was black. "Oh I'll spot him, don't worry," I said.

'So we're coming over Tara Street Bridge and there he is. You'd have spotted him a mile away. Nowadays you might see twenty black people on one street in Dublin. But this was 1980. A black person stood out in the crowd.'

I don't really know what I was thinking. There was certainly no profound reason behind going back there. We could have gone to the sun, to Spain, the Canaries or whatever. But Bochum was the only 'foreign' place I had been to. I suppose I felt I'd know my way around.

To be honest, we made our own craic. Maybe it was an exorcism of sorts for me. I don't really have a steadfast theory. I certainly haven't been back since. Germany was foreign and, in my mind, that made it exotic.

Back home, meanwhile, completely unknown to me, Billy Behan had a plan.

8

BECOMING A SAINT

John Young and I were now a kind of a package, the two Dalkey United players who most people assumed were certain to outgrow junior football.

Soon enough, the invites began to arrive from League of Ireland clubs offering an opportunity to try out at the higher level. The deal was that we'd spend a week training with better, harder players and see how we survived it. I didn't know it at the time, but for Paul McGrath, this was part of a long-term strategy to bring me to Old Trafford.

Alerted by Billy Behan to the fact that I seemed to have all the raw materials for a career in professional football, Matt Busby had taken a discreet interest. He suggested to Behan that a season in League of Ireland would answer most lingering questions about my toughness, both physical and mental.

Those questions were now more relevant than ever.

I was comfortable in life. I wasn't being stretched. The great, compelling dream of making it as a pro in England had, largely, disappeared. Life was too good now. I had a family, a job, a girl-friend. I was still competitive, for sure. But ambitious?

John and I did a little circuit of League of Ireland clubs. Two big fish from a small pond, innocently strutting our stuff. Both of us feckless, irreverent, immature, always giggling, always messing.

Home Farm was our first port of call and it lasted a single evening. Dave Bacuzzi was the manager in Whitehall. He lost patience within an hour. 'If you two came down here for a laugh, ye can piss off home again.' And that's precisely what we did.

Next stop was Bohemians, one of the great, old giants of domestic football in Ireland. They were managed at the time by Billy Young and the physio was a man who would, down the line, have a massive role to play in my career as an international footballer. His name was Mick Byrne.

That night at Dalymount Park, though, John and I were like kids after an overload of chocolate. It never seemed to occur to us that this might be a gilt-edged opportunity. I remember I had a little confrontation with one of the Bohemians players when I inadvertently sat in his dressing-room spot.

It was all a little heavy and unwelcoming and, getting the bus back to Crumlin that evening, my mind was made up that whatever colours I might end up wearing, they wouldn't be the red and black stripes of Bohs.

An approach to Jimmy Shields at Shamrock Rovers was firmly rebuffed and, for a time, it looked as if Billy Behan's plan to 'blood' me in League of Ireland football wouldn't even get off the ground. It was then that St Patrick's Athletic came into my world.

Frank Mullen: 'We were having a lot of trouble getting a club to take Paul. Then, out of the blue, Tommy Cullen got a phone call. It was from the St Patrick's Athletic chairman, Paddy Becton. They were interested in Paul. So he came out one day with Pat's manager, Charlie Walker, to have a look. And Paul played brilliantly.

'We went into the club afterwards and Charlie wanted to

know how much we wanted. We weren't looking for money. But we made it quite clear that Paul was earmarked for Old Trafford. That, if Pat's took him, United was still where he was headed. Any other deal would be totally opposed by us.'

Charlie Walker: 'I'll always remember it was a hot day. Between the heat of the sun and the dust rising off the park, it was as if no one wanted to play football. I remember this Afro head. He did a few little things in the match that really impressed me. Little things that no one can put into you.

'I didn't go near him. Just spoke to a few of the lads in the club to see if they'd mind me talking to him.

'Then I found out where he lived. On Keeper Road, in Crumlin. We used to train in Brickfields, just down the road from there. I went up and his mother answered. Terrible nice woman. We got chatting. "Where's the boy?" I said. She explained to me that he was in bed because he worked nights in security.

'The granny was in the kitchen. We're talking away and, next thing, in comes Paul. I hadn't any money to offer 'cos, as a club, we never had any money at the time. But I suggested he come and train with us, see what he thought. If he didn't like it, he could just walk away.

'And the granny pipes up, "You listen to that man . . ."'

St Patrick's Athletic was a big club in decline, playing out of Richmond Park in Inchicore. The nearest they had come to a trophy in many years was finishing runners-up in the FAI Cup in 1980. They had just lost two of their biggest names – Barry Murphy and Jackie Jameson – to Bohemians.

Pat's, then, would not quite have had the lure of Bohemians or Shamrock Rovers. But they certainly had some terrific players. Dave Henderson was as good a goalkeeper as I've played in front of, and people like Joey Malone, Fran Gavin, John Cervi, John Cleary and Synan Braddish were all really smart, streetwise footballers.

I knew if I did well with them, Charlie would make me one of the handful of semi-pros on the Pat's books. That would mean some kind of signing-on fee, a weekly wage of £25, and a win bonus of £8. I thought it would be easy.

The plan was that I would play out the remainder of the season with Dalkey, enabling me to represent the Leinster Senior League in the Oscar Traynor Trophy, an interleague competition that the LSS went on to win in that summer of 1981. It also meant I would have the 'luxury' of pre-season in which to become acquainted with my new teammates.

What should have helped further was that Billy Reid was joining (from Fatima) with me, but, contrary to urban myth, my early days in the League of Ireland were to prove an absolute nightmare.

Fran Gavin: 'I remember clearly the first night he came up training because, at the time, I was the quickest player in the club. I had been a long time in football as a semi-professional and, by and large, nobody beat me in sprints. Anyway, Paul came up this night and left me for dead. Unbelievable.

'He was just such an athlete. I had never seen anything like it. But we knew absolutely nothing about him before he came up. He just arrived with Charlie. He was playing junior foot-ball, but we were League of Ireland players. We never both-ered looking at junior football. To us, it was just a different scene altogether.'

Charlie decided to try me as a striker and I just couldn't hack it. I did score a couple of goals early on and remember thinking 'This is great. I'm playing with a good team, getting a good service. There'll be plenty more where they came from.' And Charlie moved quickly, singing me up as a semi-pro. But the goals dried up and my confidence began to waver. The pace of the football, the skill and savvy of the players all took me by surprise. I was hardly getting a touch in games.

After a while, Charlie switched me to midfield. It made no difference. I felt out of my depth. I was hating every minute of it. I had no touch, no timing. I was making no contribution. Increasingly, I could hear grumbles rising from the bank on the Camac side of the ground, where Pat's real hard-core fans assembled. I could sense, too, a brewing impatience in the dressing room.

It came to a head one Sunday afternoon, when Limerick were the visitors to Richmond Park. About an hour before kick-off, Charlie called me over for a chat. He had a way of whispering what he had to say. 'Look Paul, the directors aren't happy with you. You've failed up front, you've failed in midfield. You're going back to centre-half today, and if that doesn't work, the next move you'll be making is out of this club.' With my confidence at such a low ebb, I remember thinking that this could well be my last game in the red shirt of St Pat's. I just wasn't doing it for them.

But the switch to centre-half meant that I would be playing directly alongside Joey Malone. Now, Joey was the main man in a dressing room full of strong characters. He was the talker on the pitch, a really good player who kept everyone else going.

From the moment I slotted in beside him, I just acquired a completely different sense of presence.

Fran Gavin: 'I was centre-half at the time and the switch meant I had to move to right full. After that, I think we went virtually unbeaten until the time came for Paul to move on. At centre-back, he was incredible. Because he had all the play in front of him.

'He was a great man at getting the ball and going forward with it. And he could mark three people at once. I mean no one could get by him. But Paul was very quiet at the time.

He didn't socialise, didn't go out for a drink with us or anything like that. And, at the time, there was a big drinking scene in the League of Ireland. Especially the night after games, we'd all go for a few drinks.

'Everybody did.'

I loved the physicality of the football. There were some hard men in that league and they wouldn't spare you. I especially remember one game against Athlone Town and a fella called Frank Devlin. It was real war between us. I enjoyed every minute of it. The more aggressive the opponent, the better I invariably played.

In later years, Ron Atkinson would always thump me on the chest just before we'd go out, to 'wake' me as he put it. Ron's view was that that was what I was going to get on the pitch and I'd better be ready for it. So a big striker inclined to leave his elbow in my face was, sometimes, exactly what I needed. I needed anger. I needed something to get me wound up. To get me focused.

From that Limerick game on, I just thrived alongside Joey. The national newspapers started taking an interest. One journalist, Karl MacGinty of the *Evening Herald*, took to calling me 'The Black Pearl of Inchicore' and the name began to stick. Speculation was fizzing again that some English clubs were interested. A lot of nice things were being written and said.

One huge game for me that I remember vividly was a clash with Shamrock Rovers. Matt Busby had come over from Manchester for the game, reputedly to watch Rovers' striker, Liam Buckley. I was a huge admirer of Buckley's but the moment I heard Sir Matt was in the crowd, I was on a mission to blot out the 'Hoops' attack.

We beat Rovers 3-0 that day and I often thought after that, if Liam had banged in a couple of goals, he might have been the one on his way to Old Trafford.

★　★　★

I loved the attention. I started getting the newspapers on a Monday morning to see how the journalists would rate my latest performance. The assessment of old, experienced scribes like Charlie Stuart in the *Irish Press*, Noel Dunne in the *Irish Independent* or Peter Byrne in the *Irish Times* always seemed to carry added weight.

There were also a few kind mentions from the legendary Con Houlihan on the back page of the *Evening Press*, which – in my eyes – amounted to the ultimate endorsement. I remember, too, a glowing piece written in one newspaper by Turlough O'Connor, a man I admired hugely when he was a really smart, intelligent centre-forward with Bohemians in the seventies.

Now the general consensus seemed to be that England was the proper stage for my talent. In a matter of months, I had been transformed from a brewing misfit into some kind of strolling colossus. I was slightly startled by the pace of it all.

Then, one Tuesday, I arrived home from work to find Charlie Walker in the living room. He had, as he put it, 'a bit of news'. It turned out that there were firm offers on the table from Manchester City, Luton Town and Watford. But, more importantly, Manchester United wanted me on a month's trial.

The decision was easy. I wanted to try my luck at Old Trafford.

To be fair, it would probably have suited St Pat's a bit better to get some immediate cash. By taking the United option, I was, effectively, just stepping out of the Pat's dressing room for a month, with no guarantees. But Charlie didn't try to pressure me. He understood the lure of United.

So I signed off on a miserable March Sunday at Richmond Park, going for a celebratory drink with the lads. And something a little strange clicked inside me. I hadn't touched alcohol in two years. Not since the first trip to Germany. Now I decided to try again.

The Pat's players were unequivocal about my month's trial. 'You won't be back Paul. There's no way you'll be coming home.' So we started the celebrations there and then. Joey didn't drink pints.

He had a kidney complaint and couldn't cope with the volume of beer.

So he was drinking a short. Someone asked me what I'd have. 'I'll have whatever it is that Joey's drinking,' I said.

And that was the moment I was introduced to the strange, perfumed taste of Southern Comfort.

9

UNITED

First impressions?

Ron Atkinson is a creep. I can't stand the man. He's looking at me like I'm something congealed on the heel of his shoe. He's abrupt, hostile, talking at me in little gun-bursts of words. It's a hapless mismatch and I'm sinking.

Manchester United are offering me a take-home pay of £101 a week. I've been making more than that in Dublin. The lads from Pat's are outside the door. I ask to speak to them. 'Be my guest,' he says.

I need someone batting for me here. Charlie Walker goes in and makes the effort. 'Em, about the money Mr Atkinson . . .'

'He's not happy with it?'

'Well, do you think maybe . . .'

'Send him back in.'

I shuffle back to the guillotine. He's looking at me with absolute contempt now. I'm a jumped-up nobody from Dublin being offered the chance of a lifetime. And all I'm thinking of is shillings.

'You're not happy with it?' he sneers.

'Well . . .'

'Piss off back to Dublin then.'

'No, I didn't exactly say . . .'

'That's our offer. If you're not happy with it, piss off.'

'Em, so, where do I sign?'

I was twenty-two and being offered the chance of a career with Manchester United. To walk out of that room without signing would have been like leaving the lottery office without the cheque.

The previous day, I had taken a phone call from John Givens. He was secretary of the Professional Footballers' Association of Ireland. He could see this coming.

John Givens:'I phoned Paul in his digs. I had decided to come over and, at least, be available to him. I said, "Paul I'm coming over to help you tomorrow. Don't sign anything until we go through it together."

'Paul's reply to me wasn't exactly convincing. "I'll try," he said. The next morning, I rang Atkinson's office only to be told, "You're too late. He's signed!"'

There was a small battalion of people from St Pat's with me, none of them really qualified to bat on my behalf. Ron knew exactly what he was dealing with.

Charlie Walker: 'I didn't like Ron Atkinson's attitude. He was sitting in this high chair. He was going on about how, at twenty-two, it was very late for Paul to be joining United. And he went on about Paul's earring. I remember getting thick with him. "He doesn't play with his ear," I said.

'There was some fella beside him taking notes. "What happens if he gets a cap?" I asked. "And what happens if he's sold for big money?" Atkinson turned to me. "You fucking Irish!" he said.

'"You fucking English!" I replied. I think we got £30,000 for him in the end.'

I couldn't have known at the time that Ron Atkinson would become one of my favourite people in football. A real man's man who got to see the best and worst of me over the next decade and more. During the course of the month's trial with United, I had spoken to him occasionally without ever really getting any sense of feedback.

Because of some problem with my registration, I actually sat out the first few reserve games, watching enviously as Barry Kehoe ruled the roost. Barry was a real livewire footballer from Dundalk who had travelled over with me and – in many ways – kept me sane.

I have an abiding image of him actually pushing Ray Wilkins out of the way to take free kicks in a reserve game. Barry absolutely thrived during that month, but he never did get offered a contract. Unfortunately Barry was diagnosed with a serious medical condition which ruined his chance of a career in professional football. Tragically, he passed away some years ago.

We were put in digs in Chorlton, the area where Sir Matt Busby lived. The house was a tall, three-storied building run by a lovely woman called Bet Fenham. It was a house held specifically for Manchester United players. Kevin Moran had only recently moved out into his own place, but there were three other Irish guys there – Ashley Grimes, Phil Hughes and a cocky sixteen-year-old who looked like someone in his mid-twenties. His name was Norman Whiteside.

The Fenhams were lovely people who looked after the United players as if they were their own sons. Norman shared a room in the attic with Hughes, who was a young goalkeeper. In time, I got a room on the second floor to myself. Bet used do all our ironing and cooking.

The joke among us was always that we got a very varied menu with Bet. You usually had a choice of boiled eggs, poached eggs, fried eggs, eggs with soldiers . . . Just eggs everywhere. Sometimes, we'd sneak out to get a Chinese. To be fair, Bet and her husband, Tom, were very good to us. They let us live our lives. If we came in late at night, nothing would be said. The girlfriends would even be allowed to stay over on occasion. We were treated as young adults and expected to behave responsibly which, most of the time, we did.

Norman Whiteside: 'I remember sitting in the digs and he came walking in to be introduced to us. This big, six-foot-plus lad from Dublin. And me being from the Shankill Road in Belfast, I just turned around and said, "Big man, it's bad enough being a Catholic, but being a black one . . ."

'That broke the ice a little. It got a laugh.'

For whatever reason, Norman and I clicked immediately. He was very grown up and irreverent for someone his age. He knew the ropes. You just felt that here was a kid who would never be intimidated by anything that professional football could throw at him.

To begin with, the journeys to and from training were real marathon affairs. We'd have to walk quarter of a mile or so to catch a bus to White City. From there, we'd get another bus to Old Trafford. Then, finally, a minibus to the Cliff. Norman eventually worked out that, if the four of us pooled our bus fares together every morning, we could have a taxi waiting for us outside the door instead.

In the end, we got it all down to a fine art. We'd have our jeans spread across the bedroom floor, ready to be stepped into. From the moment the taxi driver beeped his horn outside Bet's to the point of actual arrival at Old Trafford took almost exactly fifteen minutes.

My friendship with Norman was hard to explain. Once out of the orphanage system, I had converted back to Catholicism for no particular reason other than to keep my ma happy. I didn't have any strong feelings on religion. You might have imagined that a Dublin Catholic and a Belfast Protestant would have tiptoed around one another to begin with.

I mean, in school, I had been brought up on a diet of the Easter Rising in 1916. I felt *very* Irish. Ostensibly, at least, Norman and I existed in different worlds.

But nothing could have been further from the truth.

Looking back, you could say there was a slightly odd dynamic between us. I was twenty-two, Norman was sixteen. Yet, he was unmistakably the senior figure. Norman just had this air of calm and confidence about him. Everyone was talking about him.

He showed me the ropes and, almost instantaneously, we became great friends.

My first opportunity to pull on the famous red shirt arrived in a reserve game at Newcastle. It went fine. We won 1-0. I didn't do anything spectacular, but there was one moment that caught everyone's eye. A moment of apparent brilliance that was, actually, pure fluke.

I lumped this ball forward from the back. It wasn't a pass at all, more a clearance. But the ball just dropped to Norman on the edge of the square. He let it bounce once, then BANG. Buried it with an unbelievable volley.

Next thing I know people are running towards me, congratulating me on the pass. And I'm thinking 'Yeah, not a bad delivery ...'

Norman was just phenomenal. You could give him the ball with two defenders tight on him and he'd just hold it, knock them away. They couldn't get near the ball. He was very similar to Mark Hughes in that respect. You could knock the ball to him in any position. He always wanted it and could always hold off tacklers.

I often think that young people today probably haven't seen

enough footage of Norman Whiteside in action to appreciate just how good he was.

We got the coach back down to Old Trafford after that game and, from memory, had a few beers on the journey. Just as we arrived, Ron Atkinson was coming out of the stadium. He walked straight across to Norman and asked him how I had done.

'Absolutely brilliant,' said Norman, proceeding to waffle on about this 'amazing' fifty-yard pass I had hit for the goal.

The month actually came to an end without me knowing United's verdict. It had just been announced at home that I had been voted the Soccer Writers' Player of the Year and I was about to fly to Dublin to accept the award. No one seemed inclined to tell me anything.

Barry had already been let go at this point and I became convinced that I was going to follow. I mean Barry had been absolutely brilliant. I was haunting Norman with my worries now. 'I know they're going to let me go, I just know it . . .'

And there was Norman, six years my junior, trying to reassure me. 'Nah big man, you're safe . . .'

Then, just as I was about to leave, the reserve team coach – Brian Whitehouse – shouted after me, 'See you back here on Monday!' Just a throwaway line that changed my world forever.

Ron Atkinson: 'The first time I actually noticed Paul, I was looking out the window of my office in the Cliff. He was taking part in a training session and there was something about him. He reminded me of Ruud Gullit. I mean you didn't look at him and think "What a great player!" It wasn't an instant thing.

'But I'd sort of pursued Gullit a little when he was younger and there was something of the Dutchman in the way Paul moved. Funnily enough, many years later I was speaking to the Dutch goalkeeper Hans Van Breuckelen in Australia and he said of McGrath, "You know something, he reminds me of Gullit . . ."

'Anyway, Paul played two or three reserve games and did OK. Not sensational. Then he played a game against big Mick Ferguson, the Everton centre-forward, in a Central League game and did exceptionally well. That was when we said, "Yeah, we've got to take him."

'The day of signing? I tell you I've done big transfers in my life but, to this day, I've never seen anything like when he came into my office. It was like a small Third Division crowd that came in with him. There was Charlie Walker and what seemed like half a dozen uncles. Kids and aunts nearly.

'And he had an earring in. So I've gone, "Hey big man, I've seen them all. I've seen Neil Franklin, I've seen John Charles and Billy Wright, all the great centre-halves. And they didn't wear earrings. Get that out." He just said "Grand" and I never saw it in again though, by all accounts, it did come out occasionally on Saturday nights.

'I can't remember the actual deal. But he would have been on one to measure up to players on his level. Put it this way, he'd have been on more than Mark Hughes and apprentices like that.'

I was absolutely blown away when Matt Busby turned up in Dublin's Gresham Hotel to present me with my award. It was gradually beginning to dawn on me that he had taken more than a passing interest in the events leading up to my signing for United.

From what I remember, the deal wasn't just a flat £30,000. St Pat's received a further £15,000 when I made my international debut three years later. They also got to stage a benefit match against United in Dublin.

So, I returned to Manchester and commenced my career as a full-time professional footballer. The season was coming to a close and all the talk in the reserves was of an end-of-season trip to Vancouver, San Diego and Seattle on the horizon. A few reserves would be joining the first-team squad on their travels.

About a week before the end of the season, Ron called me into his office to confirm that I would be one of the lucky ones. I was exultant. But Norman, it would transpire, ended up with even bigger fish to fry.

Having made his first-team debut in April, he would come home from that two-week trip to be called into the Northern Ireland squad for that summer's World Cup finals in Spain. He was about to make history as the youngest player ever to play in the World Cup finals.

Me? I didn't even make it to Vancouver.

The final reserve game of the season was against Sheffield United at Bramall Lane. A clumsy tackle from the opposing centre-forward unleashed a dart of pain in my right knee that would, over time, become pitifully familiar. I had never been seriously injured in my life before but, suddenly, I was facing my first cartilage operation.

Initially, we didn't know that. I just remember saying to Brian Whitehouse, 'Brian, my knee's knackered, it feels like something pretty bad is happening inside it.' Brian was a lovely guy who could see panic written in my expression. 'Don't say anything, just see how it settles,' he said. 'No point ruling yourself out of Vancouver if it's fine in a couple of days.'

But something told me that it wouldn't be. Sitting on the coach coming back from Sheffield, the knee swelled up badly. I was distraught. The idea of travelling to somewhere as exotic as Canada in the company of first-team players had me completely smitten.

But, much as I wanted to stay silent, I knew I was in trouble. This was more than a little twinge. Something drastic had gone wrong. So, reluctantly, I held my hand up, and sure enough, tests confirmed the cartilage damage. I was told I could go home for the summer, but to report back early for the operation.

It was really odd to find myself back in Crumlin during that summer of 1982, watching my new mate Norman make a global name for himself in Spain, where Northern Ireland had a terrific World Cup, reaching the quarter-finals and beating the hosts 1-0 en route, on a famous evening in Valencia.

He was a phenomenon really, not just the youngest player to play in a World Cup, but also the youngest to play for United's first team since Duncan Edwards, and soon to be the youngest player to score in an FA Cup final.

My mother was bursting with pride at the thought that her son had become a Manchester United player. She went straight into McBirney's, a big drapery store in the centre of Dublin, and bought me a grey, pin-striped suit as well as some other clothes, more suited to a banker than a professional footballer.

The cartilage operation meant that I missed the beginning of the new season. In hindsight, I was too star-struck to be unduly concerned. Suddenly, I was rubbing shoulders with household names like Bryan Robson, Lou Macari, Steve Coppell, Gordon McQueen, Frank Stapleton and Kevin Moran.

I was especially excited to be in such close proximity to Moran. He was a real hero in Dublin where his swashbuckling displays with the county's Gaelic football team had earned him iconic status. That team, managed by an intense, taciturn man – Kevin Heffernan – completely charmed the city through the mid to late seventies.

After a lengthy period in the wilderness, Dublin won three All-Irelands in four years and their rivalry with Mick O'Dwyer's Kerry, perhaps the greatest Gaelic football team ever seen, became massive box-office material at home.

Kevin played centre-back for a side that became known as 'Heffo's Army' in the All-Ireland finals of 1976, 1977 and 1978. To me, he seemed just about the biggest name on United's books in that autumn of 1982.

More importantly, he was hugely approachable too. From the moment I arrived at United, Kevin seemed to take an interest. He was always offering advice and encouragement, always open to a conversation. Over the years, he probably became the one guy in football I'd always listen to, even if the advice on offer was precisely the opposite to what I wanted to hear. He was a godsend to me.

Kevin Moran: 'We would have gravitated towards each other because, being from Ireland, there was a natural bond, a natural affinity. I always did that with the Irish lads. I mean, from the outset, there was a great bond between Norman, Paul and me. We would discuss everything. We were totally open with one another about money, contracts, that type of thing. Other players wouldn't dream of letting you know what they were earning. But we were completely open. We hid nothing from one another.'

Frank was another who kind of took me under his wing. And I remember Anto Whelan was at United around that time too. So there was this mini Irish community, if you like. I didn't feel isolated in any way. I didn't feel homesick.

The knee responded well to the operation, and soon I was pushing my way into what Big Ron referred to as the 'magic circle'. This was, essentially, his first sixteen. If you weren't in that group, you didn't exist. Stuck in the reserves, you could feel invisible.

But push into the magic circle and, suddenly, you were eligible for win bonuses. You were A Player.

Frank Stapleton: 'In a very short period of time, Paul was pushing to get in the first team. I didn't really know anything about him, other than the fact he was from Dublin. You could tell he was shy. I think he was a little bit overwhelmed by all

112

the players at Old Trafford. He wouldn't engage people in conversation. In that sense, it was probably good that he started with the reserves.

'But once people saw just how good a player he was, the esteem they held him in just started to grow. And Paul's confidence started coming through. A lot of people look at Paul and think that he's totally laid-back. But he had a lot of determination too. And he just got better and better. He was becoming too good for the reserves.

'And the better he got, the more he felt able to strike up friendships with different people.'

I made my debut for United in a lopsided fund-raising match at Aldershot, alongside the likes of Robson, Whiteside and Hughes. Soon after, I got a run in a Milk Cup game on a wretchedly wet night at Bradford.

But my League debut arrived on 13 November, a home game against Tottenham. We won 1-0. I was relatively unfazed by the experience. Looking back, I have very few vivid memories of it. I don't recall being in any way petrified beforehand. Quite early on in the game, Chris Hughton came attacking down our left flank and I had to stop myself gaping in admiration.

Chris was an Irish international at the time and, just momentarily, I was a little star-struck at the sight of him approaching. But he pushed the ball a little too far ahead of him and I remember just dinking it over his head, then passing to a teammate. There was a kind of collective 'Ooooooh' from the crowd and, in that moment, I was hooked.

This was where I wanted to be.

Charlie Walker: 'I went across for that game. It was the first time I was ever taken into the VIP lounge at Old Trafford. Who comes across to me after the match? Only the famous

Matt Busby. And in his Scottish accent, he says, "That's one hell of a lad you've sent us there."

'The following week, a parcel comes to my house from Paul. In it were his shirt, knicks, socks, tie-ups, everything from the Spurs game. I was thrilled. But it was too big a present to keep for myself. So I gave the gear to a school in Greenhills and told them to put it in a frame.'

I was still well down the pecking order at United, though. When everyone was fit, the battle for the centre-half positions wouldn't really involve me. Gordon McQueen was the fastest player at the club. Martin Buchan was this immaculate, Mr Gentleman figure, who never seemed to make a mistake. And Kevin was, well, Kevin.

These guys were serious players, miles ahead of me in terms of positioning and nous. They were class acts. I loved watching Buchan play especially. It was like a one-man tutorial on the art of defending. The man had ice in his veins. He simply didn't make mistakes. And he had this aura about him, always dressing impeccably off the field, carrying himself like a statesman.

Gordon was a much more attack-minded footballer. Anything thrown into our box, he just met it head-on. He'd compete ferociously and, off the field, proved a great character who could bury you with his one-liners. One of the biggest early boosts I got at United was when Ron pitted me against him in a training-ground sprint and I won.

'Fuck McQueen, he's even quicker than you . . .' Ron purred. His surprise was understandable. I had this lazy-looking run. I know for a fact that people would look at me sometimes and wonder if I was seriously intent on actually getting to a ball. Gordon, by comparison, was physical and hugely combative.

Beating him in that sprint worked wonders for my credibility. It also fed my ego. I felt I was getting noticed now.

Of course, Kevin's fearlessness was legendary. He would literally put his head anywhere to protect his team. But he was also a hugely intelligent footballer, a guy who could read a game brilliantly and seldom, if ever, made the wrong choice of pass.

Compared to these, I was a complete novice, still learning my trade. There was no question of marching nonchalantly into that United first team. Ron made it clear that I would have to bide my time. In that 1982–3 season, I would make fourteen League appearances for United.

But I still had some distance to travel.

Ron Atkinson: 'I do remember playing him in a game against Stoke. He didn't do very well actually. I think it was against big Brendan O'Callaghan and he gave Paul a bit of a towzing. I mean the first six months he was with us, you knew he was a player. But you never knew he was going to be quite the player he became.

'You could see he'd got good ingredients. But he was no overnight sensation. It would take him eighteen months to two years to actually establish himself.

'I do remember that season, I played him right side against Luton. He scored two goals in the first twenty minutes. But he was useless. I mean I went down and said, "Paul, go centre-half . . ." He was all over the shop. I think I pushed Kevin into midfield.

'He might be the only player who ever scored two goals in about twenty minutes and the manager's changed him.'

I remember that game, and Ron was spot on. Despite the goals, I was absolutely rubbish. The thing is you couldn't bluff it at that level. You were either at the pace of the game or you weren't and, on that particular day, I wasn't.

Ron Atkinson: 'There was another game where I decided to have a look at him as a sitting player in midfield. He said, "What do you want me to do boss?" I said, "Well, just play the position like Ray Wilkins does!" So the game starts and he's galloping here, there and everywhere.

'At half-time, I said to him, "When have you ever seen Ray Wilkins play like that?"

Paul just looks at me. "Suppose, if I'd said play like Bryan Robson, you'd have just sat there," I said. You had to smile.'

So, though dipping in and out of the magic circle, I stayed very much on the periphery of things with United that season. It was a decent campaign for the club, finishing third in the First Division and staying unbeaten at Old Trafford. We also finished runners-up to the mighty Liverpool in that season's Milk Cup, losing the final only after extra time.

But the big story was winning the FA Cup.

I featured sporadically in that Cup run, but was very much, surplus to requirements the day of the final against Brighton. That was a massive disappointment.

Ron Atkinson: 'We had a problem on the right-hand side for that Cup final. And Paul could have come into contention for that if he hadn't played that game against Luton. But, after what I saw against Luton, I just couldn't go with him. So he didn't make the Cup final "cut". I decided to give Alan Davies the nod instead.'

A few of us weren't even on the coach travelling to Wembley because, with TV cameras on board, there was a dearth of space.

It meant that some players were in these black limos behind the coach. Laurie Cunningham was one of them. Now Laurie was a fantastically gifted footballer. But his career was blighted by injury

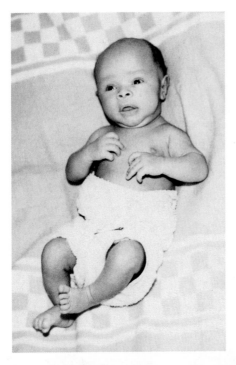

'Picture of Innocence',
striking a pose for my
first photo-shoot,
Ealing '59.

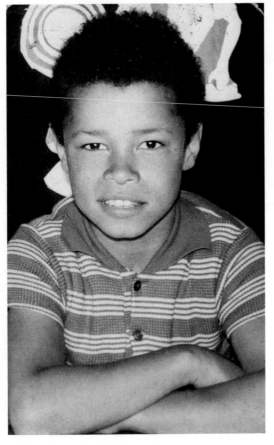

'Steel in the Smile',
ready to take on
the world at the
age of eleven.

'Mother and Son', a
treasured day at the
sea-side with Betty.

Brothers in Arms,
with fellow orphan
Danny Maguire.

'Dressed to Kill', striking a
pose with Betty on the day of
my Confirmation, Dublin '71.

'Theatre of Dreams', practicing on the pitch we dug with our own hands at Glensilva.

'Cool Dudes', 'Gramps' and me on O'Connell Street in Dublin after taking in a movie at The Ambassador.

'Red Devil', one of
the first shots of me as a
Manchester United player.

'One for All...', combining with old buddies, Robson, Moran and Whiteside,
to keep Everton's Graeme Sharp at bay.

'A Player', that's me in the middle of the second-row for a pre-season shoot
at Old Trafford before the '86/87 season.

'Eyes Left', something's caught my attention elsewhere as we celebrate the
'85 FA Cup final win against Everton at Wembley.

'Trouble Brewing in those Knees', an ominous sign of things to come as I resort to crutches in September '84.

'Green Giants…', chilling out with Ronnie Whelan during 'Euro '88'

'Smooth Operator…' Yet appearances can be deceptive. Underneath the surface my demons were tormenting me.

'Green Man…' Me in early action for Ireland. Little did I know what an extraordinary journey we would have under Jack Charlton.

and, tragically, he would die just six years later in a horrendous car accident in Spain.

Laurie would certainly have been on the coach if he hadn't been so honest. He had come to United on a three-month loan after an unhappy period with Real Madrid and Ron was clearly keen on him. The day before the final, Laurie had a fitness test on a suspect thigh at Roehampton and seemed to come through with flying colours.

But he still felt slightly impeded by the injury and told Ron, knowing that his honesty would cost him a Wembley appearance.

So Laurie was sitting next to me on the way to the stadium and his frustration was palpable. Eventually, he just told the driver to stop. 'I've had enough of this,' he said. 'I'm going back to the hotel.'

It briefly occurred to me that I might do the same, but the lure of Wembley was just too powerful. I wanted to be part of the occasion, even if I wasn't going to have an active role to play. I wanted to walk the pitch beforehand, drink in the atmosphere. To me, this was football's Mecca.

So, they brought us to seats directly behind the dugout from where I watched United struggle to a 2-2 draw against underdog opposition in a game that went to extra time, Ray Wilkins and Frank getting the goals. In fact, Brighton would have won the Cup but for a point-blank save by Gary Bailey from Gordon Smith in the second period of added time.

Five days later, however, the boys made no mistake, winning the replay 4-0 and I happily immersed myself in the celebrations. I was one of the boys now, waving from the open-top bus, swigging back champagne, breathing deep the collective sense of glory.

There were no clouds in my world. Just a nagging voice somewhere deep in the subconscious, cutting me down with that same old, relentless sarcasm. '*Deep down, you know they're going to see through you, don't you . . .*'

10

A PLAYER

In the four seasons I was part of Ron Atkinson's first-team squad at Old Trafford, we never finished outside the top four in the First Division.

We won the FA Cup twice and had a name for playing the kind of flamboyant, attacking football that felt true to Manchester United's heritage. But we never won the League. Despite many promising opportunities, we always seemed to come up hauntingly short on the home straight.

This led to a little cottage industry of theories. United, clearly, had some of the best players in English football at the time but, over the course of a season, would inevitably come up short of the consistency shown by Liverpool and (in 1985) their Merseyside neighbours, Everton.

The frustration was enormous. United hadn't won the League since 1967, yet – less than forty miles away – Liverpool were able to accumulate titles almost on cruise control.

Ron eventually lost his job in November 1986, forced out by a run of poor form that culminated in a heavy Milk Cup defeat at Southampton. It was said at the time that he had 'lost the confidence' of the players. As far as I was concerned, nothing could have been further from the truth.

I had grown to love Ron. His off-the-cuff style might have created the illusion of ambivalent leadership, but he was as committed and passionate a football man as I've ever come across.

What he *did* do was treat players as grown-ups. His rationale was simple. If you delivered for him on a Saturday, he wasn't inclined to pry into how you lived your life between games. This led to an impression of rampant indiscipline in the United dressing room. And the impression became hugely exaggerated over time.

Ron didn't take prisoners. If you messed up, he'd let you have it with both barrels. Put it this way, the United dressing room wasn't exactly a gentle place to be when games were lost that shouldn't have been.

Having overcome a certain degree of stage fright, I certainly settled happily into the life of a professional footballer. Though I missed home, Gramps and a few of the other lads from Dalkey were coming across pretty regularly, and I had even decided to formalise my relationship with Jacinta by investing in an engagement ring. It wasn't exactly a purchase made with excessive pomp or ceremony. Gramps was over at the time with his girlfriend, and we just got the bus into the Arndale Centre, where Jacinta picked the ring of her choice.

I was sincere in my belief that she was the girl for me, yet it wasn't the most practical of decisions. We were seeing less and less of one another now, and the better I got to know Manchester, the more comfortable I became socialising in the city.

I wasn't exactly a man about town, but I did come to realise that being a Manchester United player brought its share of attention from members of the opposite sex. Pretty quickly, Jacinta and I just drifted apart. In hindsight, with her still living in Dublin, the relationship never really stood a chance.

My salary was reviewed after that first season, and with the offer of more money, I stupidly agreed to a long-term contract. My new wage was £500 a week. Decent money at the time, no question, but roughly just a quarter of what the likes of Bryan Robson were on. Worse, I was tied to it for seven years.

For a club of their size, United were notorious for penny-pinching.

Norman Whiteside: 'Ron wasn't too generous with the club's money. We seemed to have meetings after meetings about bonus systems and schemes. The feeling was, well, you're not going to walk away from Manchester United are you? When it came to wages, they were dreadful. Some people, though, ended up on a hell of a lot more than others. And I think, over time, Paul just felt that he was being crapped on.'

In August 1983, I went to Majorca with United on a pre-season tour. Though we trained each day, the atmosphere was quite relaxed. I didn't hold back. On our first night there, I got extremely drunk and ended up in a fight with this group of US marines. When I awoke the following morning, my clothes were in tatters and I was sporting an angry black eye.

But for Gordon McQueen, I would – apparently – have taken an even worse hiding. The lads didn't spare me afterwards.

'You plonker Rodney, couldn't pick a fight with just one person, could you? Had to take on the whole American army!'

The same thing happened to me on another pre-season tour in Holland. We were let out for the night and I was in this club with Arthur Albiston and Scott McGarvey. Again words were exchanged with somebody and I took the bait, not realising this chap had half a dozen mates around the corner.

So I'm giving it plenty of 'C'mon, let's sort this outside . . .' when his friends arrive from behind and, right there in the club, give me an unmerciful kicking. Needless to say, I was unavailable for selection for the upcoming game, sitting on the sideline in dark glasses.

Ron Atkinson:'I think Paul's doing himself a bit of a disservice here. My memory of the Amsterdam incident is that some guys had tried to rob Scott McGarvey's Rolex and McGrath just stepped in and sorted it. I mean you'd never see him lose his temper, but he was a strong boy. I heard he took down three or four that night.

'First I heard of the incident in Majorca was when the lads came down for breakfast. It was the talk of the place. "Hey, McGrath cleaned out the American navy last night!"'

The night before we came home from that trip to Majorca, I met Claire. She had been staying in the hotel with one of her girl-friends. Gary Bailey and I were sitting at the bar in the disco this night when they walked in. I noticed her immediately.

Now, I still had my black eye and didn't exactly have the confidence to play Romeo. But Gary got talking to her friend, and Claire and I gradually got drawn into the conversation. She was quiet and reserved and extremely pretty. I was smitten.

That night we ended up strolling together on the beach and exchanging phone numbers.

Claire: 'Paul was quite drunk, but very charming. He kept saying to me, "I'm going to marry you, you're the girl I'm going to marry." At the time I had a very serious boyfriend at home. The United team went home the next day and I didn't think anything more of it.

'I was living in nursing accommodation at the time. When I got home, he'd managed to track down that accommodation and pinned a little note to the door saying "Please ring me!" And I did.

'We arranged to meet a couple of weeks after that and he stood me up! I was training in a school of nursing in Chorlton, where he still lived in digs. We used to get a coach to the school and back and I missed the coach that evening because Paul had said he'd give me a lift. I waited for an hour and he never came.

'Then he rang me about two weeks later and said that he had had the flu! Gave me all these excuses. I should have been warned then.'

The romance blossomed pretty quickly. By January 1984 we were engaged and the following August, exactly a year after our first meeting, Claire and I were married. The ceremony took place in a registry office, just the two families present and Norman acting as best man. Afterwards, we had a big reception at the Ashley Hotel in Hale, all of the United lads turning up for the 'afters'.

Those pre-season escapades might give the impression of a life already hurtling dangerously close to burnout, but that simply wasn't the case. Claire's arrival into my world brought a great deal of structure and serenity. By now, Norman was head over heels with his future wife, Julie, too. If anything, we were slipping into pipe-and-slippers mode.

True, I had bought myself a BMW, but it wasn't exactly cutting-edge engineering. Actually, it was this old, repulsive yellow thing that was shaped suspiciously like a Lada. Norman and I would drive around Manchester in it, though I didn't even have a licence. We felt a bit like gangsters cruising the hood.

You could say I wasn't the most accomplished of drivers. For weeks, I complained about how the engine shuddered every time I pulled away from traffic lights. One night, I think I was fiddling with tapes when a light turned green, so I said to Norman, 'Just sling it into first there.'

Next thing, I put my foot down and my yellow Beemer went

screaming down the road like something from *The Dukes of Hazzard*. Turned out I had been putting it into third gear all along! I was serious about my football, though, and by and large wouldn't countenance a drink from Monday to Saturday. Claire and I were living in a flat in Didsbury, but then Christopher was born that December and we moved into a house in Sale owned by the club.

Alan Brazil had been the previous occupant, but we were only there for maybe three months before switching again – with great excitement this time – into our plush new home at nearby Madeley Close in Hale.

Christopher was a large baby (nine pounds, four ounces), delivered by emergency Caesarian section while I sat chewing my nails in the waiting room. That same night, in the bed adjacent to Claire's, the daughter-in-law of Nobby Stiles also gave birth to a bouncing boy. What did they call him? Christopher, of course.

There was terrific slagging between the two new mothers as Nobby arrived to see his first grandson. A kind of point-scoring competition began between the relatives of Christopher Norbert Stiles and those of the eminently more handsome Christopher Eric McGrath.

I adored the whole idea of parenthood. Perhaps because I never had a father myself, I wanted to be there for my own kids. To be a protective presence. Maybe it didn't quite work out that way over time, but it was certainly what I intended.

Claire: 'Paul was an excellent dad. He was really hands on, changing nappies, nursing them to sleep, feeding them. To be fair, all through the years, he's always been very caring.

'When Christopher was born, he had the whole hospital in fits of laughter. The nurse was telling me that she took Christopher out to Paul, wrapped in a blanket with a little hat on. So he's holding his son for the first time, when Christopher suddenly opens his eyes. Paul immediately panics, putting his hand over the baby's face.

'The nurse asks, "What's the matter?"'

'Paul replies, "He'll go blind if he opens his eyes this soon!"'

'He'd never had any dealings with babies, you see. He thought they were like puppies. Over the years, Paul was actually the softest dad in the world. He always gave the boys whatever they wanted. He was never good at discipline.'

By now I was a fully fledged member of the United first-team set-up. Under Ron, we were always a decent Cup side. It was as if we thrived on the nervous energy of knockout football. In the League, we tended to slip up in humdrum fixtures. I mean look at United's record against Liverpool back then and it is astonishingly good. But we could follow up a win at Anfield with a defeat at home to the likes of Coventry or West Brom.

The start of the 1983–4 season had seen us beat Liverpool 2-0 in the Charity Shield and win eight of our first eleven League games, including victories over Liverpool again and a triumph against Arsenal at Highbury. I remember Ray Wilkins, especially, being on fire at the time.

Ray was one of my favourite people at United. A real class act as a player, but also one of those senior pros who always offered encouragement to less experienced members of the team. I never once remember Wilkins bawling out someone for making a mistake. It just wasn't his style. On the contrary, he'd always look for the positive.

When I was just breaking into the team, Ray was a massive support. I might just make a simple tackle, pass the ball ten yards, but he'd be on to me immediately. 'Fantastic Paul, absolutely fantastic. Keep it going big man.' I never forgot that. In fact, in later years, I tried to follow Ray's example when dealing with younger players.

Sadly, that League campaign petered out quite timidly with us winning just two of our last ten games to finish fourth. And, for United now, fourth was nowhere.

The highlight of the season would be a fantastic run to the

European Cup Winners' Cup semi-finals, in which we beat a Maradona-driven Barcelona along the way. Sadly, a late Paolo Rossi goal in Turin would edge Juventus past us into the final.

The 1984–5 season followed a similar pattern, flattering to deceive in the League (fourth again), beaten in the UEFA Cup quarter-final by Videoton of Hungary.

But redemption arrived in the FA Cup.

Six years after hearing my mother tell that nurse in St Brendan's that that silent, damaged kid slumped in front of her was 'going to play at Wembley some day', I finally got to fulfill the prophesy. More importantly, I was relevant all through the 1985 campaign, even scoring in both the fourth and fifth round victories over Coventry and Blackburn respectively.

I had finally become A Player.

Kevin Moran: 'I specifically remember the game against Blackburn. It was at Ewood Park, a freezing cold night. The ground was rock hard, absolutely rock hard. It was a real tricky game for us.

'Paul was just coming through at the time. He played in midfield for us that night and scored the second goal. I don't think he had played in the position too many times before, but his performance that night was just awesome. His strength, his power. Everything about him.

'The one thing I quickly came to realise with him was that he never knew or understood how good he actually was. That came through so much. He didn't think that he had the ability everybody else said he had. He had this lovely humble, under-stated manner about him.

'I used to say, "Paul, you should be getting that ball and going forward. You can do so much more with the talent that you have." His reaction was always, "Aah no, I'll just get it and give it . . ."

'He had what very few players have. It's what we call an overdrive. It's the ability to be running at high pace with someone and all of a sudden, from nowhere, it's like a fifth gear kicks in. Boom, the turbo comes on. And he could just wipe out the opponent to get there.

'He also had guts to burn. People used to say that I was brave, mainly because I had a name for getting cut quite often. Paul just didn't get cut because he was better in the air than me. But he was every bit as brave as I was. He'd never shirk a tackle, never shirk a header.'

It would take us two epic semi-finals against Liverpool to get to Wembley that year, a late, extra time Paul Walsh goal pulling us back to parity in the first game at Goodison Park. We fell behind in the replay at Maine Road only for second-half goals from Bryan Robson and Mark Hughes to secure our place in the 1985 final against Everton.

It was a game that would secure its place in FA Cup history, if not for the reasons we might have hoped for. And I played a guilty hand.

Actually, the contest itself was, for the most part, relatively dull and undramatic. Everton were a serious team at the time, about to break Liverpool's stranglehold on the League. On the day, they had plans for us and we had plans for them. It led to a pretty lethargic stalemate.

I had certainly been nervous in the build-up, fretting a little at the scale of the stage I was now stepping on to.

Frank Mullen: 'He was a bag of nerves before that final. There was a chief superintendent at Wembley called Pat Fanning. He was from Mayo. We knew one another through the police federation and the garda association. Through Pat, I literally got an access-all-areas badge at Wembley.

'So I was in the dressing room when United came in with the Cup. Paul was so thrilled. Because, before the game, he didn't want to play, he was that uptight.'

The final was actually meandering to one of the dullest goalless draws in Wembley history when, with roughly ten minutes remaining, I mishit a back pass, offering Peter Reid a clear run on the United goal. Kevin Moran immediately sprang to the rescue, but mistimed his tackle a fraction and Reid went down on the edge of our box, as if hit by sniper fire.

Kevin was promptly sent off for his challenge, the first player in history to be dismissed in an FA Cup final.

Ron had to rejig things frantically, withdrawing Frank Stapleton to play alongside me at centre-back. And, to be fair, Frank was just magnificent. He slotted in as if he'd been a defender all his life.

Frank Stapleton: 'I was astonished when Atkinson said to me, "You go play centre-back." I stalled for a second, as if to say "Why me?" I mean Bryan Robson had been a centre-back in his time. I had only played the position once before, in the 1983 League Cup final against Liverpool. We had a horrendous list of injuries that day.

'So, reluctantly, I said "OK", went in beside Paul and told him, "Right Paul, you've got to start talking here because I've never played this friggin' position before." I was warning him that my instinct would be to wander, to let people slip off my shoulder.

'I said, "You pick up Graeme Sharp, I'll mark Andy Gray." I felt I'd have no problem with Gray pace-wise and would be able to compete with him in the air. Paul just said, "Grand, that's great Frank!" I knew that, for whatever reason, he always liked marking Sharp.

'So we just got on with it. Most of it is a blur, to be honest. It was just a matter of making sure that we didn't make any mistakes. It was a battle and we got through it. It was easy to play alongside Paul because you always knew that people were never going to run away from him.

'People said that he didn't talk. But he did. He would pull people around, give the right instructions. You couldn't survive on a pitch like that without talking.'

With ten minutes of extra time remaining and the tie seemingly headed for a replay, Norman struck. His goal would go down as one of the greatest ever seen in the history of the competition, a run down the right wing, a jink inside Pat van den Hauwe, then – using the Everton full-back as a kind of human shield – curling the most sublime shot beyond the reach of a partially unsighted Neville Southall.

It was an astonishing goal that completely shattered Everton and lifted a huge burden of guilt from my conscience. I had been entirely to blame for Kevin's dismissal. If we'd lost the final, I'd never have forgiven myself.

Funnily enough, I have an uncomfortable memory of the celebrations. You know that moment when the winning team gathers for the group photograph and they're bouncing together as if on some invisible trampoline? When they're singing something imaginative like 'championeeee, championeeee'? I just felt incredibly self-conscious at that moment. That old voice, somewhere deep inside my head, still goading. '*You don't belong here.*' I've often looked at the video since and I can detect the unease in my expression. Even at that moment, low self-esteem was tugging me down.

Outrageously, Kevin was prevented from climbing the podium to receive a medal afterwards, but sanity eventually prevailed and he did subsequently receive one. We all felt for him. He didn't deserve that place in history because he was a scrupulously fair player. Hard, no question. But never malicious.

The function was held in the Royal Lancaster Hotel on Hyde Park, a regular stop for United at the time. The BBC presented *Match of the Day* live from there that night and we had a hell of a party. One abiding image is of Jimmy Hill holding court in a circle of players, among them a completely revved-up Norman.

Every time Jimmy expressed an opinion, Norman would pipe up, 'Well that must be right Jimmy, 'cos everyone knows you know your football.'

Kevin Moran: 'That night, I got a load of this "sorry for your troubles" stuff from different people. I remember saying at the function, "Look, I'm no different here from anyone else." I was just delighted we had won. Family and friends took over. I remember I gave my shirt to an uncle.'

The following day we paraded the Cup from an open-top bus through Manchester, and this time, at least, I felt entitled to wave. Just three months earlier, I had made my international debut for the Republic of Ireland. No question, I was A Player now.

Now all I needed was that Championship medal . . .

11

DRINK CLUB

I don't read very often but, last year, I got my hands on a book about the New York Mets baseball team that won the World Series in 1986.

It was called *The Bad Guys Won!* and chronicled the behind-the-scenes mayhem as a group of 'arrogant, insane, rock and roll party all night' players managed to win the biggest prize in base-ball. I couldn't put the book down. The Mets of 1986 broke every behavioural rule imaginable.

They drank, they brawled, they wrecked airplanes, trashed hotels, insulted fans and played the most offensive pranks on one another. They were the bad guys of American sport. Dysfunctional, vulgar, utterly unscrupulous. Yet, they won.

Reading the story, I was struck by a thought that, in 1986, Manchester United were pretty much seen as bad guys too. Nothing on the scale of the Mets, admittedly, but we were depicted as the heavy boozers of the First Division. The team supposedly pissing away its future. Caring too little and, habitually, coming up short.

That image, deserved or otherwise, almost certainly cost Ron Atkinson his job in November of that year. It also led to pretty deep historical divisions in the dressing room. There were those who drank and those who didn't.

I, of course, was a drinker.

How big a drinker? Big enough, I imagine, to be deemed a roaring drunk by the abstemious standards of today. But, back then, different attitudes prevailed. Beer was as much a part of most footballers' lives as pasta is today. Pre-match curfews rarely extended beyond forty-eight hours.

At United, we had our school of boozers and we considered ourselves pretty accomplished at it too. We didn't get messy. If there was a lock-in, say, at Paddy Crerand's, it never ever dissolved into drunkenness. We could hold our drink, you see.

But anyone who imagines that a group of players perpetually in party mode could finish third, fourth, fourth and fourth again in the English First Division cannot ever have experienced ninety minutes of seriously competitive football. It wouldn't happen because it couldn't.

By and large, we confined our drinking to Saturday nights and Sunday lunchtimes. If there was no midweek game, a session might start after training on the Tuesday, sometimes rolling all the way through into Wednesday morning. By today's standards, that's not very professional, I know. But, by the standards of the mid eighties, it was commonplace.

Maybe part of our infamy of the time came from the fact that Norman Whiteside and I spent so much time sidelined through injury, we effectively took it as a licence to drink.

I mean I made just nine League appearances during the 1983–4 season and improved to only twenty-three for the 1984–5 campaign. This despite the fact that, when fit, I was now considered a first choice centre-back.

Injured, I think both Norman and I would drink as a way of escaping. You can feel a bit lost when you're no longer particularly relevant to the first team dressing room. And, over time, I suppose I allowed this feeling to eat into me a little too much.

Eventually, I would quite literally drink whenever I could. It started off with bottles of lager. But, later in my career, I graduated to stronger stuff. Vodka, whatever. When you were sidelined, you'd really have nothing else to do. What else was there? Snooker? Golf? I wasn't a golfer. I could take snooker in small doses. I didn't have hobbies.

To be fair, the hard stuff was still a long way down the line in the mid eighties. At United, to me at least, everything felt rational and normal. The main men in our school of boozers were Norman, Robbo, Kevin, big Gordon and me. We could drink for hour upon hour without anyone ever looking remotely drunk (or so we thought). It never became stroppy or argumentative. We just enjoyed one another's company. Used it as a means of unwinding.

But, to this day, opinion remains divided on exactly where we stood in the annals of boozy football teams.

Ron Atkinson: 'Listen, we couldn't live with the Liverpool lads as drinkers. I used to stop Robbo going out with Terry McDermott. "He's a bad influence on you." I'd tell him. I mean has there ever been a fitter player than Bryan Robson? He'd tell me when they were going out. "Gaffer, I'm taking the boys out tonight." It might be Tuesday, if there was no midweek game. Or a Sunday lunchtime. I'd have no problem with it. There was a collectiveness there.

'To be fair, I can never recall Paul coming into the club in any sort of state that he shouldn't have been in. You might look at him sometimes and think "Hello, he's had a late night . . ." But he used to do all the training with United.

'This thing about the drink culture is always coming up. And it's always Robson, Whiteside and McGrath. Gordon Strachan told me he went out with them one time and they put him in the boot of the car!

'But, when I give after-dinner speeches now, I always say

that – seeing as how they were usually my three best players – maybe the other lads should have been out with them. Hey, they did it at the right times.'

Paddy Crerand's the Park was one of our more regular haunts in Altrincham. Most of us lived in Sale, which is pretty close. That's where you'd find the Little B, a good place for Sunday lunch and one of our regular watering holes I remember too, one great session we had in the Circus Tavern, the smallest pub in Manchester. It was run by a chap called Terry Corless, who would have known a lot of the United players.

Terry had a rule that he never let anyone stay after closing but, this particular night, for some reason he relented. The pub only served bitter and, though most of us were lager or Guinness drinkers, we settled in for a great night. It all felt very civilised, very sane.

Another regular haunt in the centre of Manchester was a night-club called Bavardage. We had some terrific nights there, especially after midweek European games. Again, there was never a sense of betraying any trust or responsibility. We worked hard, then we drank.

Kevin Moran: 'Our drinking was never ever frowned upon or clamped down on. I can never remember Ron calling us in and having a go at us over drinking during the week. Never. It was accepted. It was part of the game generally. You ask Ronnie Whelan about Liverpool. They had some of the best drinkers you'd ever come across and they won every single thing, Championships, European Cups, the lot.

'I know other United players will express a different attitude. But week in, week out, the best three players we had were invariably Robson, McGrath and Whiteside.

'Personally, I think the perception was exaggerated. I know Norman and Paul would have done a bit more than I did. I wasn't really one for having a few pints after training. I couldn't be arsed. But the odd time it might happen. And, when it happened, it was a good session.

'We never ever did it before games, though. Never ever did it at the wrong time. I always had a rule myself. Thursday night, I could go to the pub for a couple. But I'd never kick on after that. Maybe two or three drinks, that would be it. I'd never see myself going on to a nightclub or anything like that.'

Maybe, without knowing, I was deeper into it than the others. I do remember an end of season trip to Swaziland. It was the only time Ron actually turned on me, calling me a 'bloody disgrace'.

I came down from the room this day and Ron was sitting out by the pool with John Gidman and Arthur Albiston. It was a beautiful setting and a beautiful day. The lads were in their tracksuits, but they had beers in front of them. I think it was John who turned to me and asked, 'What are you having big man?'

Without thinking, I immediately replied, 'Oh, I'll have a beer.'

I remember sitting there, getting the drinks in, thinking 'This is magnificent.' Ron had gone off to do his own thing. We were playing Tottenham that evening in a tournament game. But this was end of season. It didn't really matter. Get a few waters in before kick-off and we'd be fine.

That, at least, was how I read things.

What I hadn't realised, of course, was that John and Arthur were both injured. They wouldn't be playing. In hindsight, I remember them looking a little startled when I had asked for a beer. But Giddy just shrugged his shoulders as if to say, 'Presumably, he knows what he's doing.'

Trouble was, one beer led to a dozen. And by kick-off, I was buckled.

My performance against Spurs that night was absolutely abysmal, yet somehow we managed to bring the game to penalties. Under normal circumstances I wouldn't have dreamt of taking one, but we simply ran out of takers in the end. By process of elimination, my time had come.

Tragically, everything would come down to my spot kick. If I managed to beat Ray Clemence, we won the tournament. Up I stepped, trying to look nonchalant, like someone who had taken (and scored) hundreds of penalties in his career. No pressure. Did I pick a spot? You're having a laugh.

All I concentrated on was making a clean connection. It was too much to ask, though. Not alone did I fail to beat Ray, I barely reached him with my effort. The ball just trickled harmlessly into his grasp. He could have pulled out the *Racing Post* and checked a few cards while he was waiting.

On the sideline, Ron was apoplectic with rage. He absolutely lacerated me afterwards for my lack of professionalism, telling me – not unreasonably – that I was indeed 'a bloody disgrace'. And he assured me that I'd be reporting back early for pre-season. I'd never seen him so angry.

But, twenty minutes later, all would be forgotten. One of the things I loved about Ron was the fact that he never held grudges. Once he bawled you out, it was over. He never stayed bitter.

A lovely memory I have of that trip is of all the United team in an exclusively all-white nightclub when two bouncers came across and warned the other players that, if either Remi Moses or myself 'clicked', we weren't to leave by the front door. Remi and I, of course, were black. It wouldn't be considered safe for either of us to be seen leaving with a local white girl.

The boys immediately asked the DJ to play a special request. Next thing, Paul McCartney's 'Ebony and Ivory' came on and everyone linked arms in a show of solidarity. That's one of my fondest memories of life on the road with United.

There was actually a great bond in that team. A real sense of loyalty. It's something that I loved about the sessions that we'd have. This feeling of being part of a genuinely tight group. But maybe drink was feeding an illusion. Maybe it suited me to believe that those sessions were, somehow, nurturing.

Frank Stapleton: 'Everyone keeps talking about Liverpool being just as bad for drink and I don't really believe it. I mean I'm sure they had drinkers, but I don't think they went on huge binges. Just go through the individuals.

'You didn't see Hansen out. You didn't see Lawrenson on a binge. Dalglish didn't drink. Souness liked a glass of champagne, but he was a dedicated footballer. You're talking about the mainstay of their team there. Binge drinkers? I don't think so. It's an image they were quite happy with I think, having people believe they were on these sessions. But they knew when to stop.

'At United, we had players who should have won the League. Just look at the quality. Ray Wilkins, Bryan Robson, Remi Moses, Steve Coppell, Norman, Paul. We definitely had the squad.

'But we found ourselves in winning positions on a couple of occasions in the League, only to lose it. I'm not saying that was necessarily down to how certain people were behaving themselves, but you could see what was going on. Towards the end, it got really, really bad. Players were just running riot, more or less doing what they wanted.

'It was never checked on.'

After a while, I would have been conscious that I was actually drinking far too much. If I was going anywhere with Claire, I'd have to have a few drinks before we even went outside the door. We were getting invited out a lot, going to parties all over Manchester. Claire always begged me, 'Look, please don't get drunk tonight.'

I rarely listened. I'd have enough on board before we'd even arrive to be maybe just two more drinks away from drunkenness. Looking back, it was very tough for her having to put up with that. Everyone else could arrive at a party stone-cold sober and just enjoy the night. I needed to be on a fast track to oblivion.

I was, certainly, better able to hold drink in those early days. When I was just out with the lads, I'd make a point of always trying to stay reasonably straight. It was the manly thing to do, you see. Match them drink for drink without making a show of myself.

Of course, it didn't always go to plan.

I do remember a night out with Norman, when we were drinking in a place near Wilmslow. It was the early hours by the time we left and we just couldn't get a cab. So we walked in the freezing cold to Frank's house.

Frank Stapleton: 'I was between houses at the time, living in rented accommodation in Wilmslow. It was about four in the morning when the bell went. I went down and it was Paul and Norman. The two of them were out of their heads. Paul had been to the house once before. My lad, Scott, would have been good mates with his lad, Chris.

'I said to them, "What the hell are ye doing here?" It turned out they'd been in this hotel halfway between Manchester Airport and Wilmslow. So they had walked maybe three or four miles on a country road to get to my place. I remember, I was telling them to be quiet. The kids were upstairs in bed. Had to drive them both home in the end.

'That was the problem under Ron at United. You were off from Tuesday lunchtime until Thursday. And the lads who were drinkers would go straight out on a binge on Tuesday lunchtime until all hours Wednesday morning.

'I mean, in all the time I was at Old Trafford under Ron Atkinson, I never did a full day's training. Even in pre-season, we did half days all the time. I had been used to working morning and afternoon every single day with Arsenal. Even on Thursdays, at the end of training, Don Howe would have us out doing shuttle runs in the shale car park at London Colney and we'd then have a five-a-side in the indoor gym at Highbury on Friday mornings.

'At United, we'd just have the odd physical day. Just a bit of running maybe every two or three months. It was a different concept. And, when you look at Paul's situation, I think someone even stronger than him would have been lured into the drink culture. I mean other people did get dragged in.

'It didn't help Paul's situation. Actually, it probably made it a lot worse.'

There were certainly two camps in the dressing room: those who did and those who didn't. I do remember that, when Arnold Muhren left for Ajax, he did a big newspaper article heavily criticising the drinking at United. Arnold very rarely drank. Having been brought up in Dutch football, he thought our social habits a little excessive, to put it mildly.

People like Arnold and Jesper Olsen were coming from a very different culture and mindset in terms of preparation. They just couldn't understand our approach to the game.

Kevin Moran: 'Ron Atkinson was very much off the cuff. He just wanted to come down and join in the five-a-side. He was old school. "Ah, put the cones away and let's have a game ..." Forget the technical stuff. He was dying for a game himself. I suppose you're talking about a different era, a different time.

'You look at the levels you've got to go to for coaching

badges now and the difference is so huge. I remember talking to Jesper about it and he said he'd never seen anything as bad in his life. But, when you don't know anything better, what do you judge it on?

'I could judge it when I went to Spain subsequently and was introduced to warm-ups that lasted three quarters of an hour. Just the warm-ups! And really technical training sessions. Dave Sexton used do that at United before Ron. But Ron never did.

'He probably thought. "Sure, look at that other shower [Irish expression for 'that other crowd'] down the road who don't do anything . . ."

'I mean, I'd ask Ronnie [Whelan] how Liverpool trained. "Five-a-sides," he'd say.

"That's all ye do, five-a-sides?"

"That's all."

'People were always looking at Liverpool and wondering what the secret was. The secret was probably just having good players and getting them to bond and play together. I mean, at the start of every single season, we would think "This is going to be our year, look how much that we've improved . . ."

'You knew that you were capable of doing it. Because our track record against Liverpool was awesome. But I'd rather lose the battle and win the war. Which is what Liverpool invariably did.'

Frank Stapleton: 'I remember one season [1983–4], with ten games to go, we were two points clear at the top. We beat Arsenal 4-0 at Old Trafford on Easter Saturday. Then there was a free week, for the FA Cup I think. And we ended up going away on a trip to Majorca. It was a jolly.

'Most of the lads didn't want to go. We just wanted to stay and train, concentrate on the next game. I thought the timing was wrong and tried to get out of it. I didn't want to go. But Ron just wanted us to get away. We were out there for close to a week, did a little bit of training. Nothing much.

'When we came back, we lost 2-0 away to the bottom team, West Brom. And, after that, we went into free fall. It was just so disappointing.'

We certainly wouldn't have been drinking day in, day out. I mean you had to be able to train for a start. In those days, I was expected to take a full part in all of the physical sessions, my knees not yet having been declared protected species.

The routine, generally, was that you wouldn't drink within forty-eight hours of a game. Hand on heart I can say that that rule was rarely abused. You still had to walk the walk, you see. You still had to play.

But injury changed everything. When injured, that forty-eight-hour rule would just cease to apply. If there was no game to play, there was no restriction. If there was no restriction, there was no closing time. That was the mindset.

I especially loved Sundays in Paddy Crerand's. If it was cold, there'd be a big fire on and we'd sit there with all the punters, pretty much drinking through the day. At night, a little Irish music would start up. No one ever bothered us. It felt safe and warm, a lovely sanctuary from the stresses of big games, frustrated fans and – maybe more than anything – brittle knees.

But the further I got into my United career and the more problematic those knees became, the more enthusiastically I imbibed.

Ron's reign as United boss was brought to an abrupt conclusion in November 1986. Another promising League position had been squandered the previous season, United again slipping to fourth, despite winning our first ten games. For a time, people had actually been telling us we were certainties for the title.

But injuries to Robbo, Gordon Strachan, John Gidman and a career-ending ankle problem for Remi Moses led to a gradual unravelling of confidence and our form just tailed away. Unknown to us, Ron – devastated by the slippage – had actually offered his resignation to the chairman, Martin Edwards.

The offer wasn't accepted, but Ron would have come to the start of the 1986–7 campaign knowing that United needed another fast start. As it happened, we left the blocks at a crawl.

Maybe pre-season offered an ominous portent.

We went to play a tournament in Amsterdam where, as we gathered one night for our evening meal, it was discovered that seven players were missing. Ron immediately did a roll call and, to his utter amazement, all of the so-called 'drinkers' were present and correct.

The most unlikely of culprits emerged, people like Gary Walsh, Jesper Olsen, Terry Gibson and Clayton Blackmore.

Boy did we milk that moment when they came down for breakfast the following morning. It was the revenge of the big hitters. Robson, McGrath and Whiteside, sitting there, clucking their tongues, grinning smugly about this 'disgraceful behaviour'. Needless to say, Ron was not amused.

He was already frustrated by the fact that five of the first-team squad had just returned from the World Cup in Mexico, needing operations. That was a handicap our squad just couldn't absorb. We would lose our first three League games, then draw at Leicester, trounce Southampton 5-1 before losing another three on the trot. We were joint bottom after eight games.

The final straw arrived with a shocking 1-4 hammering in a Littlewoods Cup replay at Southampton. Two days later, Ron was sacked.

Norman Whiteside: 'Yet again, I was injured. I had just come into the Cliff to do a few laps and was on my way up to the physio's room. Next thing, Ron pulled up in the car. He'd just been to Old Trafford. He called me over. I could see he was nearly in tears. "I've just been sacked!" he said.

'He said he wanted everyone to come back to the Cliff, so that he could tell them. The boys were all in the other training ground on Littleton Road.

'So I went up there and called over the reserve manager, Brian Whitehouse. "The boss wants everyone back, he's just been sacked," I said. So we all went back and Ron just went around, shaking everyone's hand, wishing them well for the future.

'That night, he held a party in his house in Rochdale. I went to it and so did Robbo and Strachan. And that night he told us he had heard that Alex Ferguson would be taking over.'

I didn't go to the party. Not sure I was even invited, actually. Maybe Ron just wanted to keep Norman and myself apart. If so, he was probably wise.

I was desperately sorry to see him leave. In fact, I felt it was a measure of the man that he brought us all in to tell us the news himself. If it had been me, I think I'd just have disappeared without saying anything to anybody. But Ron would never shy away from things. Like I said before, he was a man's man.

I know that Alex Ferguson took issue afterwards with the fact that Ron invited players to his party. Alex felt that this wasn't exactly helpful, given United had a game that weekend. But, to the best of my knowledge, the only players who went to Rochdale that night were those already on the injured list.

There was certainly no question of him trying to sabotage Alex's first game.

Ron Atkinson: 'I get on well with Alex, but I just think that when you take on a job, you shouldn't be critical of what's gone on before you. And he has made reference to the drink culture at United before he came. It's too easy to blame that. I mean it wasn't as if they were out on Friday nights.'

My own view is that the one thing we lacked at United under Ron was a prolific goalscorer. Probably the first one that came on the scene in the eighties would be Brian McClair. I mean Frank wasn't prolific. He was a fantastic leader of the line, but he wasn't prolific. Norman was a scorer of great goals, but he wasn't prolific either.

We never had anybody that could guarantee you twenty to twenty-five goals in a season. Someone to score tap-ins, if you like. We certainly got goals from midfield. Robbo could be depended upon for ten goals a season. He was phenomenal. Strachan would get a few. We'd get the occasional goal from defence too, but we didn't have what you'd call 'a goal-machine' striker. Liverpool did. They had Ian Rush who seemed to score for fun. To me, that was the difference between us.

I still love Ron. Always will. And United were certainly no New York Mets in the mid-eighties. But we *were* big boozers and I was one of the biggest. I was a pretty mixed up young footballer when I joined United in 1982. Drink offered escapism. And, over time, I became an expert at escaping everything around me.

By the time Ron left, I was probably floating somewhere in my own, private world. And something had to give.

12

POLAR OPPOSITES

The first training session with a new manager is always an exercise in bluff.

Bluff on his side, bluff on the players' side. The great comfort blanket of a footballer's life, the clique, is suddenly threatened. Gossip takes over. Paranoia too. Everyone begins second-guessing the likes and prejudices of the new man.

In Alex Ferguson's case, we felt prepared for the impending war. Gordon Strachan had worked under him at Aberdeen and painted pretty graphic images of a hard, taciturn man who liked to control everything and everybody within the boundaries of his football club.

Now maybe Gordon wasn't the most objective of voices. He could clearly tap into some kind of troubled personal history with Fergie that now persuaded him his days with Manchester United were numbered, even though by all accounts they were still in regular contact.

'Ach, that's me buggered then, I'm on my bike . . .' was the gist of Strach's response to Ferguson's appointment in November 1986.

We certainly knew things were about to change. The image of United as a club of boozers was now rampant in the game. Under

Ron Atkinson, we had never finished lower than fourth in the First Division. Trouble was, we never finished higher than third under Big Ron either.

United, now, had gone nineteen years without a title. The dressing room was depicted as nurturing a kind of dockers' bar mentality, some of us – obviously – being bigger culprits than others. And the whole world knew our names.

Ferguson was officially appointed on a Thursday, and the following day, we assembled in the gym at the Cliff to meet him. It was an unremarkable meeting. He said little beyond the customary 'We're all in this together' kind of stuff, mindful I suppose that we were playing Oxford away the following day.

Rightly or wrongly, I came to an immediate conclusion that he didn't rate me.

Fergie picked me in midfield for the Oxford game, then took me off after about an hour. We lost 2-0. I was convinced he was trying to prove a point and I discovered from a subsequent conversation with Bryan Robson that he *did* express doubts about my ability or, maybe more pertinently, my discipline.

The following Monday, back in the gym, Fergie offered us the first glimpse of that fabled hairdryer. He laid down the law in no uncertain terms, eyeballing those of us perceived to be heavyweight drinkers and insisting that from now on things would be done his way and his way only. I always thought we played really entertaining football in Ron's time with United, football that – in a sense – mirrored his personality.

Now a whole new era was dawning and we all felt a bit like errant schoolboys about to be whipped into shape.

Sir Alex Ferguson: 'The big mistake I made on my very first day was deciding to play Paul in the centre of midfield against Oxford. He wasn't in great shape from the night before. When I took him off, he looked surprised. I don't think he'd been

145

taken off too often in a game of football.

'If I'd known he'd been out the night before, I'd have played him centre-half. But there were a lot of players injured. And I decided to try to stabilise things. So I played Kevin Moran and Graeme Hogg at centre-back with Remi Moses and Paul sitting in the centre of midfield. It didn't work.

'I already knew a little about the drinking through Gordon Strachan so, that Monday, I said to them, "Look, I've a difficulty here. You see, I can't change who I am. So you all need to change who you are!"

'There was a sense of amazement in the place. Some of the younger kids looked a little startled. I remember coming out and saying to myself "I don't think I've done the right thing there . . ." But I couldn't go back on it.

'My main intention was to tell them who I was rather than trying to find out anything about them. Then I had a chat with Robbo. He was as much a party animal as any of them. And his attitude was, "Well, the lads like a drink, but they can always do it on a Saturday."

'And I said to him, "Tell me what it is that ye're doing on a Saturday? Because you've not won anything. Is that not the answer? Winning things?" I mean they used to go on about Liverpool, with all their trophies, drinking like hell. But there's a distinction there. A winning team, you can turn a blind eye to everything.'

Alex made it clear from the outset that he would run every aspect of the club. And in many ways, you had to hand it to him. He worked nearly twenty-four hours a day. Every night, he seemed to be watching a game somewhere. Norman Davies, the old kit man, used to drive him around and he'd say, 'Alex would see floodlights on and want to know whose ground it was in case there was someone worth looking at there.' I doubt he was ever at home.

In hindsight, you can't but admire the dedication of the man but, at the time, all I could see was a cold, autocratic figure who was hell-bent on taking the laughter out of the dressing room.

I was also unnerved a little by what Robbo had told me before the new manager had even seen me play. Something along the lines of Ferguson saying, 'McGrath, I'm not happy with him . . .' Robbo said he'd fought my corner and I've little doubt he did. But, to me, this was a manager who wanted to see the back of Paul McGrath.

To begin with, though, the changes were superficial. Fergie brought in a stricter dress code. He insisted on hair being short. My liking for wearing an earring was pretty forcibly frowned upon too, though I never wore it on club duty. He had an abruptness in how he spoke to you. There was almost a sense of being lectured.

Now, I've always had an aversion to people barking at me, trying to put me in my box. I sense it goes back to the orphanage days. This thing of being talked down to. Or, at the very least, suspecting that was happening.

The moment I sense someone do that, I turn rebellious. I mean I can see what Alex was trying to do. Things had to change. But from the moment he raised his voice to me, I'm afraid we were on a collision course. I stopped listening. This invisible armour would come down. My eyes would glaze over. I'd sit there thinking 'No one speaks to me like that. You can try, but you're not going to dominate me.'

Fergie would be incandescent. I could see the exasperation in his eyes. He wrote in his autobiography, *Managing My Life*, that he found me 'unreachable'. And, in some respects, I was. United might have had a reputation for dysfunction at the time, but I felt happily cocooned in the belly of it.

Now Alex wanted to rewrite the rules.

Claire: 'I didn't see the drinking as anything abnormal. It seemed to me that that was what they all did. But, when Alex Ferguson came in, things started to change. Paul just took an instant dislike to him. Not a personal dislike, but a dislike of his rules. He was just so different to Ron Atkinson. Ron used go out for drinks with the boys. He knew all the wives' names. It was like an extended family.

'Whereas Alex came in and changed it all. He didn't want the wives or children around. He was less inclined to say hello. He was clearly trying to bring in a sense of discipline that was obviously needed. Paul used to come home from training in a stinking mood. There might have been a row about his hair or his earring.

'At the time, Paul had his hair permed ridiculously. It used to hang down over his collars and he thought he was the trendiest thing. But, once Alex came, everyone had to have their hair short. So they just seemed to be rubbing one another up the wrong way all the time.'

Frank Stapleton: 'I couldn't see that people were going to last long if they continued drinking. Because Alex wasn't going to tolerate it. And he had the backing of the board to do whatever he wanted. At the time, Norman and Paul were very good players. Excellent players. But what Ferguson didn't like was unreliability. He didn't want this situation where one week they were very good, and the next week very poor. Especially if it was because of other things.'

Norman Whiteside: 'The way Ron operated, he didn't give a hoot what you did off the park as long as you performed on the Saturday. That was it. He didn't really care if Robson, Whiteside and McGrath were drinking because we were the first names on his team sheet. Why? Because we performed for him every week.

'There's no doubt he'd hear stories about us being out and about. But he wouldn't come running around the pubs trying to find us. Fergie would. He'd go from one end of Altrincham to the other, dipping his head into pubs, asking, "Have they been in here? Where are they now?" I wouldn't say that Ron didn't care. He just let us get on with it, being adults. Or maybe not, as the case might be . . .

'So, by the time Alex came, some of us had been labelled. You could see that from the first day he arrived. He'd turn up at your house, unannounced, checking up on you, doing the detective work. I remember one evening I had just bought six cases of wine. I had this wine rack, sunk into the wall, that could take eighty-eight bottles.

'So I'm putting all this wine in the rack and I just happen to look out the kitchen window. And there's Ferguson and Archie Knox coming up my drive. I don't think they saw the wine.'

The biggest difference was the feeling that you were being constantly monitored. That he didn't quite trust you. Training became a lot tougher. You knew you were being scrutinised. The teams he picked were pretty much shaped by what he would see in training.

But it would be wrong to say we were in any way intimidated. We weren't. If anything, we took the view that here was a guy coming down from Scotland to one of the biggest clubs in the world and trying to convince people that he was up to the job. True, he had been successful at Aberdeen.

But this was another world. We were big shots. We were United. As far as we were concerned, the new manager was more on trial than any of us.

So the drinking didn't stop. There was no overnight revolution.

In a sense, we just became a little more secretive. You had to be on your toes a bit. Did it stop us going out? No.

To begin with, there was virtually no change in personnel and – thereby – no great change in habits. Hard though it might be to imagine in today's game, United just didn't have the funds to finance an assault on the transfer market. Maybe that, too, made some of us feel impregnable.

Sir Alex Ferguson: 'The difficulty I had first of all was that I was trying to establish myself at a massive football club that had really gone backwards. Not just in terms of where the first team were at that time, but the whole club. It was one of those situations where I was going to sink or swim by my own decisions. And I had to establish some sort of discipline and authority from the word go.

'My first season there, the chairman says to me, "How many players do you think we need?" I said, "Eight!" He nearly fainted. He said, "Eight? But we've got sixteen internationals here . . ."

'I said, "Well you asked for my opinion. We need eight. We need energy. There's no energy in this team. This is a team that's grown old together Mr Chairman." I mean, up front, Frank [Stapleton] was gone. He was inclined to drift out to the wing all the time. Peter Davenport just wasn't an aggressive centre-forward. I had bought Terry Gibson from Coventry and the move was too big for him. I just didn't have the ingredients to make Manchester United a big club.'

I remember one of our first trips under Alex took us to the Middle East. Lads got stuck into the beers, and eventually he pulled us all into a room. 'That's it,' he barked. 'You've been on it all afternoon. I said you could have a drink, but I didn't expect you to do that.' He read us the riot act, ordering everyone to be in their rooms by seven.

Seven o'clock came and went. Eight o'clock. No movement. Then a lot of the lads went out, down to a local nightclub and stayed there till about four in the morning. For some reason, I didn't go. But Alex got wind of it. Next thing, he turns up in the club, marches the lads out and makes them walk all the way back to the hotel, maybe a mile and a half at four in the morning!

There were a few of the more senior players among the culprits. All along the way, he kept saying to them, 'Fucking hell, ye're supposed to be the backbone of this team. The ones to lead. And look at ye . . .'

Sir Alex Ferguson: 'The perception that I was always lecturing would probably be one hundred per cent right. There was no real communication. That's where my lack of experience would have come into it, you see. Although I had the experience of Aberdeen, that was an easy club to run. They were young lads, all grew up together. We had great success, but I was never confronted with a problem. So my management skills were probably not up to dealing with a Paul McGrath. Today, I think I would go down a better route in trying to get through to him. The arm on the shoulder, fatherly type of thing.

'But I was just working from scratch, if you know what I mean. I had no individual campaign for Paul McGrath, Norman Whiteside, Kevin Moran or whoever. I was only thinking of one thing – Manchester United. And how I could get this ship back on an even keel.

'At that time, when I'd see Paul sitting there, knowing I wasn't getting any response, it probably created a sort of war of attrition. I mean I tried to devote a lot of time to both Paul and Norman, to get them to come round. By the finish, I think they must have been in the manager's office more times than any other players in the history of Manchester United.'

That first season under Alex carried little hint of what he was going to achieve with United in years to come. Our League form improved sufficiently to lift us up to eleventh by the end of the season. Maybe the most momentous achievement was a 1-0 Boxing Day victory against Liverpool at Anfield, secured with a late goal from Norman.

But even that had to be tempered by an acknowledgement that, under Ron, we tended to have the Indian sign over the perennial champions anyway.

There was also a third round FA Cup victory over neighbours City, and a hot-tempered 2-0 League victory over Arsenal at Old Trafford that brought the Londoners' unbeaten run of twenty-two games to an end. But, by and large, the season petered out a little timidly.

If the Messiah was among us, he was still dressed as an ordinary man.

13

TROUBLE

To the untrained eye, I started the 1987–8 season as one of the pillars of Manchester United Football Club.

I was floating through life. Football seemed easy. During pre-season, I had been selected in the Football League side for the Mercantile Credit Centenary Classic at Wembley against the so-called Rest of the World. We won the game 3-0 and my performance against Diego Maradona was widely acclaimed.

In the dressing room afterwards, I felt ten feet tall. The boys were full of it. 'Diego fucking who?'

Our other two stars of the day had been Bryan Robson and Norman Whiteside, sharing the three goals between them. It was quite a compliment to English football, but an even bigger one to United.

Fergie must have had very mixed feelings that day as he watched us swap jerseys with Maradona, Platini and Co. In a star-studded team that included the likes of Peter Shilton, Liam Brady, Peter Beardsley, Ossie Ardiles and Chris Waddle, the three United boys stole the plaudits.

Yep, the three drinkers.

By now, Norman had his own fan club up and running from an office in Altrincham. Robbo was England captain. I was a fully fledged international too, feeling much more a part of the Irish set-up since Jack Charlton took the reins. There was a genuine sense of a big season pending for all of us.

We started relatively promisingly too, and all was fine in my world until we travelled to East London for a game with West Ham on 25 October.

Sir Alex Ferguson: 'I can still see it to this day. Paul had this really nonchalant way of defending. He could just sally through a game. A ball would come into the box and he'd just back-heel it to safety. This day at West Ham, he tried it and somehow managed to do his knee.

'It was a desperate blow because it would keep him side-lined for five months. And, by then, we had improved the players' fitness levels. For a while, Paul was terrific. Then this happens and he's gone from October til March. I'll always remember, he came back and played about three games.

'But we had an Easter Monday visit to Anfield coming up. And I dithered over whether I should play him or not, because Rush and Dalglish were a handful. I just wasn't sure that he was ready for them. I played him in the end and he was absolutely magnificent. Honestly, he just walked through the game. Never gave Rush a kick.

'And, of course, Ian Rush never would score against United while McGrath was playing. We actually gave Liverpool a bit of a doing that day, came back from 1-3 down to draw 3-3. I know that doesn't sound great defensively. But McGrath was superb. It told you a lot about him.'

Not long after I broke down at Upton Park, Norman followed me into the medical room. He was having serious problems with his knees too, and it was around this time that our reputation as a 'terrible twosome' began to gather steam. Paddy Crerand's bar, the Park in Altrincham, remained a favourite haunt.

Paddy was very loyal, very protective. He'd cut the nose off anyone trying to imply that we might ever have left his place under the weather. By and large, we didn't.

But it was a strange and difficult time. Being injured, you just felt totally disenfranchised from the dressing room. The team pushed on without us. Results were good. Fergie had brought in Brian McClair from Celtic and, much to our surprise, Viv Anderson from bitter rivals Arsenal. We were staggered by Viv's arrival; even more staggered when Alex invited Norman to show him around Manchester.

McClair was the natural poacher United had been missing and Viv had the competitive streak that Fergie always coveted in a player. Looking in from the outside, United seemed to be doing just fine without me.

In December, Steve Bruce arrived from Norwich for £850,000. He might have been bought with the intention of forming a long-term partnership with me but, by now, my glass was always half empty.

I suppose I started drinking to blot out the worries. Norman did much the same. We became soulmates. Out of the loop, you felt invisible. There was talk of an end of season clear-out. From positions of strength, both of us now felt increasingly vulnerable. So the barstool became the shrink's couch.

'You're safe, I'm the one he's gonna offload . . .'

'Big man, you're raving. He's not stupid. He wants to build his team around you.'

'Nah, he doesn't fancy me. Robbo told me what he said.'

'You're wrong . . .'

'No, trust me, I know. Hasn't liked me from day one.'

'Hey, I'm the one still waiting for a new contract.'

'Bollocks, that's a formality.'
'Somehow I don't think so.'
'Anyway, how's the clock?'
'Only twenty-five to . . .'
'When you're ready Paddy!'

Norman Whiteside: 'Remember you're talking about twenty years ago. It was just different in those days. You had a drink and worked it off in the gym the next day. We were injured so the opportunity was always there. We had no game to work up to. It meant you could be out seven nights a week if you wanted.

'You shouldn't of course. But we took advantage of our situation. It's the opposite now. When you're injured, you have to work even harder to keep yourself fit. But we didn't do that. Maybe it was our downfall.

'Twenty years ago, the injured ones were the ones sent out to do all the charity functions. Actually, when Fergie first came, he insisted that all the injured players go up to Old Trafford to meet guests at lunchtime. We'd have to report back to the Cliff in an hour and a half.

'So you're sitting down at Old Trafford with the à la carte menu, ordering what you like. Beef stroganoff, all sorts. I started piling on the weight.'

Approaching Christmas, I bounced back into the headlines for all the wrong reasons. Claire was heavily pregnant with our second child, Mitchell. She had already had two miscarriages since Christopher's birth in 1984 so I had every reason to be an attentive husband.

But I was still months away from playing again and the frustration was becoming complicated by boredom.

This particular day, I rang Norman to see what he was up to. Code for checking out if he was available for a session.

It was a few days before his wedding and they'd been erecting a marquee in his garden for the function. His future father-in-law, an engineer, had supplied his own workers to do the electrics. As a thank you, Norman took the boys to the Four Seasons hotel for a drink. 'Come down and join us,' said Norman when I phoned.

Bingo. Boredom sorted.

The Guinness flows and, by closing, Norman's fiancée – Julie – has arrived to collect him. I'm offering anyone and everyone a lift home. Funnily, no takers. Julie takes one look at me with the car keys in my hand and offers to drive me home. 'Nah, sure I'm grand. Only live down the road.'

My bluff is called on a bend entering Hale. I clip the kerb. That's when everything slows and gets a little silly. I'm going to crash into someone's garden. I let go of the steering wheel and it starts spinning like a frisby. Do I feel fear? I feel nothing. I just put my hands up to protect my face and wait for all the ripping, smashing sounds to end. I wait for silence.

The next thing I know, there are people helping me out of the wreckage and lying me on the ground. Their faces look ghostly with concern. And I'm laughing. Every time I attempt to sit up, a little geyser of blood goes spurting from my head. It's hilarious. To me, at least.

'Watch this, oooooooooh, hee hee hee . . .' Hysterical.

Claire: 'The first thing I knew, an ambulance man rang me. I'll never forget his words. "Do you want to sit down?" My heart missed a beat. "Oh my God, what's happened? He said that Paul had been in a crash, but that he was OK and had been taken to Woodenshaw hospital.

'So I went over and found him sitting on a gurney, drunk. He wanted to go home. But the police came and took a blood sample, which he wasn't too happy about. I was so furious with him. We only lived about a mile away from the hotel. "Why didn't you phone me? "I kept asking him.

'I then discovered that Julie had offered him a lift. But he was just pig-headed and drove, presuming it would be OK. The car was an absolute mess. But, luckily, the main impact was on the passenger's side. If it had been on his side, he wouldn't have had any legs left.

'And the people in the house were lucky too. Because it was a fairly substantial garden in Hale and the house was quite far back. He'd gone through the hedge and only a tree stopped him ploughing into the house.'

Norman Whiteside: 'Julie and I stopped for fish and chips on the way home. Almost as soon as we got into the house, the phone goes. It's Claire, telling me he's in hospital. So Julie drove me over straight away and I remember the police hanging around, waiting to interview him.

'For some reason, the rumour actually got out that I had been in the passenger seat and had run away from the accident. You only had to see the car to know that, if I had been in that seat, I'd be dead.

'The next day I head into training and walk into the medical room. Jim McGregor, the physio, comes straight over. "You'd better go and explain yourself to the boss," he says.

'"What do you mean?"

'"You were out with Paul McGrath last night, weren't you?"

'"Yeah."

'"And he's not well, is he?"

'The story had reached the training ground even before I got there. So I went straight in to Alex and explained the situation. All about the boys from the marquee, how Paul had joined, how he had gone home alone. He wasn't happy.'

I could see the disgust on the manager's face when he came to see me. I tried to be flippant. 'How are you?' he asked. Oh grand.

Not a bother. Even then I wasn't really absorbing the seriousness of what had happened. The fact that I could have killed someone. That I was about to be banned.

I could tell Alex was sickened with it. He was thinking exactly what any other rational human being would be thinking. 'What if someone's child was walking along there?'

Sir Alex Ferguson: 'What sickened me was that someone had offered to run him home and he wouldn't take it. That's what annoyed me. It angered me. I mean I used to sit him down, read him the riot act and Paul would sit there shaking his head. "Yeah boss, I know. Yeah, I'm sorry."

'Norman would hold his hand up and admit that whatever he'd done was "fucking stupid". But I couldn't get to Paul the way I could get to Norman. I don't think he maybe realised what he was doing to himself. It was one of those situations where I felt I could never get through to him.

'Actually, I wasn't getting through to him. But he was such an affable, unaffected, pleasant young man. He would sit and just nod his head to you. If I could have got him to lose his temper, I probably would have got more out of him. But he wouldn't lose his temper.'

Quite rightly, the accident led to me losing my licence. I was ashamed. Now I needed to be driven everywhere. Couldn't even collect Christopher from playschool. The stigma of what I'd done really began to depress me. It just touched an inner nerve.

My reaction came straight from the textbook of cop-outs. It always did. I drank. And drink just compounded the self-loathing.

I kept having flashbacks to the accident, to my feelings of complete helplessness just before the point of impact. I kept thinking of the randomness of my good fortune that no one happened to be walking on the pavement at that moment. I hated what I'd done and what I was becoming.

One day, it got too much for me. I remember feeling that I had reached the end of my tether. Looking in the mirror, I didn't have the faintest respect for the man I saw looking back at me. I was a potentially lethal drunk. I was pissing my career away. I was endlessly at odds with Alex Ferguson.

I can't remember actually taking the decision. It just happened. Just a blizzard of voices in my head, all of them goading. Then a small hill of paracetemol on the table in front of me. A large glass of water. Sleep. Peace. Freedom.

. . . People shouting.

'Paul, *Paul*, Jesus Christ PAUL . . .'

Claire: 'I knew he had got really down in the dumps over losing his licence. He was furious with himself. But I didn't realise the extent of it. We had to get him straight to hospital and have his stomach pumped. It all happened really quickly. He was back home within hours and we just decided to keep it quiet. He was very remorseful. Annoyed that he had done something "so stupid".'

I just wanted to draw a line under it afterwards. In a sense, delete it from the memory. We told no one. I went back to playing football again, being 'normal'. I was like someone who had done something indiscreet at a party. It was a closed book. A family secret.

And a secret that, down the line, would carry echoes.

Meanwhile, the speculation continued to mount about who Alex might be bringing in as new signings. In March, he was said to have made a move for Danish international Michael Laudrup, from Juventus. The suggestion was that Norman might go to Italy in part exchange. In the end, Laudrup went to Rangers, but all the newspaper talk continued to undermine Norman.

We both started to wonder if our troublesome knees and turbulent lifestyles meant that Whiteside and McGrath might be becoming surplus to requirements at Old Trafford. United had stopped negotiating with Norman on a new contract, and in March he announced his intention to leave the club at the end of the season.

I knew that my old mate was in emotional turmoil. He no more wanted to leave United than I did. But there was a palpable sense of distance growing between us and the management.

I vividly remember that 3–3 draw at Anfield, more for Norman than for me. He was brought on as a substitute when we were 1–3 behind and arrived like a hungry lion released from its cage. There was anger in every step. The first casualty was John Barnes, shaken up by a high elbow. The second, more significantly, was Steve McMahon, Liverpool's self-styled 'hard man', upended by a heavy Whiteside tackle. The effect of Norman's arrival on the whole United team was startling. He took the game by the scruff of the neck. Liverpool, admittedly, took a less sanguine view. Former Anfield favourite, Tommy Smith, accused Norman of being so late on McMahon, that he wondered how he ever managed to catch the coach for United's away trips!

Our performances at Anfield may have been lauded in the media, but they didn't alter our sense of growing unease. By now, I had also expressed a desire to move on. Terry Venables had shown an interest in bringing me to Tottenham and I didn't exactly hide my enthusiasm for such a move.

Before a home game with Luton, my name and Norman's were both jeered during the team announcements. I was growing increasingly uneasy.

United had me tied to a long-term contract, paying me less money than some of the reserve team were now earning. I effectively didn't have a relationship with the manager. And I was drinking for fun. If I had been out on a Wednesday, I would wake up feeling so bad that I felt I had to have a drink just to get through Thursday.

That feeling would, then stretch into Friday and suddenly I'd be drinking on the eve of a game. Knowing that what I was doing was wrong. Knowing that my direct opponents were probably on strict pasta diets all week. Knowing that I was cheating the people around me.

When fit, Kevin Moran and I had invariably been first choice centre-backs. It was a decent partnership. But both of us were injury prone. We just couldn't seem to get any kind of extended run together. Ultimately, Kevin would leave Old Trafford on a free transfer that summer, moving to Sporting Gijon in Spain.

His departure served only to deepen my unease at the changing face of United.

Kevin Moran: 'That [bad luck with injuries] was our biggest nightmare when you look at the number of games we missed. I mean we were effectively the numbers one and two centre-halves at United for the guts of five years. Graeme Hogg might come in at times and do the odd stint, but we were the first choices.

'And, for whatever reason, we could never string a consistent partnership together. I know that upset Alex more than anything. He wanted consistency there. If you want consistency in any position as a manager, it's with your two centre-halves. That's what he got subsequently with Bruce and Pallister.

'They hardly missed a game between them for four and a half years.'

United finished the season as runners-up, nine points adrift of Liverpool, but apparently now in shape to mount a serious title challenge. There were rumours that Paul Gascoigne could be joining and that Mark Hughes might be on his way back from Barcelona. The sense of a new dynasty was beginning to find discernible form.

But I departed for the European Championship finals in Germany, not knowing if I would return a United player.

14

BREAKING POINT

Over time, injury becomes a state of mind for the sidelined footballer.

The first thing you lose is the capacity to be hopeful. People forget you. The rituals of rehabilitation just wear you down. You pine for the open spaces of training, the banter, the aggression even, when all you see – day after unending day – is the medical room, the table.

You are like a cartoon character that has been erased from the page. Rubbed out. Deleted.

I came back from Euro '88 knowing that my right knee needed serious attention. Between pre-season and Christmas, I would undergo three operations to try to repair the damage. Always, it seemed, some kind of complication kicked in. I was seeing more of the physio, Jim McGregor, than I seemed to be seeing of my family.'

Deep down, I had begun to worry seriously about my future in the game. After one of the operations at Whalley Range Hospital in October, I was warned that my career expectancy might now be dramatically curtailed. The most pessimistic opinion – and the one jangling around my brain – was that I could be on the scrap heap within a matter of months.

Even the obligatory teasing of the English contingent over their defeat to Ireland in Stuttgart had a certain tameness to it now as I began to withdraw a little into my own private world of frustration and self-doubt. As luck would have it, Norman was side-lined too with a collection of injuries, ranging from Achilles to ankle that would keep him largely inactive for more than six months.

Sir Alex Ferguson: 'That last season Paul was with us, I had to make up my mind about where Man United were going. I went to the chairman and I said, "Look, this team is never going to win the League." For a start, there were too many of them too old. We had quite a few players in their thirties, and I've always felt with players in their thirties that, if they've never won anything, it's hard to galvanise them to win their first ever trophy. And that was the situation we were in. So we decided to just have a cull. Sell as many players as we could.

'People say, "Maybe if you'd been more patient with him . . ." You know, if I had more experience, I'd probably have handled it better. But that wasn't the issue. The issue was to establish a discipline in Manchester United Football Club that I could recognise.

'So I had to do that. Because I was saying to myself "Where am I going with this team?" That was my biggest difficulty. I simply couldn't see us winning the League with it. So I said to the chairman, "Look, unless we get an influx of young players who are hungry enough . . . I mean they might not win it in their first or second seasons – but they'd be young enough to win it in their third . . ."'

I did make a brief argument for my case to be reassessed, returning as a substitute in the 3-1 Old Trafford defeat of Liverpool on New Year's Day. The day before, I had completed an A team game against the same opposition at the Cliff.

By now, Steve Bruce and Mal Donaghy were manning the centre of United's defence, but Alex had indicated an interest in trying me as a sweeper behind them once I had regained full fitness.

Looking back, he was being extremely fair to me. Even if, deep down, the decision had been taken to offload me, his public utterances suggested that I still had a future at the club.

Twenty-four hours after the Liverpool win, I played all ninety minutes of a 0-1 defeat against Middlesbrough at Ayresome Park. It was just my seventh first-team game of the season and I looked to be on the road to redemption. But three games in three days? Was I pushing my luck a little?

When I awoke the following morning, my right knee was extremely stiff and sore. I reported this to Jim McGregor the following day at training and, when there was no improvement overnight, spoke to Alex about it on the Thursday. In hindsight, there was no defining call made on my availability or otherwise for that Saturday's FA Cup third-round tie with QPR at Old Trafford.

That said, personally, I felt there was no way I could play the Cup game.

I didn't train that week, opting instead for more hours of infernal treatment in the medical room. By the Friday, the team was named without me and I took this as confirmation of my own view that I would have no involvement against QPR. Was I drinking? Absolutely. I felt that I was off duty, that my only role at Old Trafford for the Cup game would be strictly that of spectator. Time would reveal, of course, that Alex took an entirely different view.

Norman, who was also injured, had asked me to go on Granada's

Kick-Off programme that Friday as a favour for someone he knew and, after some persuasion, I agreed. It wasn't my thing but, loosened up by a few jars, I reasoned that I'd get through it OK. What followed is embedded in the files of football infamy.

Norman Whiteside: 'I was doing a mate of mine a favour. Terry Smith, formerly of the BBC, had moved to Granada and wanted the two of us on live the night before the FA Cup game. Paul thought he wasn't playing. So we went to the Axe and Cleaver pub in Dunham. I was driving, so I only had about two pints.

'From there, we went to Old Trafford. I remember Elton Welsby was presenting the programme. Paul didn't really like doing this kind of stuff and I think he walked up to the Trafford bar on the corner. I didn't go with him. He must have just downed a load of doubles because, when he came back, he was just giggling and making faces. "Coooooeeee . . ." All this kind of stuff.

'So we go on the programme and, clearly, we look a little the worse for wear. The two of us get labelled big style. People are phoning the club, saying this was disgraceful the night before a game.

'I know to this day that I wasn't over the limit. But it must have looked dead funny, I admit. And it's stuck with us to this day. "Whiteside and McGrath, pissed on the telly . . . what's this club coming to?" It's still shown every now and then as an example of footballers behaving badly.

'We both got fined two weeks' wages, which I wasn't happy about. If I had been drunk, I'd just have handed the fine over, no problem. But Fergie wouldn't believe me.'

Blissfully unaware of the storm brewing, I turned up to Old Trafford on the day of the game, expecting to have more treatment on my knee, then take a comfortable seat in the stand. But, with injury piling upon injury and a sudden dose of flu ruling out Lee Sharpe, it suddenly emerged that I was expected to tog out.

Alex had seen the television interview and was unimpressed, to put it mildly. He lambasted me for embarrassing the club in such a way. But now he needed me. With a predominantly young team lining out that afternoon for United, he felt that the sight of a more senior pro togging out might boost the youngsters. And he was supported in that view by assistant Archie Knox.

I couldn't believe it. If I played, I knew that an already bad situation would only worsen. As I protested, Alex grew apoplectic. Bad enough that I had done my little cabaret act for TV. Now I was declaring myself unfit to help out a seriously depleted team.

Ultimately, the tension was only defused by Jim McGregor's intervention. He said that he couldn't be held responsible for what might happen to my knees if I played. He said that for all he knew, there was the potential to wreck my career that afternoon and he couldn't have that on his conscience.

It was only then that Alex relented. But his anger was undiluted. Norman and I were to report to his office that Monday.

Sir Alex Ferguson: 'The whole week, him and Norman had been on the sauce. It was quite funny in a way, when you look back. Because, all week, I was getting phone calls from people in different pubs all over Manchester. When they'd leave the training ground, they'd go somewhere and I'd get a phone call. Then they'd go somewhere else. There was a trail leading right back to where they lived.

'I must say, at the time, I was disgusted by their behaviour. It was hard for me. Because I felt the whole thing was coming in on top of me. And I was thinking "Well, I'm going to have to do something . . ."'

This had been the final straw. That Monday, I strode into Alex's office, bracing myself for nothing more than another fine and a rap across the knuckles, only to find a few unexpected faces present. There to greet me was club chairman, Martin Edwards, secretary, Ken Merrett, and most worrying of all, PFA chief, Gordon Taylor.

Gordon actually took me off to one of the directors' offices for a private briefing. This was no ordinary summit. United had decided to cut their losses. They were proposing that I retire from the game, receiving a £100,000 insurance payout (roughly two years' wages) and a testimonial game in Dublin. I was only 29-years-old and still felt I had many years left as a professional footballer.

Norman, meanwhile, was dispatched to the famous sports rehabilitation centre in Lilleshall for a month. His future was also on the line.

Sir Alex Ferguson: 'Paul was a much more natural athlete than Norman. He could still train when his knees were injured. Norman couldn't. Not being the quickest, he depended on his sharpness, on being really bright up top. But I couldn't get to Paul the way I could get to Norman. I tried to devote a lot of time to them both.

'There was one morning, the two of them had been in some bar down in the meat market. A place that opened at four in the morning or something like that. And they came straight in from there to training. Of course, by the time they come in, somebody's phoned me. You could tell they were pissed, just the smile on their faces. "Och, we've had a great night . . ."

'And so you go through the whole process again. Fine them a week's wages. It didn't matter, didn't mean a thing. Norman would make some effort to explain himself. But, with Paul, I could never get anything back. Just "Yes boss, no boss . . ."

'Talking to the physio, the feeling was that his knees wouldn't last more than two or three more years, if that. But my biggest fear was what was going to happen to the boy himself.

'In the end, him leaving United had nothing to do with his ability. It was to do with how I was going to change Manchester United. And there was a ruthlessness about it. But I had to be ruthless. I felt if I don't make my mark, I'm going to die here. And if I don't do it quickly . . .'

Norman Whiteside: 'Basically, they wanted to split us up. I had piled on a bit of weight and they wanted me away to Lilleshall to lose it. But Paul was first into the meeting. I couldn't believe it when I heard they were offering him the door.'

To begin with, the offer attracted me. I was sick of the endless cycle of injury and argument. The prospect of pushing £100,000 into my pocket and walking away held its attractions. I always seemed to be arguing with the manager. Always coming at things from a different planet.

His attitude was that I should be thrilled just to be wearing the shirt of Manchester United. I *was* thrilled. I was very proud to wear it. But I also felt exploited.

On roughly £50,000 a year, I was one of the poorest paid players on United's books. It wasn't that I was looking for parity with the likes of Bryan Robson. But I felt I should at least be a little better off than the higher paid reserves.

Eventually, some kind of protective inner voice kicked in to the negotiations for my 'retirement'. I reasoned that a testimonial in Dublin would probably come my way anyway, courtesy of the Football Association of Ireland. If United were offering me a game, it should have been at Old Trafford.

Under colder analysis, their offer was actually pretty poor. I had, after all, five years left on my contract.

For one of the few times in my life, I decided not to take the easy option.

I have to admit I felt a terrible coldness to the discussions too. A definite lack of empathy. It was as if I was just a piece of meat being weighed on a scale. I could tell they didn't envisage an argument. One hundred grand. Lot of money in 1989!

I discussed it with Claire and friends like Norman and Robbo over the coming days. Their opinions more or less backed up my own gut instinct. So, I spoke to the PFA again and they said they'd back me whatever option I chose. Eventually, having been advised to stay away from the training ground, I made an appointment to see Alex. And told him I wouldn't quit.

Sir Alex Ferguson: 'On reflection, Paul was quite right to speak to the Player's Union. We had given him the option of the insurance claim based on the diagnosis we were getting on his knees. But he was absolutely one hundred per cent correct to do what he did.

'In a way, it told you the game meant something to him. Because sometimes you wondered if he had a real passion for it the way that other players would have. He obviously did. But it was getting that passion out.

'I mean I had tried getting people to talk to him. Even Sir Matt [Busby]. I phoned Paul's wife. I remember making a comment to her once that he was driving me mad. And her response was, "He's driving *you* mad?"

'I knew there was some family situation between Paul and Claire at the time. Some marital problem. And that was the sort of situation that you're always afraid to step into as a manager. From my background in Govan, I always remember my dad saying – say you heard a fight going on next door – it was

nothing to do with us . . . If it was a family thing, you turned
a blind eye . . .'

Claire: 'I do remember having one serious conversation with
Alex Ferguson. He was asking me did Paul have any problems, because he always seemed to be so bolshy when they
spoke. He wondered if I could pinpoint something. I remember
saying to him, "He just doesn't like being told what to do.
It's always been the same."

'There wasn't really a lot else I could tell him. Paul just
wasn't one for taking orders. Maybe, again, I was naive. But
I thought we were blissfully happy. To me, we were young
and in love. We had a good, happy life. Paul would come
home most afternoons after training and play with the two
boys.

'As wives, we were all in the same social circle. We partied
together. I thought things were fine.'

Sir Matt would stop me in the corridor and chat away in a lovely,
unaffected way. No matter what scrape I might have been in, he
was always encouraging, always telling me not to worry about
anything outside the game. It may have seemed that I took no
notice, but the reality is I was completely awestruck.

I could hardly speak in his presence. I found the idea that he
was taking the time to speak to little old insignificant me quite
incredible. And he seemed to take a genuine interest. I mean I
look back and actually have a lot of sympathy now for Alex
Ferguson's position.

Maybe the problem was that, even before a ball was kicked, I had
it in my head that he wanted rid of me. Call it drink, call it whatever you want, I think Alex just decided that there were certain
people who weren't going to be at the club much longer. I was one
of them. Norman was another. Even Robbo might have been one.

But the difference between Robbo and us was that he could play his way out of anything. He literally could. I mean, at that point, Norman and me were getting injured a lot, and when we tried to play our way out of trouble, we couldn't. We couldn't muster what Robbo had. Maybe it was genius.

But the moment he was back on a football pitch, no matter what his preparation, he just brought something to everyone. He could step up to the plate. He always wanted the ball. I always wanted the shade.

It may surprise people when I say this, but in hindsight I wish to God I had a stricter manager at United when I first got there. I mean I loved Ron. But he would almost drink with you outside the game.

I even wish that Alex had brought me into his office the day that he arrived and said to me, 'Look son, I would love you to be at this club for the next seven or eight years, to get your testimonial, whatever you want, because I want you here playing for Manchester United . . .' Maybe I'm naive in thinking that that kind of pep talk might have brought the desired reaction.

But I believe I might have listened. Trouble was, every time I walked into his office it was always in a fractious atmosphere. Basically I felt that I was being lectured from the very first moment that I spoke to him. And something within me just railed against that.

From the moment we met, there was a voice inside saying 'I'm not going to get on with this fella . . .'

Sir Alex Ferguson: 'I used to sit with Sir Matt and we'd talk about George Best. I would ask him about George so that I could relate to United at the time. And he'd say to me, "We just didn't know how to handle that [the hype] at the time. We never had press at the training-ground doors. Ever. Although we had all these great players – Duncan Edwards,

Bobby Charlton, Paddy Crerand, Denis Law – we never had any press at the training ground. Then, all of a sudden, this young, skinny lad from Belfast comes in, and next thing, there's press everywhere. Photographers with ladders up so they could peer over the training-ground wall and get shots of George arriving. We had to get security. We had no idea how to handle it . . ."

'George in many ways had similar problems to Paul. I think he was a boy who was vulnerable to the same things. Go into a bar, get a drink, chat away, then disappear into oblivion. They can't get out.

'I mean I was always conscious – and I was trying to get this across to Paul – that there was absolutely no personal issue between me and him. But players maybe don't under-stand what decision making is. Decision making is not done for you and it's not done for me. It's never done for me. It's done for the club, because somebody has to do it. There is always a bigger picture.'

By the end of the season, I had played twenty first-team games, two fewer than the previous season. It wasn't an impressive batting average. By and large, I was now missing every second game for United.

I vividly remember travelling to London for a game against QPR. Again I was injured and, as such, again felt free to indulge.

On this occasion, I was rooming with Jim Leighton. Jim was a goalkeeper and a good, honest pro who Alex signed from his old club, Aberdeen, in the summer of 1988. I often think that some of the guys who roomed with me over the years must have wondered – at times – if they were being punked. Or being caught on *Candid Camera*.

This time, Jim had every reason to suspect that Jeremy Beadle was about to jump out of the wardrobe. I can still see the look of disgust on his face as I launched a one-man attack on the minibar.

Sitting on the end of my bed, I went through every single drink in the fridge. Whisky, brandy, vodka, gin, wine, champagne, beer, everything. The only drinks left untouched were the non-alcoholic stuff. And all the time I'm chatting to Jim, as if what I'm doing is the everyday act of a normal, perfectly rational human being.

As the alcohol hit, I wouldn't have any qualms about what I was doing. It'd be a case of 'I don't feel so good at the moment and this is what's going to help me get back on an even keel . . .' The more I drank, the less I felt a need to explain. Eventually, my attitude would be 'I don't give a toss. No disrespect, it's got nothing to do with you. This is just what I do when I'm in this sort of humour. If it offends you, too bad . . .'

Finally, I'd be drunk and cavalier and that's when the annoyance of a roommate would kick in. In Jim's case, I just remember his face. He was repulsed by what he saw. It was as if he was looking at an animal.

Alex had made it clear to me that if I didn't accept the insurance option, I could have no guarantees of first-team football at United. After the optimism of the previous season, we had slumped to a disappointing eleventh in the First Division. He was clearly under considerable pressure.

My attitude was that I would see out my contract in the reserves, if need be. United could either sell me or keep paying me for the next five years. I wasn't for turning. There were rumours that both Swindon and Blackburn attempted to get me on loan, and an even more intriguing story that Kenny Dalglish was interested in taking me to Liverpool.

My performances towards the end of the season had certainly improved sufficiently to alert clubs to the fact that, when fit, I was still a pretty decent footballer. Trevor Francis was reputedly ready to part with £600,000 to bring me to QPR. I also spoke to Billy McNeill at Celtic. Even Manchester City expressed an interest.

But Alex was adamant that no one was leaving Old Trafford and even ordered me back for pre-season four days early, despite the fact that I had been involved in World Cup qualifiers for Ireland into early June. He didn't want me to come back to haunt him with another big club.

It was during those four days that Graham Taylor finally came into my life. I was at a barbecue at Bryan Robson's house when Alex phoned to say that he had given Taylor permission to talk to me about a move to Aston Villa.

I formally left United in the first week of August, two days after Norman signed for Everton.

Hand on heart, when I look back at that time now, I have to say I would have thrown out Norman and me. In fact, I would have done it a hell of a lot quicker than Alex did. I would have had me, Norman and maybe one or two others out of the club. So he did the right thing. Both for Manchester United and for me. Time has proved that.

I mean Alex brought in Gary Pallister who was magnificent for the club. Was that a bad move?

Contrary to general perception, I like Alex Ferguson. I've seen since that he's a decent man and I'm glad that all the hostility is gone between us. He invited me to his testimonial dinner. He encouraged me to come to Old Trafford on match day and do some corporate work. Anytime I meet him, he's extremely friendly.

A few years back, I had been to the gym at Mere Golf Club and was driving out when I noticed Alex on a green with his son. He spotted me, stopped his game and came across for a chat. That's how we are now. Civilised and grown up and letting bygones be bygones.

Just wish it had happened earlier.

15

GONE FISHIN'

Jack Charlton is standing behind me, his arms clamped around my waist.

I peer down at the reflection in the water. It's like looking at a cartoon. Think *Scooby Doo* goes *Finding Nemo*. Jack's talking. 'Now, listen, what you've got to guard against . . .'

I'm going to burst here if I'm not careful. There's snot bubbling in my nose. I'm going to wet myself. Going to fall down crying. My eyes sting and my throat hurts. I'm trying to swallow it away.

Jack's got a grip of the fishing rod. 'Always remember, Paul . . .' He's lost in the lesson and I'm standing there, thinking 'Beam me up Scotty'. Jack's swinging the rod like a whip. He's telling me that trout are clever. 'Always pick a target when you cast . . .'

I can hear the sniggering from the bushes. The bastards have come down from the hotel. They're loving this. Roll up, roll up. Big Paul goes fly-fishing. Jack's completely swept up in the detail. He's got hold of my thumb. 'You want your fly to float as if there's no line attached . . .'

I'm here because I don't play golf. Because Jack believes I need another interest. Something to get me down out of the room. To pass the time. And now I'm the afternoon cabaret. I can hear Andy Townsend's voice and Mick Byrne telling him to 'Ssssshhhhh . . .' I'd swear I can hear someone taking photos too. They're slaughtering me.

'Remember trout have an inner ear . . .'

Almost involuntarily, I hear myself say, 'Oh yeah Jack, I see what you mean.' And I look at the reflection in the water again. My face is that of a giant fish. Laughing.

It's a heavy, overcast June day in 1993. Jack's forgiven me again. I am back in the fold after missing a World Cup qualifier in Tirana. We are billeted in the Nuremore Hotel and Golf and Country Club on the outskirts of Carrickmacross in County Monaghan.

Around the time we had been due to board the flight from Dublin to Albania, I was skulking across the tarmac in Cork airport, liquor humming through my head, pursued by an RTE camera crew. I ended up in Tel Aviv, a kind of random destination to a week of epic chaos.

Jack's forgiveness has taken on a routine shape here. He's gruff and hostile and – in spite of himself – ever so slightly paternal. I suspect that he is tired of this, though. The Nuremore is surrounded by lakes and rolling countryside and, on my arrival in the hotel, Jack summons Mick Byrne to take me on a five-mile run. Jason McAteer, who has also just joined the squad, will accompany us.

Mick is the Irish physio, confidante, agony aunt and all-round best friend of the players. He knows that Jason and I need different things now. Jason is a whippet who runs on sickeningly light feet. I am old and tired and damaged.

We jog to the first hill and, once out of view, Mick and I revert to a genteel walk. Jason bounds away towards the horizon and beyond. By the time Mick and I get back to the hotel – running the last 200 metres, naturally – Jason is showered and sitting in the lobby. Jack's standing by the door as we enter.

'How'd it go Mick?'

'Yeah really well boss, Paul's in good form.'

'How come Jason's back so long?'

'Took off like a lunatic, Jack. We thought about goin' with him, but Paul's knees . . . you know the story.'

And he did. Jack always knew. I won seventy-three of my eighty-three international caps during his ten years as Irish manager, and in that time he forgave me a range of sins that most parish priests wouldn't encounter in a lifetime. He became a friend and I like to think that I repaid that friendship over time.

But we didn't make the most auspicious of starts.

Jack's first game as Irish boss was a friendly against Wales at Lansdowne Road in March 1986. I was late joining the squad for no particular reason. Just strolled in with everyone already standing in a circle, listening to the introductions. Jack spotted me skulking on the edge. I think he saw in me an opportunity to lay down a marker.

So the new manager went through the new arrival for a short cut. 'That's the last time you'll breeze in here late son . . .'

It was a surreal introduction. We got up on the Monday, pulled back the curtains and Dublin was under a good six inches of snow. It was obvious we couldn't train. We were staying in the airport hotel, and Aer Lingus had a small gym right beside it. So Jack took us into this tiny, cramped gym that had the feeling of a church hall. Comical session. One of the most bizarre I've ever been involved in.

He starts this drill where he calls out different colours and we have to react in a different way to each one. No ordinary colours either. Must have been colours peculiar to the Ashington of his childhood.

So it's 'Puce . . .' hop on one leg, 'Turquoise . . .' jog on the spot. We're pissing ourselves as we run. I'm doing the circuit and thinking 'This man's with the fairies. He can't be the next manager of Ireland . . .'

And yet, instinctively, I love it too. It's different. Quirky. It's a breakaway from the deadening repetition of conventional training, a respite from the monotony of laps and sprints and running cones. And at least we're laughing.

But it's not exactly scientific and Frank Stapleton injures a knee in the session, immediately ruling him out of the Welsh game. Frank is our captain. Jack comes to me and says he thinks I'm too good to play centre-half. He wants me in midfield. No worries there, I assure him.

'Oh and by the way John,' he says to me, 'you can bring the ball out. You're the captain.'

'Actually Jack,' I correct him, 'the name is Pau . . . oh shit, did you say captain?'

Frank Stapleton: 'Paul came straight over to myself and Liam Brady. He said, "Look, I'm not a captain, I don't want this. I just want to be left to do my own job." He was mortified. So we went to Jack and told him that Paul felt the captaincy would be too much pressure for him.

'Jack didn't have any problem with that. But he kept getting confused with the names. Paul was being called John, presumably after the old Southampton defender John McGrath, and there were three Byrnes in the squad: Pat, John and Mick. Jack just couldn't get his head around them.'

Oh that was a pantomime. 'Now, what I want from you Mick is . . .'

'Actually, it's John, Jack . . .'

'Who the fook is Mick, then?'

'That's me Jack.'

'And I'm Pat, Jack.'

'Pat fooking who?'

'Pat Byrne.'

'Aw bugger . . .'

Some days I was John, some days James. I'm convinced Jack was doing it deliberately. It was as if he wanted me to get annoyed and correct him. But I never did after that first meeting. I just had a suspicion that this was all part of Jack's grand plan.

He liked us to think of him as scatty. He was old school, flat-capped and walked around the training pitch with hands clasped behind his back. Every now and then he'd pull a player aside and start telling him what he wanted from them. He'd dispense some information.

And, gradually, the mischief would hit you. Jack wanted us to see him as a 'make it up as you go along' manager. And he was anything but that.

This dawned on me quite quickly. On the eve of one game in Dublin, he beckoned me over to the side of the pitch with his customary greeting, 'James, over here!' Dutifully, I ran across, having long since decided that I would happily be called Mary if it meant I was in the team.

Jack put his arm around me. 'Now Paul,' he started, 'when you shake hands with these guys tomorrow, don't fucking flinch. Look them straight in the eye. Give them that smile of yours. . .' His voice began to tail off as I realised he had called me by my name. Finally. He knew exactly who I was after all.

I wanted to play the game for him there and then. At that moment, I just felt twelve foot tall. And I suspect that Jack had choreographed it.

Always he would tell me to come armed with 'that smile'. To give 'a real man's handshake' in the preliminaries. I suppose it was a means of subtle intimidation. Under Jack, Ireland became a pretty physical team and at no point were we inclined to retreat from the reputation.

When I think of what we went on to achieve with him, I'm a little tickled by my own initial reaction to the news that he had got the job. The selection fiasco has gone down as one of the more infamous chapters in the history of the Football Association of Ireland. Without attempting to recycle the detail, let's just say that Bob Paisley topped the first ballot at that FAI Executive meeting with as many votes (nine) as the three other candidates combined. He needed one more vote to be elected.

Of the other candidates, Liam Tuohy was eliminated first, then John Giles. Eventually, it was a straight fight between Paisley and Charlton. And Jack won that fight 10-8! Someone who originally voted for the Liverpool legend had mysteriously changed their minds.

Apparently, Jack was completely flabbergasted when a journalist rang to tell him he had a new job.

I remember feeling mildly outraged that the new manager wasn't even Irish! And yet he was replacing a native Irish boss who I always suspected had fundamental doubts about me.

I won my first seven caps as the reign of Eoin Hand was beginning to taper. Eoin will always be regarded as an unlucky international manager. He was in charge of Ireland at a time when we had the core of a potentially great team in place. People like David O'Leary, Mark Lawrenson, Ronnie Whelan, Liam Brady, Frank Stapleton and Gerry Daly were all regulars in that side, but they seemed endlessly jinxed by dodgy referees and the concession of late goals.

I was into my third year at Old Trafford by the time Eoin called me up for international duty. In many ways, he had been in a slightly awkward position. Not only was he manager of Ireland at the time, he was also in charge of St Patrick's Athletic in the League of Ireland, my old club in Dublin.

A clause had been inserted in the contract bringing me to United in 1982 that, if I graduated to the Irish senior team, St Pat's would get a bonus. There was a feeling that Eoin maybe felt slightly compromised by that clause.

Eoin Hand: 'That became an urban myth. I would put my hand on a Bible and say that it didn't affect my thinking in any way. As far I was concerned, I wore two separate caps. My view was simply that Paul would be capped when he was ready. He was still feeling his way, adjusting to professional football.

'And the international game was even sharper again. It could be lightning quick in the final third. There was just a different pace to it, a different thinking. I did get a bit of slagging about the St Pat's connection at the time. But the idea that I was reluctant to cap him because of the financial bonus coming to Pat's was absolute nonsense.

'Myself and my assistant, Terry Conroy, were convinced that Paul was going to be a big star. But he still had to learn his trade. When he came in first, he was quite nervous. I don't care what anybody says, Paul McGrath did not become a sensation overnight.'

My call-up arrived in February 1985 when Eoin included me in the squad for a prestigious friendly against Italy at Dalymount Park. I made my first mistake even before pulling on the training gear. It seems ridiculously naive in retrospect, but rather than stay with the team that first night in Dublin, I decided to sleep in my mother's house in Crumlin.

My simple reasoning was why waste a hotel bed when my Ma lives relatively nearby?' Eoin, naturally, wasn't impressed.

Eoin Hand: 'We sat up until about three in the morning waiting for him. I couldn't believe it. All I was thinking was what the hell is McGrath playing at here? Eventually, I gave up and went to bed. Next morning, I get hold of him. I'm spitting fire.

'"Paul, what time did you come in last night?"

'"Aah, I didn't come in till this morning."

'"Hang on a second, we assemble here."

'"But I don't see the sense in that. Sure I live in Dublin!"

'I had to explain to him the whole principle of getting together, of bonding, of gelling as a unit. I had to tell him that, on international duty, it wasn't up to him to decide where he'd sleep for the night. But it was obvious he didn't think he was doing anything wrong. It was genuine naivety.

'I remember I called over Frank Stapleton, who was captain. Told him what had happened. And Frank's response was, "Yeah, Paul's a bit laid-back about things like that. Even with United!"'

The Italy game was big box office in Dublin. This was the side of Bergomi, Conti, Tardelli, Rossi and Altobelli. There was still the core of the team that had won the World Cup in 1982, and on the night, Dalymount would be drastically overcrowded.

I was named on the bench, but nine minutes into the game, Mark Lawrenson had to come off with a dislocated shoulder and he was ferried straight to Jervis Street Hospital. My heart was thumping from the second he pulled up. This was my moment. It felt as if all my years kicking a football had carried me on a natural path to this day, this game, this green shirt on my back.

Dalymount was a tight, old-fashioned little ground (sadly soon to be demolished) squeezed in amongst the shops and terraced houses of Phibsboro on Dublin's Northside and there was a sense of good-humoured chaos in the stadium.

Even the Italians seemed genuinely tickled by the scenes as the crowd began to spill onto the edges of the pitch, some of them sitting literally close enough to get in a tackle. It was chaos, but smiling chaos. Italy went on to win the game 2-1 with goals from Rossi and Altobelli, Gary Waddock netting the Irish score. Me? I did OK. Nothing spectacular.

Two more international friendlies quickly followed, against Israel in Tel Aviv and England at Wembley. I started both. But if I thought I had now arrived as an international footballer, the England game was to provide a rude awakening.

Eoin took me off at half-time and I was absolutely seething. Now I realised I hadn't been playing well. Why? I honestly can't say. Maybe my concentration just wasn't right. Essentially, my job was to mess up the opposition midfield as Eoin had picked Mick McCarthy and Mark Lawrenson as his centre-backs.

I had no issue with that. We were inundated with quality centre-halves. I mean Dave O'Leary was on the bench that night.

So I saw my role as bungling into tackles and giving the ball to our more skilful players like Ronnie Whelan and Liam Brady. I never had the talent of a Brady. I never professed to have it. In fact, looking back, if there was a loss of concentration on my part that night at Wembley, maybe it was because I was a little star-struck by the quality of my own teammates.

To me, Brady and Whelan were unbelievable talents. I vividly remember playing one game at Lansdowne Road when Ronnie fizzed this astonishing pass across the width of the pitch, the ball skimming the grass for every inch of its journey. It was so graceful, it left me standing there, completely lost in admiration of the skill required to do that.

I literally had to talk myself out of the trance. 'Fuck's sake, concentrate . . .'

At Wembley, I just didn't seem able to get into the general mix. It wasn't that I was standing off anyone. I would have relished the idea of getting stuck into my United teammate, Bryan Robson.

But for some reason I didn't get into that game, and to my disgust, Eoin came to me at half-time and said he had seen enough. O'Leary was going on.

In many respects, I probably felt unworthy. Back then, it was the norm for there to be minibars in the rooms and my routine would be a couple of stiff vodkas on arrival, just to settle nerves before going down to meet everyone. How else could I be expected to rub shoulders with Brady, Lawrenson, Whelan and Co? These guys could see straight through me, or so I felt.

After Wembley, the next three games were World Cup qualifiers and I started all three on the bench. We beat Switzerland 3-0 in Dublin, but on either side of that recorded disappointing scoreless draws with Norway at home and the Swiss away. Our World Cup dream was over.

It meant that the final qualifier, at home to Denmark (which I started), was effectively a dead game. Just as well, too. The Danes demolished us 4-1. It was an appalling experience as the lightning-quick visitors ran us ragged with the pace and cunning of Michael Laudrup, Preben Elkjaer and my own United colleague, Jesper Olsen.

There was a shocking atmosphere in Lansdowne that November day. Eoin had taken a pounding from certain sections of the Irish media, and now the crowd saw fit to follow suit. Coming off the pitch, he was spat at by a few imbeciles whose concept of patriotism left something to be desired.

Were we repulsed by it? Hardly. We didn't even know it had happened.

The final whistle had triggered a near stampede to the Irish dressing room, most of us desperate to get off that pitch. It was much later that I heard what Eoin had endured. I felt sickened.

We knew, though, that change was imminent. Quite reasonably, Eoin had remained loyal to old soldiers like Tony Grealish and Gerry Daly. Now that his time was up as manager, it was assumed that the new man would bring in new bodies as well as new ideas.

I had liked Eoin. I loved the way he tried to bring people together. The sing-songs, the laughter. It may sound simplistic, but when people talk of the special spirit of an Irish dressing room, I believe Eoin Hand understood as well as anyone how to create that spirit. He wasn't ever overtechnical or self-important.

He encouraged lads to do things together. Train, play, drink, sing, fight, laugh. He got people to come out of their shells. On only my second time linking up with the Irish team, I ended up singing rebel songs in Israel, accompanied by John Devine on guitar.

When I think about that, when I realise the depth of insecurity I carried with me through my entire football career, that image borders on the surreal. Then again, six pints of beer can loosen a lot of inhibitions.

Eoin Hand: 'Paul was so quiet usually. You had to drag things out of him. Sometimes it was like trying to pull teeth. I felt I had an excellent relationship with him, though. I would certainly never have perceived him to be a messer in any way. There was never a single incident after that first morning.

'Actually, as a team, I thought we were too quiet. I suppose that's the reason I brought in Mick McCarthy. To get a stronger message across. Because McCarthy was a mongrel. I mean Brady wouldn't have a go at Lawrenson and Lawrenson wouldn't have a go at O'Leary. McCarthy cut through all that. He was in there, effing people out of it. "You didn't track back you lazy bollocks . . ." He'd even say it to Brady, if need be. Mick McCarthy was actually the bit of rawness that we needed.

'Paul was totally different. Class personified and a wonderful athlete, but wouldn't say boo to a goose. You could see he was going to be a big star, but I knew I wasn't going to be Irish manager to see it.'

Jack's arrival didn't bring any drastic change (apart from our knowledge of exotic colours). There were certainly a few new faces, Jack immediately availing himself of the so-called 'grandparent rule' to recruit the Oxford United pair, Ray Houghton and John Aldridge.

But that first game against Wales was lost to a solitary Ian Rush goal. We then went to Iceland for a triangular tournament towards the end of May and – beating the hosts 2-1 (yours truly getting the second goal), then Czechoslovakia 1-0 – managed to win the first piece of silverware ever won by a Republic of Ireland team.

That tournament is probably most famous as the one that sealed Dave O'Leary's two-year banishment from the Irish squad, Jack taking umbrage with Dave's decision not to forsake a family holiday for the charms of Reykjavik.

At the time, though, it generated a real sense of achievement among the players. After years of habitual underachievement on foreign soil, we were coming home with a trophy. Some of the officials were so chuffed, we might have been bringing home the Jules Rimet itself.

But this was no revolution. As the subsequent European Championship campaign evolved, we again looked destined to end up as grumpy bridesmaids. Two excellent away results – 2-2 against Belgium in the Heysel Stadium and 1-0 against Scotland at Hampden Park – were undermined by scoreless draws at Lansdowne in the return games.

We also lost to Bulgaria in Sofia, so winning the final qualifier – against Bulgaria in Dublin on 14 October 1987 – looked as if it had salvaged nothing more tangible than pride. Kevin Moran and I got the goals in a resounding 2-0 victory, marred by the late dismissal of an absolutely outstanding Liam Brady.

The atmosphere had been electric in the ground – a palpable sign, I suspected, that Jack was winning the crowd over.

But that night we just drowned our sorrows, resigned to the fact that Ireland had – again – just come up short of qualification. Bulgaria still had a home game to play against Scotland in November. If they avoided defeat, they would be going to the Euro '88 finals in Germany.

I was lying on a bed in Manchester's Whalley Range Hospital when the face of Irish football changed so dramatically. Booked in for another knee operation. Just emerging from the anaesthetic, fog still behind the eyelids. Nice room. My own TV. Attentive nurses.

I'm watching the news. Picking up half sentences. It's garbled. Something about Sofia. Scotland. Gary Mackay. Jack Charlton. Ireland. It's all connected. Scotland winning, Mackay goal, Ireland qualify for the European championships. Did they just say . . . ?

Then the phone on my bedside locker rings. I pick it up and a voice on the end of the line says, 'Jaysus, can you believe it?'

16

TEETERING . . .

Graham Taylor could never have imagined the damaged goods he was investing in when he signed me for Aston Villa in the summer of 1989.

He wasn't so much taking on a gamble as a lost child. I was in turmoil. The drink and the knees were almost trivial side issues when set against a brewing emotional crisis. Leaving Manchester United terrified me. In many ways, I had been cocooned there, surrounded by friends and fellow drinkers.

The rows with Alex Ferguson had probably brought out hints of paranoia too. The victim mentality. I convinced myself that he was being vindictive, that he could not bear to see me go to another big club like Tottenham, my preferred choice. Villa had barely avoided relegation in the closing days of the season just finished, and looked to me like a club haplessly settled in down-the-table mediocrity.

Having rejected United's efforts to nudge me into retirement, my own vanity was now kicking in. I wanted to prove a point to United and Ferguson. But how the hell was I going to do it scrabbling in the basement of the First Division?

In many ways, the move took place in spite of me. I had become slightly disconnected from everything and everybody. As a Manchester United player, I had found several new social opportunities presented to me, and I wasn't being faithful to Claire. The structures holding up my social excesses were beginning to come apart. Now I was headed for Birmingham and a dressing room of strangers.

One of the hardest things a footballer has to do in his career is present himself for training that first morning at a new club. Naturally, you feign nonchalance. You strut almost.

But you're outside the circle. You're starting from scratch. It's like a kid moving to a new school. You're second-guessing everyone. You're monitoring cliques, identifying leaders. You're praying for acceptance. You're trying to laugh at the right jokes, radiate the right savvy.

But, in football, the scrutiny runs even deeper.

Because the biggest exam is still ahead, even if you breeze through training. The dressing room is the beginning, not the end. It's the supporters that will make or break you.

Now, to an Aston Villa fan, my CV wasn't exactly promising. For starters, I was coming from United. That defined me as a Big Time Charlie beyond the environs of Old Trafford. Then there were the knees, by now deemed to be as fragile as cut glass. And to cap it all, my age. I was six months short of thirty. Everything about me roared 'old pro, coming for the shillings'.

So I feared the worst from the Holte End.

Graham Taylor: 'It's in my diary that I went to see the Republic of Ireland play France in a friendly at Lansdowne Road on 7 February of that year. The game was scoreless, but I remember being really struck by McGrath's presence in the Irish defence. I thought to myself "You might have problems big man, but you sure as hell can play."

'I saw him again that May in a World Cup game against

Malta. Same thing. He just cruised for the ninety minutes. It was soon after that that I heard Alex Ferguson had decided to move the drinkers out of Old Trafford – Robson, Whiteside and McGrath. So I made a few enquiries . . .'

Ron Atkinson: 'I was manager at Sheffield Wednesday when United tried to pay Paul off. So I rang Alex. I'd just sold a centre-half to Stoke. "Tell you what I'll do Alex," I said, "I'll give you £150,000 for Macca and we can build that figure up, based on appearances." Alex wanted £450,000, but he said he'd have a think about my proposal.

'Lo and behold, about a day later, Graham Taylor rang me. He says, "You worked with Paul McGrath, tell me about him." Now I'm against a wall. I suppose I could take the cunning route and say "Wouldn't touch him with a barge pole Graham . . ." then sign him within a week. But, in conscience, I couldn't do that. Graham and I went back a long way. So I was straight up.

'I said, "Graham, I'll tell you what I've offered. And, if you're asking me what he's like as a lad, the Paul McGrath I knew was a smashing fella. Wonderful player. Very quiet. But I genuinely don't know the severity of his knee problems."

'I suppose it worked out well for me in the end because, of course, I eventually inherited Paul when I took over Villa two years later.'

Graham Taylor: 'The deal was done on a Sunday afternoon to keep things nice and quiet. Paul and Claire came up to meet myself and Doug Ellis. I was very conscious at the time that Claire did most of the talking. Paul just sat there, didn't say anything at all. I didn't mind. I was actually quite pleased that his wife was there. In my time at Watford, I had always encouraged players' families to get involved in the club. Even the children.'

Claire: 'I did all the talking because Paul just wasn't confident enough. We had gone up on the train a few times to meet Graham. He was such a nice chap, even brought us to his house to meet his wife. It was all very relaxed and nice.'

The emotional thing of leaving Old Trafford was really getting to me. My brain was in overload. I knew I had been drinking more than was healthy at United. That was somewhere there in the subconscious. I wasn't saying it to anyone. And, to be fair, I had warmed to Graham Taylor almost immediately. My salary was almost triple what I had been on at United. And, even at that, he turned to me and said, 'I'll squeeze a bit more out of the chairman for you if I can.'

I was astonished at the civility of it all. I had become used to the manager's office as a place of attrition. This was like stepping into someone's front room and negotiating the price of a few paving stones. It was friendly and laid-back. There was a genuine sense that these people valued me.

And yet . . .

Graham Taylor: 'The first inkling I got that something wasn't quite right came the day Paul signed. We had arranged a joint press conference at Villa Park to unveil Paul, the Danish defender Kent Nielsen, as well as an addition to the coaching staff, Denis Booth.

'I drove down to collect Paul and Kent from the Moat House Hotel in West Bromwich, right next to West Brom's ground, the Hawthorns. Paul sat in the back of the car and wouldn't shut up from the moment he got in. He just prattled on for the whole journey. And I just couldn't reconcile that with what I had seen during the negotiations. It just didn't add up.

'Much later, when I had gotten to know Paul, I asked him if he'd been drinking that day. And he told me he'd gotten through the best part of a bottle of Southern Comfort before he even got in the car.'

I know it was disrespectful. But I also knew that to get through that unveiling at Villa Park, I needed that bottle of Southern Comfort. The moment I saw those microphones and cameras, the teddy bears, mascots – and more than anything, maybe, the faces of the supporters – I knew I'd go to pieces without some kind of help. I suppose I needed what I needed that day.

My mindset would be very simple: I know this is wrong. I know it flies in the face of the commitment I have just made to this club. But I'll pay them back. That was what I always believed. Just indulge me this and I'll make sure that I repay you.

I suppose any reasonably intelligent person would know that, if you stop drinking, you're improving your chances of success, whatever the walk of life. But I was in denial. I remember my first game was a pre-season friendly against Hibernian. Graham played me in midfield alongside Gordon 'Sid' Cowans, who had just returned from a spell in Italy. It went really well, and for some reason the supporters seemed to take a shine to me. If anything, that compounded the denial.

Physically, pre-season had been desperately tough. My condition wasn't great and I suppose it had showed in some of the sessions.

'Sid' Cowans: 'Graham Taylor worked us hard in pre-season. Really hard. I remember one of the first sessions, he made us do six laps around the training ground. Paul just tagged on at the back. He couldn't do it. And from that moment on, he just seemed to go to the gym and do his own thing.

'The lads didn't care, because they quickly saw how good he was and how important he became to the team. Normally in that situation, there might be an attitude of "This fella's taking the piss . . ." But Paul wasn't taking the piss. He genuinely had a problem with his knee. We all knew that.

'But he was such a wonderful player, we needed him in the team on a Saturday.'

I had reckoned it would take me up to seven decent games to win the supporters over. But the Hibernian game convinced me that maybe I could do this the way I had started out.

Graham Taylor: 'So we start the season. Now I knew I couldn't afford another campaign fighting relegation. I'd sold Alan McAnally to Bayern Munich for £1.1 million and Martin Keown to Everton for a tribunal-set £700,000. I'd bought Nielsen for £500,000, Paul for £425,000 and – a little later – brought in Adrian Health as a squad player from Espanol for £300,000. Kent and Paul were my serious investments.

'We open with a draw at Nottingham Forest, then we've four successive home games. We draw with Liverpool and Charlton, lose to Southampton, then beat Tottenham. We then go to Sheffield Wednesday and lose 1-0. Next up is QPR at home. That was the game when I realised I'd signed an alcoholic.

'We lost 1-3 and Trevor Francis got all three Rangers goals. Five minutes from the end, Paul fell down in the penalty box. And I whispered to Jim Walker, "Just go in and tell him all I want him to do is stand up." Because I could see then I had a big problem.

'I mean we had won one of our first seven League games and I was in a bit of trouble here.

'I remember going into the dressing room after and looking at Paul. He wouldn't look at me. I knew then that I'd got a problem. I mean I had heard that he liked a drink, but I hadn't realised I had actually taken on an alcoholic. I was very, very disturbed.

'I remember I sat the players down and spoke about having respect for people. As I was speaking, I never took my eyes off him. And he wouldn't look at me. I was talking about the respect you have for people, how you work for one another, how the trust between me and them was so important and how, if we were going to lose, there was a way that you had to lose. And everything I said was for him. I was angry.

'One week later, we play Derby at Villa Park. Now there was a bit of a background to this game. That morning I get a phone call from the club's commercial manager, Abdul Rashid, telling me there's a board meeting after the game in the visitors' dressing room. I smelt a rat immediately. Why was the commercial manager informing me of a board meeting?

'I rang the club secretary, Steve Stride. I could see what I was being set up for. "I'm not having this," I said to Steve. "Sod you, I'm not going to be treated like that. I'll pack it in now."

'So I was actually ready to resign before that Derby game rather than let them sack me if we lost. But Steve talked me out of it. "I'll get to the bottom of this," he promised.

'As it happens, we beat Derby 1-0. Should have lost 1-5. Dean Saunders ought to have had a hat-trick against us. Now Paul hasn't played anything better against them than he did against Trevor Francis. It's just this time he's got away with it.'

Jim Walker: 'With about a quarter of an hour to go, Paul's gone down injured. We're 1-0 up, but struggling. Just hanging on. I run in and Paul says, "Jim, you'll have to take me off. I'm seeing double." I knew that he'd been drinking. At the time, he was staying in digs quite close to me in Walmley. His landlady used to keep me up to speed on his movements.

'I said, "Paul, I can't bring you off now mate." I knew

Graham's situation and what might happen afterwards if we didn't win. He said to me, "Every time I go to head the ball, I'm seeing two balls Jim." He was deadly serious.

"'Well," I said, "just head them both!"'

Those games with QPR and Derby were horrendous. Trevor Francis was effectively at the end of his career. He was QPR's oldest player. The goals he got against me were ridiculous. I remember thinking to myself 'This can't be happening . . .'

In the Derby game, I think Dean Saunders nutmegged me a couple of times. He was a tricky little so and so. But I was conscious of how it looked. Villa must have been wondering what on earth they had brought upon themselves.

It wasn't that I was actually drinking before the game. I wasn't. But I was certainly drinking too much generally. My head was all over the place. I remember having the sensation that something was beginning to slip. A feeling I'm familiar with now. I wasn't in good form. I just had this sensation of something calamitous coming down the line.

Those close to me can tell when this happens. I become more introverted than normal. I lose focus. And that's what was happening out there. I just wasn't able to focus. My head was gone. That's really the only way I can describe it.

Graham Taylor: 'At the beginning of October, we go to Wolves in the second round, second leg of the Littlewoods Cup, draw 1-1 and go through. Paul does his hamstring. Now that's followed by an international week. Paul flies over to Dublin for the Republic's World Cup qualifier against Northern Ireland. The hamstring isn't that bad but, sensibly, he doesn't play.

'What happens next? He goes missing. Absent without leave. Now I'm getting the team ready for Luton Town away. Kent

Nielsen's been struggling with the pace of the First Division and, after a brief spell of playing Paul in midfield, he's now at centre-half beside Derek Mountfield. But there's no sighting of him anywhere before the Luton game. I bring Kent back into the team.

'People are asking about McGrath and the official line is "injury, injury". We beat Luton 1-0, and eight days later beat Manchester City 2-0 away. It was some time during those eight days that Jim rang me to say he'd had a phone call.'

Jim Walker: 'I was sat in the training ground and the phone rang. I didn't often answer the phone, but I was the only one there that Monday. So I answered and Paul's eldest son, Christopher, was on the end of the line. He could have been no more than four or five at the time. This was, like, about four in the evening. There was a nanny with Christopher, but she couldn't speak very good English.

'Between them, they were trying to tell me what was happening. Christopher was talking about his daddy and "a knife". While I was talking to Christopher, the girl screamed. Christopher said that Paul was bleeding. I told them to get an ambulance and immediately rang the club doctor, Barrie Smith. Then I got in my car and headed straight to Manchester, not knowing what I was going to find . . .'

17

RESCUED ...

I knew I was in trouble with Villa. I could feel this pressure begin to build and just couldn't see a way out. In my memory, the house is completely empty. I'm sat on the end of the bed and Graham Taylor has just phoned to read me the riot act.

I'm drunk and ashamed. All the kindness shown by Villa has been thrown right back in their faces. I'm a bum who can't be trusted. All that hot air about proving Alex Ferguson wrong? Give me a break. Ferguson was right after all.

Did I seriously want to kill myself? I don't think so. But I do remember thinking there was something drastically wrong with me. I vividly remember the Stanley knife and the blood pouring onto the floor. Come to think of it, I remember the au pair's scream too.

I'm pretty sure I didn't want to die. But I did want someone to help me.

Claire: 'I came home to be told that Paul had hurt himself. The ambulance hadn't arrived yet. I went up to the bedroom and he was sitting on the end of our bed in floods of tears.

It was the first time I'd seen him cry. I'm kneeling down in front of him, saying, "Tell me what the matter is, tell me . . ." And he's sobbing his heart out.

'And I'm thinking "I don't know this man." I mean I'm there, he's my husband and I don't know why he's crying. I've no idea. There had been no warning signs. We were living what I thought was a normal life, and next thing, I find him like this . . .'

Dr Barrie Smith: 'It was very difficult. I was a hospital consultant, and when Jim rang I was doing a ward round with my junior doctors. Next thing, I get this call. What do you do about it? Paul's in Manchester, I'm in West Bromwich. I had enormous difficulty in trying to establish the situation because I had to go through the hospital telephone system and I couldn't get an outside line. Remember, we didn't really have mobile phones at the time. The whole process of communication was difficult.

'So there was a lot of toing and froing. I tried to ring Cheshire ambulance service while Jim was on his way up to Manchester to get them to go to the house. But I wasn't even sure where Paul lived. It was all very muddled. I remember I spoke to Paul's wife at some stage a little later and I thought she said over the phone, "He's dead!"

'Eventually, I got to speak to the doctor in the casualty department Paul was brought into and ascertained that the wounds were relatively superficial. Immediately after that, I contacted a psychiatrist – Dr Liebling, a keen Villa fan – and I arranged for Paul to be taken directly from Manchester to the psychiatric unit where this doctor worked.

'The press never got to know any of this, which was remarkable. They had rumours alright. I remember going to the next Villa game and they were trying to extract information. It would have been a huge scoop, of course. One of the club officials was offered something like £2,000 by a press man outside the stadium. It was that sort of situation, but we were batting it away.'

It's a blank. Like an out-of-body experience. I don't remember who was around me or anything they said. Even the actual act of cutting my wrists. It's all so matter of fact . . . just a case of 'Em, this might get me a bit of help . . .'

Some things I subsequently did to harm myself were more serious. Far more serious. And yet, the thought that I cut myself in front of Christopher . . . well it's not very brave, is it?

The problem with depression is that you can actually convince yourself you're helping your kids by doing something stupid like that. That they'd be better off with you out of the way. I know a lot of people will read this and find it a little repulsive. 'So you did that at home in front of your kid . . . ?'

Believe me, I can relate to that view.

I remember nothing of the hospital or of Jim coming in to collect me. All I know is that I felt relieved that things had come to a head. That I was going to get some help at last. That I could stop pretending I was OK.

Claire: 'Looking back, it was a massive thing for him to leave United. Maybe more so than any of us realised at the time. He felt he had left under a cloud. When I saw him sitting on the end of the bed, crying, he just looked like a lost little boy. He kept saying, "Everything is on top of me . . ."'

Graham Taylor: 'I can remember the phone call clearly. I'm at home, in the family room, and Jim tells me that Paul's messed around with his wrists. So I've now signed a player for £400,000 who, on his seventh game with the club, is drunk on the pitch. Who I suspect is drunk again for his eighth game, but gets away with it.

'Then he goes missing on me and does this. I remember putting down the phone and thinking "Fuck's sake, have I got problems here . . ."'

Jim Walker: 'When I got to the hospital. Paul was OK. Very woozy, but not in any danger. I was relieved because I actually considered the possibility I was driving up to see a corpse. I asked the doctor what would he say to me bringing him back to Birmingham. All I wanted to do was stop the press finding out. He said, "It's up to you, but you're taking a chance."

'So I took the chance. Dr Smith had arranged for him to go straight into the Priory in Edgbaston. From memory, he slept for the entire journey down there.'

Graham Taylor: 'I never visited Paul in the Priory. I couldn't be seen. He was in under an assumed name. If I had gone down to visit, the press would have been all over it. "What's Graham Taylor doing up there?" So Paul is off the beat effectively from that international week for the guts of a month. Yes I'm upset. But look at my run.

'Five wins on the trot. Nielsen is alongside Mountfield in the centre of defence and we're not conceding many goals. In fact, we concede one goal in the games he misses and move up to seventh in the table. It's been a dicey time. Only 14,000 at Villa Park for the home game with QPR. A lot of pressure. But, suddenly, we're moving,

'While he's in the Priory, we start bringing Paul in for treatment on his hamstring. The kit man, Jim Paul, used to collect him, then bring him back. The other players don't know what's happened. I never even mentioned it to another member of staff. Because it had to stay in-house. There had to be some trust along the line.

'During this time, Paul starts coming to my office. He starts talking. Just gets his treatment and comes in for a chat before going back to the Priory. This happens maybe three or four times. And he starts opening up to me. About his background, about his breakdown. And I'm sat there, thinking "Oh my goodness . . ."

'He spoke more than he would normally speak. It was as if he needed to get all this off his chest. And my view at the time was "Look son, there are bigger things in life than football . . ." I remember going home a couple of evenings after those chats. I shared a lot of things with my wife. I'd talk a lot of things through with her.

'And I remember saying to her one evening, "Tell you what, it's alright saying to someone they shouldn't be doing this or they shouldn't be doing that, but I think I'd be drinking too if I'd been through what Paul's been through." Listening to him, it was actually hard not to cry.

'There was something about the lad I liked. Now I'm not trying to put any halo around my head. But my view is that – as manager – I'm responsible for this person. I just felt he was a player who wanted an arm around him. He didn't want the hairdryer treatment. To be fair to Alex [Ferguson], that's probably what he had to do at United. Someone like McGrath probably had to be forfeited.

'The first suspicion I had got that something wasn't quite right was the chattering in the car. Then the game against QPR. And my first reaction was "You're letting everybody down, the players, me, everybody." I mean I couldn't actually go to him and say "You're pissed." But I wanted him to know that I was on his case. It was all about the eyes. And he wouldn't look at me. I wouldn't look away.

'But once the wrist incident happened and we began to have those talks, I realised this fellow needed help. He didn't need hammering about it. He needed help. During this time, the thing that came across to me was that he desperately wanted to stop drinking.'

I had liked Graham Taylor from the first time we spoke. He had a quirky way about him. He'd bounce up and down out of his chair, all energy and business. Even those chats in his office, they weren't all doom and gloom. He had a lovely way of lightening things. 'Ah big man, step into my clinic.'

The thing that struck me above all else was that he was interested in me. I mean he had every reason to be furious. One of his big summer signings had turned out to be a walking mess. I couldn't have argued if he was obnoxious, if he'd turned on me saying 'What the fuck are you like you dozy twat?'

But he was open and caring. I always felt welcome in his office. He'd say to me, 'Look, if you need something, come to me. We're all here to help you.' That was his attitude. He gave me his home number. I felt I could talk to him on a level I had probably never talked on with anyone else in football.

He even said to me that if I ever felt things getting on top of me again, I would be welcome to come and stay with him and his wife, Rita. I don't think I'm being melodramatic when I say that he literally rescued me from a bad, bad scene.

It wasn't just a case of giving me the time of day. He was giving me time. I was getting a lot off my chest when I'd go to see him. In many ways, I was at a point of crisis in my life and I needed someone to pull me back from it. My confidence was in ribbons. I felt intimidated by the smallest things.

The early days in the Priory, I was just mortified. I wondered how I'd ever be able to show my face at Villa Park again. I imagined that everyone knew what I'd done and, by extension, knew how weak a man I was.

Under another manager, I suspect my career would have been over. But Graham Taylor's sensitivity worked wonders. The more we talked, the more determined I became to repay him. I felt this urge inside. I wanted to play for this man. To win things.

I remember vowing 'I'm going to prove something here . . .'

Jim Walker: 'We never discussed what he had done afterwards. In a sense, it was brushed under the carpet. I knew he felt a lot of guilt. The other players didn't really know a thing. Not for a long time. But they would have been very loyal when they realised. It never came out. Not even to this day. Nobody outside the club ever got to know.

'I had to keep the medical records away from people. Nobody saw those apart from the doctor. In this day and age, I'm not sure that type of secrecy would really be possible. Certainly, it might have been different if he was still with Manchester United. But just the way it worked out . . . he went in to casualty in the evening, and before people had the chance to put two and two together, we had him out again and safely in the Priory.

'When he eventually came back to play, I remember the game was televised. Paul had to wear wristbands in case anyone would notice the damage. And everyone's asking, "Why is Paul wearing wristbands?"'

Graham Taylor: 'So I bring him back for Everton at home, 5 November. I play him in midfield, against Norman Whiteside, his old mate from United. And he's absolutely brilliant. We win the game 6-2. That was actually the game that got David

Platt into the England squad. At one point, we're leading 6-0. We just play them off the park.

'And here's the incredible thing: Paul doesn't miss another game that season. In the month he's been out, he misses Luton away, Manchester City and Crystal Palace at home. After that, he's ever-present. I mean thirty-five games out of thirty-eight. We nearly win the League. He's voted the supporters' Player of the Year.

'And no one has a clue about the background to it all . . .'

18

REDEEMED . . .

You know the movie *Speed*, where the Los Angeles police officer finds himself on a bus rigged with a bomb? And the bomb's going to explode if the bus goes any slower than fifty mph?

That was me when I arrived at Villa. I was that cop. I was Keanu Reeves, terrified of slowing. Grazing walls, crashing lights, an accident waiting to happen. Everything was frantic and a little insane. I wasn't communicating with anyone beyond the superficial stuff of dressing-room banter.

And, even then, I was largely outside the loop. Still trying to fit in, yet doing my damndest to break out. I missed the familiarities of Manchester. The sneaky little haunts. The sense of easy familiarity. I missed Norman. I missed Tuesdays and the little signals that would fly between us.

'You up for one?'

'Absolutely.'

'Little B?'

'Little B it is.'

'See ya Thursday boys . . .'

Claire and the kids were still in Manchester, while I was

effectively living in Birmingham now. To begin with, I shared a
house with Paul Birch and Adrian Heath – two little players
with a serious work ethic – and would just go home on a Sunday.
You didn't have to be Einstein to see I wasn't playing well. My
head just wouldn't allow me.

Graham Taylor had broken the club's wage structure to sign me
(I was on about £3,000 a week), and after seven games in the
League, we were hovering around the relegation zone in seventeenth place. Already there was speculation about the manager's
future. I felt a fraud.

The crash, when it happened, was almost welcome. It broke the
pretence. The denial.

Coming back, it was like some terrible weight had been lifted
off my chest. The manager, and even chairman Doug Ellis, seemed
to take an interest in me beyond what I could contribute towards
the accumulation of League points. I was surrounded by people
who wanted me to be well.

Most importantly, though, I developed a deep, deep bond with
Jim Walker.

My knees had always been an issue at United. Now Jim took
control. Over the next eight years, he would have an unbelievable
role to play in my life. He protected me, probably more than he
should have. I've no hesitation in saying that. In fact, I'd say that
at times he put his own job on the line.

In that first season at Villa, Jim took charge of everything that
I had to do. Everything fell on his back. Graham loved players to
practise little skills on Fridays – catch the ball on your chest, drop
it to your knees, that sort of thing. My knees became my get-out
clause.

'Jim, probably best if I don't chance that . . .'

'No problem Paul, I'll tell Graham. Come in here with me, we'll
go on the bike for fifteen minutes.'

'Thanks Jim.'

From an environment where my knees were treated as unsolvable problems, there was now a sense that – with protection – they could keep going for the foreseeable future. Graham trusted Jim implicitly. He wasn't fussy about the detail of my preparation, so long as I was fit to play on Saturdays.

Jim Walker: 'Graham would enquire about Paul every day. It was a strange situation. If somebody can actually be the best on a Saturday, within reason you don't care what they do during the week. Maybe that's the sign of a good manager. Other managers might have taken the view that if he's not going to train, he's going to spoil it for everyone else. He's going to create resentment.

'But that never happened with Paul. And Graham was good in that way. He knew how good a player Paul was. He didn't complicate the thing. Paul was almost the perfect centre-half really. The amazing thing is he had eight knee operations at United and not a single one with Villa.'

Dr Barrie Smith: 'Paul's predecessor at Villa was Steve Simms who came from Watford and actually had a worse knee than either of Paul's. Graham had brought him to the club with him and he did a good job for Villa. So we had seen worse.

'Now you could say Paul was almost a cripple, because he couldn't straighten his knees properly. He had a peculiar running action. The knees weren't markedly bent, but he couldn't straighten them fully. But physically he was very good. Well proportioned and muscular.'

Graham Taylor: 'When he came back, once he got back to match speed, Paul was absolutely exceptional. After the Everton game, we lose 0-2 at Norwich. Paul is substituted, but only because he's knackered. Then we thump Coventry 4-1 at Villa Park. Our next game's away to Wimbledon.

'Now this is Wimbledon at their best or worst, whichever way you want to look at it. And I come up with an idea. We're going to play 3-4-3 with McGrath, Mountfield and Nielsen at the back. So that's what we do. We go there, play ever so well and win 2-0. McGrath is outstanding.

'I remember coming away from the game thinking "That's the team!"'

I loved that system from the moment we played it. It just felt so easy. As far as I was concerned, Kent and Derek did all the hard work. I just mopped up anything that came my way. Any ball that one of us missed, the others tidied up. Kent liked to go up the pitch and had a magnificent strike of a ball. Every now and then, he'd conjure up a contender for goal of the season.

Derek was less spectacular but, if anything, more prolific. He was brave in the air and had a fantastic strike rate from corners. Me? To be honest, I used to have the cigar out. Any ball that was coming out of the air, they'd take care of it. I genuinely didn't get an awful lot to do.

Yet, I knew I was doing well. I used to come off the pitch thinking 'That didn't go too bad . . .' For me to be even thinking that way meant I must have been performing.

More importantly, the crowd had really warmed to me. All my fears about being seen as an ex-Man United player just looking for a decent pension had been unfounded. Over the years, I'd heard so many people say, 'Once you leave Manchester United, it's all downhill.' Now the opposite was actually proving to be the case.

Graham Taylor: 'It's very interesting. I remember we played Nottingham Forest. They played good stuff, but were defensive to a degree where they'd let you come onto them and try to hit you on the break. You had to think about how you wanted to approach them.

'It took me a while to work it out. They played Nigel Clough outside right and, this day, I used Paul to man-mark him. To me, a lot of Forest's football came through Clough. Great player, but he couldn't run.

'So I told Paul to follow Clough wherever he went. They were moving him all over the place to try and bring him into the game. Paul would look across at me. "Follow him," I kept saying. Anyway, we won 2-1. Cloughie never got a kick.

'Couldn't figure out afterwards why it had taken me about five years to work them out . . .'

I felt I had so much to prove to so many people. Even to the United supporters. I wanted to show them that my leaving was essentially down to a personality clash with the manager. That I was a good pro. A decent player.

I wanted to show the Villa fans that I wasn't this Big Time Charlie there to take the piss out of them. I wanted to show Graham Taylor that I recognised what he had done for me. I was a man on a mission. And Villa became a club on the rise.

After the Norwich defeat, we won ten and drew one of our next twelve League games. Included in that was a 3-0 Boxing Day rout of United at Villa Park. Eighteen games into the season, we were top of the League.

Graham Taylor: 'We went top with a 2-0 win at Tottenham. Ormondroyd scores a fantastic goal. It's the first time Doug Ellis has ever been top of the First Division. He comes on the coach, stands at the front and thanks all of the players. "You make me feel proud," he said.

'Through all of this, Paul's been absolutely magnificent. First class. It was very interesting. Paul didn't train in the main group and you might say, "Well, he couldn't with his knees." But that wasn't it. He just needed close contact. And between the physio and the manager, we could provide him with that contact. So you've got this triangle of trust, if you like.

'There was never a problem with the other players because it was recognised that he performed on a Saturday. I cannot remember one single player saying what we were doing was wrong.

'We went out of our way to protect Paul, even to the point of sending Jim over to Dublin with him for international games. Paul had this thing about him. He wanted to be one of the best players in the world, but to be able to walk down O'Connell Street in Dublin unrecognised by anyone.

'And I remember saying to him once, "It ain't gonna happen Paul. You can't have it that way son, because if you're going to be as good as you are on the pitch, people will want to talk to you off it. And that's where your problems are going to be."

'I'm very confident that he stayed healthy from that period of time where he came out of the Priory to the end of the season. We're talking about November to May. Six months, maybe. If somebody said to me that Paul McGrath had a drink in that period, I would be most surprised.'

Maybe we let our guard down a little. Our next game was home to Wimbledon. A chance to put some space between ourselves and Liverpool at the top. To signpost our intentions. We lose 0-3. Next up, Coventry away. We lose 2-0. The wheels are coming off.

It was around this time that Tony Cascarino came. He arrived in March just before the end of the transfer deadline. The feeling was that we needed a big player and it was Cas's misfortune to arrive with that label (and more especially fee) on his back.

He would cost Villa £1.4 million from Millwall and go his first seven games without a goal. The crowd turned against him. Now Cas was already a good mate of mine as well as an international colleague. He was one of the toughest, gamest centre-forwards you could come against. But he wasn't really a one-and-a-half-million-quid player.

To be fair, he never pretended to be. The word was that Villa's decision to part with such a fee had something to do with corporation tax. Not unreasonably, Doug Ellis wanted the money to stay in the game. So he paid above the odds.

All of this was little consolation to Cas who, as our League challenge began to peter out, bore the brunt of the supporters' frustration. We won only four of our last ten games, losing three. When he signed, we were two points clear of Liverpool. By the end of the season, we were nine behind.

It wasn't Cas's fault. The team generally lost a little nerve. We lost successive games against Crystal Palace and Manchester City. Cas scored in our last two games (Norwich at home and Everton away), both of which we drew 3-3. As a team, we weren't playing like champions.

Maybe part of the problem was that we knew Graham Taylor was leaving. From about the beginning of April, it became common knowledge that he was to succeed Bobby Robson as manager of England after the World Cup finals. The news didn't exactly thrill me.

It just felt like a little uncertainty was back on the horizon.

Graham Taylor: 'People ask me do I have regrets. You're either a very vain person or a totally successful prat if you say you've never had any regrets. I have to be honest, I do think what might have happened if I'd stayed with that team.

'Definitely, it's a small regret of mine that my ambition to be England manager meant that I only had one year with McGrath and that particular side. I'm not in any shape or form saying that Paul would have stayed off the drink had I stayed. I'm not egotistical enough to suggest that.

'Actually, I suspect he wouldn't have stayed off it and that it would have been a problem. But I remain confident that if he did drink, he would have got the support. Because in that year that I got to know him, I found that inside this fella was a decent man. A shy man. Very shy. And I had just sort of scraped some of the first layers of skin away to get in.

'You see people generally just didn't realise the extent of his problems.

'I remember early in the season, we played Sheffield Wednesday away. Lost 1-0. The manager at Wednesday was Ron Atkinson, Paul's old boss at United. At this stage, I had become extremely conscious that Paul had a problem.

'The custom after games was that the home manager invited the visiting manager into the boardroom for a drink afterwards. Now Ron had invited Paul in as well. And I stood there watching Paul trying to stay off the drink. I wasn't in good form. We'd won just one of our opening six games. I felt a little bit sceptical to say the least about what was happening. Ron's full of the joys of spring. He's quipping with Paul.

'"Macca, you having a drink?"'

'"No, I don't want one boss!"'

'He's got two bosses now! And he's looking at me. The only reason he's not having a drink is because of me. He knows if he has one, he might have another, then another and I might see him in a way he was confident I hadn't seen him in.

'Ron, to be fair, had got no idea that this was an alcoholic.'

Ron Atkinson: 'I hadn't an inkling. I was amazed when I subsequently heard the stories. Because it hadn't gone round the game at all.'

Our last game of the season was at Goodison Park. A 3-3 draw with Everton. Afterwards, the Villa supporters wouldn't leave the ground. Even though it had yet to be announced publicly, they knew it had been Graham Taylor's final game as Villa boss.

We all knew. Doug Ellis eventually came into the dressing room and told Graham that he'd have to go out and wave goodbye to the supporters.

It was a surreal kind of atmosphere. Celebratory almost, even though we had finished second. I suppose it had been so long since Villa last seriously challenged in the League, there was a sense that the club had now taken a major step forward.

When we got on the bus for the journey back to Birmingham, it wouldn't start. The battery was completely flat. So, we all got out and started pushing. And that's how our season ended. In a car park behind Goodison Park, every last one of us pushing a bus towards the street.

Maybe it was a portent of what was coming.

19

DOCTOR JO

Probably the last person any alcoholic footballer would want to see appointed manager of his club is a sports scientist.

Dr Josef Venglos arrived into English football in the summer of 1990 with a great raft of academic plans for the future of Aston Villa. He was, we were told by the media, 'a Doctor of Philosophy' fluent in four languages.

His appointment caught just about everyone by surprise because, to put it bluntly, no one in the dressing room had ever heard of the man. This said more about us than it did about Dr Jo.

Venglos arrived for pre-season, buoyed – much as I had been – by an epic journey that had just taken him to the quarter-finals of the World Cup in Italy. He had been manager of his native Czechoslovakia, enjoying a fine tournament that ended only with eviction by eventual winners, West Germany.

In England, needless to say, that achievement didn't exactly generate many column inches. This was, after all, the tournament of Gazza's tears and English penalty heartbreak. It was also, thankfully, the summer of Genoa, of Dave O'Leary, of Packie Bonner's save.

So I knew nothing of Dr Jo, but in many ways I didn't need

to. His arrival meant change, and in my eyes, change meant trouble.

All the support structures of my relationship with Graham Taylor were now effectively pulled down again. There could be no more 'special' arrangements. True, I still had Jim Walker to fight my corner. But even Jim was on trial now. He couldn't just presume upon Dr Jo's trust.

To be fair, the new manager established himself as a pleasant, approachable man pretty quickly. But his training methods were eccentric, to say the least. No doubt they were underpinned by some bombproof scientific formula. But they had us wetting ourselves on the training ground.

'OK boys, I want you to run across the pitch without breathing.'

'What did he just say?'

'Quickly now, imagine you are under water!'

'Sod off, he can't be serious . . .'

'Ready now?'

'Hee hee, Macca, get your goggles on . . .'

'Go!'

'Aw fucking hell . . .'

Across the pitch we'd run, choking, snorting, farting. Holding nothing in, let alone our breaths, with Dr Jo standing, watching it all with a quiet intensity.

Another of his favourites was teaching us how to roll! This one was based on ballet. The point of it seemed valid enough. If clipped in a game, a player should be able to adjust his body position as he fell, allowing him to bounce back up virtually immediately. It just needed a bit of selling.

'Say again gaffer?'

'It is about balance, the balance of the ballet dancer.'

'Ballet?'

'OK, ready?'

'Yep, ready to roll boss, tee hee . . .'

'Go!'

'Fuck boys, next stop *Swan* friggin *Lake!*'

To be fair, you could tell that he knew what he was talking about. And he understood the game. But he was too far ahead of his time. Light years ahead. We just weren't ready for his science. Worse, his laid-back manner meant that people had no fear of him. Most of the time, he just didn't get the respect that a manager needs.

Over time, Jim managed to win over Dr Jo to the fact that I did things differently. That my preparation was unorthodox. To begin with, he had been unconvinced. But if I performed on a Saturday, even science could be shelved.

Results were average from the off. I started the first eight League games, three of them wins, three of them defeats. Yet a spectacular 2-0 UEFA Cup second round, first leg win over Inter Milan at Villa Park earned Dr Jo a Manager of the Month award. It was an illusion. Villa would lose the return leg 3-0, by which time the cracks were already clearly showing.

My own relationship with the new manager took a serious dip because of his insistence on me playing in a Rumbelows Cup game against Barnsley when I didn't feel my knees were really up to it. It was after that game that I had travelled to Dublin for a European Championship qualifier against Turkey, a match I never got around to playing.

The details of the escapade are recounted later. But my reaction to crisis was nothing if not consistent. I flew back to England and went missing. I skipped training with Villa. I was cheating on Claire with a girl in Manchester, utterly convinced that no one would find me there.

Jim Walker: 'This one drags on longer than normal. He's missed a game on the Saturday. The players know he's been drinking but it hasn't broken in the media. I'm making enquiries, and somehow I hear that he's shacked up with this girl in a house in Didsbury.

'Now I'm from Manchester originally, I know my way around the area. So I drive up there to try and find him, go straight to this house and Paul actually answers the door. He looks startled to see me.

'Anyway I get him in the car, bring him back down to the training ground and put him in a cold bath. It's a day off, so there's no one else in the place. Then I run a hot bath for him, and as soon as Paul gets in, he falls asleep. Next thing, there's a knock at the door. It's David Moore, a reporter from the *Daily Mirror*.

'He says, "Jim, I've got it on good authority that Paul is out drinking and missing."

'"No he's not," I say.

'"Look Jim, I've got to tell you this information is spot on. This source has never let me down before. Ever."

'"Well, you're wrong this time."

'"No Jim, you can't keep defending him. People are getting an idea about what's going on . . ."

'So I say, "David, come with me."

'I take him inside and Paul's sitting there in the bath. I say, "Paul, this is David. He thinks you've gone missing." By this stage, Paul is a lot brighter. He looks fine. And David is mortified.

'"Jim, I'm ever so sorry. This person has never let me down before . . ."

'To this day, he doesn't know that that's what happened. So yet again, the story is kept away from the press . . .'

I returned to the fray after a short dressing-down from Dr Jo, a man clearly uneasy in the use of the verbal hairdryer. He was polite almost to the point of apologising for even hauling me into his office. 'Paul this is not acceptable, you must show respect for me and for the team.'

'I know gaffer, I know. It won't happen again . . .'

It was a kind of token exchange. He didn't know me, I didn't know him. Those simple facts fuelled a kind of resentment deep within me. Where was Graham Taylor when I needed him?

Before any significant momentum had gathered, Dr Jo was losing credibility. He just couldn't connect with the players on anything but the most formal level. There was little banter, little real sense of dressing-room fun.

In mid-season, he appointed Peter Withe as his assistant in a desperate attempt to bridge the widening chasm between him and his staff. Trouble was, there was never a sense of anger from him. He seemed to take the blame for our poor results entirely upon himself.

In this environment, players will rarely take responsibility. They go with the crowd. They take the attitude 'Well I may be playing crap, but the buck stops over there . . .' It's like a disease that eats into people. A collective abdication of responsibility.

It becomes too easy, and by Christmas I suspected a lot of the Villa dressing room had gone that way. After a 3-0 victory against Sunderland on 6 October, we had won just one of our next eleven League games. It was relegation form, and true enough, we slid towards the trapdoor.

People, of course, were saying, 'Nah, Villa are too good to go down . . .' A nice little conceit that it was easy to buy into. The truth was, of course, we weren't. Villa were hurtling towards crisis.

In a perverse way, I enjoyed the tension of scrapping for every point. The general consensus seemed to be that I was one of the few whose form was holding up. On the surface I was fine. But not for the first time, the surface didn't tell the story.

Sometimes I wonder if all the chaos in my life can be distilled down into something ridiculously simple: into the stark reality of not particularly liking the man I sometimes encounter in the shaving mirror. You see, all the emotional negatives I took from my child-hood tend to come crowding in on me when I behave poorly. The self-loathing returns.

At some point approaching the business end of that 1990–1 season, something triggered deep inside me. Maybe it was to do with the deceit now ever present in how I lived my private life. The girl in Manchester. Another in Birmingham. Maybe it was much shallower than that. Maybe it was to do with panic at the thought of relegation.

Or maybe it was nothing more complicated than resentment. Resentment that the one manager I had developed a real trust with had slipped out of my life so quickly. Resentment that United, having dumped me, were now clearly beginning to take shape under Alex Ferguson.

Whatever, I just hit a low one day in April 1991. Sitting alone in the digs in Birmingham, I started feeling angry and lonely. I was flicking between television stations, nothing registering. I needed something to take me away from this. I needed to float.

It happened in a remarkably calm, collected way. One minute I had the remote control in my hand. The next, I was opening this small bottle and swallowing tablets, two at a time. Waiting for the darkness.

Claire: 'It was Jim Walker who rang me. I must say he was the most fabulous guy. He was always phoning to let me know what was going on. Always doing so much for Paul. This day he just rang and said something about Paul having taken a lot of tablets.

'So I had to go down to Birmingham immediately.'

Jim Walker: 'I remember Claire saying, "This is not the first time he's done it." She told me about the other incident. It was a worrying time. When you take an overdose of paracetemol, if it doesn't kill you immediately, you're in danger for the next forty-eight hours. Because the paracetemol is still in your body.

'So it's not a question of "Oh, he's survived it . . ." You don't know for a couple of days. It can damage your inner organs. You're effectively still in intensive care. But thankfully, Paul came through again relatively unscathed.'

I had my stomach pumped and was booked in for another therapeutic session. My drinking was addressed at those sessions, Claire often travelling down to offer her perspective.

By now, I imagine, Villa must have been wondering what I would bring to their doors next. Dr Jo, I think, was just incredulous. Yet within the club, it was as if none of this had happened. Normality reigned. Most of the players, I believe, were never told.

Even Jim, perhaps sensitive to my feelings, carried on as though I had just been to have my teeth polished.

As ever, he became my confidant and saviour.

Jim Walker: 'My big thing was making sure that nobody found out about it. Because I thought, once they do, they'll crucify him and he won't play. He'll just pack up and that'll be the end of him. To be honest, we were all still just learning about Paul the person. Paul the footballer was doing absolutely fine.'

Dr Barrie Smith: 'Paul was an engaging character. Very likeable. But very apprehensive of people. I remember we both travelled to one game with Dr Venglos. It was a Saturday game, somewhere in the London area. We went down on the Friday afternoon because there was this supporters' club meeting that they had to go to.

'There was a presentation to be made to Paul as Player of the Year for the previous season. I was standing with Paul. And his one worry was that he might have to say something to this twenty or thirty, as I would describe them, "adoring fans". It wouldn't have mattered what he said really. They clearly adored him.

'That was the strange thing. He could go out and face Man United or Arsenal without any worries. But the thought of having to speak in public . . . In one-to-one contact, he was shy. And maybe that underpinned the alcohol and the drugs, a desire to give him that equanimity.'

Again, I slipped back into the Villa dressing room (after a one-game absence) as if the problem had been nothing more serious than a tweaked hamstring. No one said anything, but then they had reason to be preoccupied. Villa won just one of our last ten League games, shipping five goals in successive outings against Manchester City and Leeds.

After the City loss, one of the local papers went for Dr Jo's jugular. 'For God's sake GO DOCTOR JO' screamed a front-page headline.

I felt genuinely sorry for the man. He was clearly highly intelligent, but more than anything lacked the ability to connect with footballers on a smart-ass level. To match their sarcasm. To be ruthless with people who were stepping out of line. To be hard, I suppose.

We finished the season seventeenth in the table, winning our penultimate game at home to Norwich, then drawing on the final day with Chelsea at Villa Park. Everyone knew that Dr Jo's time had come and gone.

A little bizarrely, it was announced that he was to become the club's Director of European Scouting. But that was the last we saw of him.

Graham Taylor: 'When Josef Venglos came and they had the season that they had, I would have said that that would have knocked Paul back again. He was suddenly met with a situation where the fella that he was beginning to trust as a manager had gone. Yes, he'd still got Jim. But this was a new man coming in and the results weren't there.

'There was maybe a sense that Paul would have to start again if he wanted to or if he was capable of doing it. But was Paul himself capable of making the first move to Josef? I would suggest no. Therefore, what is Josef going to do?

'Everything he's coming into – new country, new environment, new way of playing, new staff – he's trying to put things into that changing room . . .'

Ron Atkinson: 'I actually tried to persuade Jo Venglos to stay. I had met him when he was manager of Czechoslovakia. I said, "Don't you do anything to make life easy for Doug Ellis." Little knowing that, two months later, I'd be taking the job.'

I can't say his departure saddened me because I certainly didn't ever want to go through that kind of season again. I liked him without ever genuinely connecting with him. The trouble was that Dr Jo never knew me, let alone understood me.

On that, I suppose, he was probably in good company.

20

OOH AAH . . .

Maybe the best place to begin is at the finish.

Gary Mackay changed my life. Without him, without his dramatic goal for Scotland in Bulgaria, the crush of College Green might never have happened. The 'Ooh Aah' chant would probably have been still-born. You see, we came home from Euro '88 as different people.

Having never previously qualified for a major finals tournament, we now had the confidence, arrogance, ambition, vanity, conceit, calm, ruthlessness – call it what you want – that all serious inter-national football teams bring to war. We became hard-nosed and expectant. We qualified for the World Cups of Italia '90 and US '94 largely because we believed it was our right to.

People hated playing us and we savoured every molecule of their discomfort. We had an army of supporters that cut an epic, green swathe across the globe without ever troubling the local police forces. We became a story bigger than football.

And I became Ooh Aah . . .

It is June 1995 and the wheels are coming off here. I am in a room in the Castletroy Park Hotel on the outskirts of Limerick. Trapped, agitated and desperate. There's a man sitting on a chair outside the door. His name is Larry. I like Larry, but right now he's a big, black cloud in my world.

Larry is my jailer. He's posted there to keep me in. If I leave the room, Larry will follow me like secret service following a US president. He'll watch everything I do, monitor everyone I speak to. Above all, Larry will set off panicked sirens if I so much as look in the direction of the hotel bar.

On Saturday, we play Austria in a European Championship qualifier at Lansdowne Road. But eyes are off the ball here. Last weekend, we drew 0-0 with Liechtenstein in Eschen and the joke in the papers is that we 'couldn't beat a ski-slope'. Everyone's a little pissed off. A little tired of this.

Jack has left us here and gone off for a couple of days to do 'promotional' work and take in a Northern Ireland game. His son, John, is left in charge. No one's really bothered. Some players have gone into town for a beer, others are golfing. Me? I'm a prisoner in this room, sitting on the end of the bed, my whole body literally aching for alcohol.

I phone reception.

'Yes Mr McGrath, how can we help you?'

'Em, could you send up a bottle of vodka please?'

'Certainly sir.'

The line goes dead and I am exultant. I've forgotten Larry at the door now. I'm just imagining the heat of the vodka in my system. The relief. The freedom.

Then the phone rings. 'Mr McGrath, I'm afraid we're not allowed to bring any drink to your room.'

My whole system convulses. I am absolutely desperate now. A bulb goes on in my head. A few weeks earlier, I'd been down to a supporters' function in Limerick. I still had the number of a guy who helped run it. His words were echoes now. 'Anytime you're down again, if there's anything I can do . . .'

I decide to park all self-respect and dial the number.

'Hi, it's Paul McGrath here. Look, I'm in a room in the Castletroy

Park Hotel and I'm absolutely desperate to get a drink, any drink. But I need it to be brought up discreetly. No one's to see it coming up.'

'What do you want?'

'I don't care, anything.'

'Well I have a couple of bottles of poitín out in the car . . .'

'Perfect.'

'OK, what's the room number?'

I am shaking violently as I put the phone down. I don't want to see another human being right now. But I want that drink. I've warned him about Larry at the door. He's got to be clever here. I've bribed him. The shirt I wear next Saturday is his if he makes this work.

It feels like an hour drifts by, then – suddenly – he's at the door. Two bottles in brown paper bags. No Larry. Where the fuck is Larry? Must have gone to the loo. Hallelujah! I barely pass this man the time of day, slamming the door shut again and frantically hiding the bottles. One in the bathroom, the other under the mattress. My heart is pounding.

I feel drunk already. I am light-headed in expectation. The relief is seismic. I wait ten minutes to make sure the coast is clear. Then I go to the mattress. The liquid is clear and in a screw-cap bottle. I open it and put the bottle to my nose. The smell is foul. No matter, I clamp it to my mouth and groan involuntarily as the poitín flows down, exquisitely burning every part of my intestine. I am safe now. I tone the taste down with a little water and drink on purposefully for the afternoon.

Later, I will go down to tea, the most contented man in the universe. Chatting, giggling, slurring my words. Every face in the dining room squinting.

There is a hell of a difference between a hungry, young team and a sated, old one. When we were new to this, there was a ferocity to the way we did things. We trained hard, played hard, partied hard. The team that went to Euro '88 didn't have an ounce of apprehension. Jack cracked the whip like a drill sergeant, barking out orders in a voice that nobody dared challenge.

But by 1995, we had all become comfortable and a little care-less. In Limerick, the lads would joke on the bus coming back from training about the coming night's curfew. With Jack out of the way, they were almost mutinous.

Of course, I'd laugh and wink and share in the general ribaldry, all the time feeling a little resentful that while they headed off in that afternoon to the Henry Cecil pub or wherever, I'd be stuck in my room with a sentry on the door. Jack might have managed to keep the Big Bad Chief of the barstool under wraps, but the other apaches were on the rampage.

The final, farcical insult arrived on the bus journey to Dublin when, after stopping off at a community centre in Ballyfermot for no apparent reason, we were then herded into Harry Ramsden's fish and chip outlet on the Long Mile Road for an official opening. Jack was a shareholder in the restaurant and watched happily as most of us took up the 'Harry Ramsden challenge', to eat what looked like a full shark in batter and a hill of chips higher than the Sugar Loaf.

The prize for meeting the challenge was a free dessert!

After Harry's we went to Lansdowne Road where, in the half-light of dusk, we partook of our final pre-game training session with all the purpose of cattle looking for shade in a meadow. The Austrians couldn't have known their luck.

The following day 'Fortress Lansdowne' fell like a house of cards, Toni Polster scoring twice late on in a numbing 1-3 win for the visitors. That scoreline would be repeated the following September in Vienna (some chap called Stoger scoring a hat-trick). A 3-0 thumping by Portugal in Lisbon two months later pitched us into an Anfield play-off against Holland.

No one said it of course, but we were beaten dockets.

In our last four competitive matches, we had conceded ten goals. The Dutch had Dennis Bergkamp, Clarence Seedorf, Edgar Davids, Marc Overmars and Patrick Kluivert. Guys you wouldn't put a penny on to win a free dessert in Harry Ramsden's.

Kluivert scored twice in a 2-0 victory. Soon after, Jack walked before be could be pushed. It was December 1995. The end of a momentous decade under Charlton . . .

Kevin Moran: 'I remember before going to Euro '88, we were staying outside Dublin in Finnstown House. The hype had really gone into overdrive. Big crowds at every training session, our faces grinning down off every billboard. For those of us on the scene a while, it was all a big novelty.

'The day before we're due to leave for Germany, we're training on a pitch in Lucan. I think we'd been out for a few beers the night before. Next thing, Paul turns to me and says he's not going.

'I'm completely lost at that moment. "What are you on about?"

'"I'm not going to the European Championships. I don't want to go."

'It's just one of those bizarre moments. It's come from nowhere. I mean you're pretty sure it's not a throwaway line. At that moment, he's deadly serious. He doesn't want to go to Germany. Looking back, I don't think any of us had an inkling about Paul's problems. Outwardly, he was just the nicest, most charming guy. But inside, he was a lot more complex.

'I remember I just let it pass. Said nothing to anybody. It was gone. Just a little passage he had to get through, then he was over it. Much later, in the middle of the tournament, I said it to him, "What was that all about Paul?" He just dismissed it. Shrugged and laughed.'

From day one, I felt a bit of a fraud with Ireland. I'd be more nervous just coming in to meet the players than I would be actually playing a game. I'm not sure what it was. Everyone used go to Mick Byrne with their problems and I was no different.

'Mick, if you wouldn't mind, could I just have the first couple of meals in my room? Just till I get my bearings . . .'

The feeling of relief when Mick would say he'd bring the food up was unbelievable. After a few training sessions, the pressure would ease. I'd appear out in the corridor in little bursts, say hello to a few people, then be gone again. It would take me a couple of days just to get the confidence up to mix. Drink was my only bridge to self-confidence.

The best part would be after the games when we'd all go out and get blathered. That was effortless. Then I felt part of the loop. A few pints could break down any barriers. The problem was if I'd overdo it.

Then I'd wake up the next day feeling a dozen times more fragile.

By 1988, the problems with my knees just compounded every other weakness. I started off being terrified that they'd cost me my place in Germany, then ended up absolutely petrified because I was going.

Jack had changed things round by then. Under Eoin Hand, there were maybe five cars available for use by players and they were invariably snapped up at the airport by the more senior pros. To a large extent, it meant that guys could make their own arrangements.

Jack got rid of the cars and insisted that everyone travel together by coach. We would go to the cinema on a Monday night and sometimes, on the way home, we'd stop for a few pints in the Hill Sixteen pub near Croke Park. The call was Jack's.

'We love you Jackie, we do, we love you Jackie . . .' the players would sing as a kind of plea for their little nightcap. Flattery usually succeeded. But, in time, I would be excluded from the round.

As Germany loomed, Liam Brady was the big story. He was

now playing with West Ham and injury, allied to a two-game suspension for his dismissal against Bulgaria, meant that Jack had to make a call on whether or not it made any sense to bring him. In the end, Jack decided to leave him at home.

I was devastated. I think we all were. The idea that we had finally qualified for a major finals tournament and would now travel without our one, genuine superstar just seemed perverse. In my view, we were going into battle without our best player. Worse, I felt that I was essentially taking his place.

Jack Charlton: 'Paul really only came to the fore for us when we qualified for Euro '88. With Liam Brady ruled out for our first two games in the tournament and Mark Lawrenson also injured, I had to find someone we could lean on. Kevin Moran and Mick McCarthy were my two centre-halves and I had been playing Mark in the centre of midfield.

'So Paul became vital to us at that time. He was the player we came to rely on. There was nobody else who could do the job I was asking him to do. He was fantastic. I felt I could have played him centre-forward, outside left, midfield, at the back, anywhere – with the possible exception of goalkeeper – and he'd have done the job for me in that position.'

Nine minutes into the England game in Stuttgart, I wrench my left knee trying to shoot at Peter Shilton's goal. I'm a passenger. We're 1-0 up courtesy of Ray Houghton's header, but it's hard to see how we can hold this. England are flooding forward. They've energy everywhere – Robson, Waddle, Beardsley, Barnes.

At half-time, I'm unequivocal. I'm barely walking. In the dressing room, Mick Byrne gets working frantically. 'It's no good Mick, I'm gone,' I say. Mick isn't listening. I start shouting at him. Bryan Robson's been floating past me in the first half like I'm a tugboat and he's a jet ski. 'It's over for me Mick.'

Jack comes over. 'We fooking need you Paul. He's OK isn't he, Mick?' Mick reassures Jack. I'm going back out. Argument over.

Mick Byrne: 'We were under so much pressure, we needed Paul's presence more than anything. He had this telepathic thing with the ball. He knew exactly where to be. Even dragging the leg, he would always be in the right place. I think even the sight of him going back out just spurred on the other players.

'That was the secret to him. By just being there, he gave the other players so much confidence. If they needed help, he was there. It's something he's never given himself enough credit for.'

How we held out is one the great mysteries of football. England just pummelled us, but Packie Bonner had an inspired day in goal. In the dressing room afterwards, I thought my tournament was over. I could barely walk. It was certainly obvious that I would have to sit out the game against Russia in Hanover.

In time, when news of my omission hit the streets, a rumour inevitably took hold that Jack was disciplining me for some alcohol-related incident. Nothing could have been further from the truth. If anything, I was one of the few stone-cold sober Irish people in Stuttgart that evening.

Even in all the hysteria (we were getting TV images of O'Connell Street as a giant carnival) there was still some disquiet among the players over the style of football Jack had imposed on the team. Long before cruel circumstance had ruled Brady out of the picture, there was a sense that Jack didn't entirely trust flair players. He wanted a rigid system in which, under absolutely no circumstances, were we to get caught in possession going forward.

It is one of my greatest regrets that I wasn't part of the game in Hanover when, despite being tagged back by a late Protasov goal for a 1-1 draw, the players offered a stinging rebuke to those who depicted us as a 'kick and rush' team. It's not stretching things to say that Ireland wouldn't have been flattered by a four-goal victory against the outplayed Russians.

Ronnie Whelan scored what looked a shoo-in for Goal of the Tournament until it was eventually overtaken by Marco van Basten's 'miracle' volley in the final.

Afterwards, there was the palpable feeling of a point having being proved.

Frank Stapleton: 'Football-wise, it was a fantastic performance. And that had nothing to do with Jack Charlton. The players just got hold of it. England was always going to be a pretty robust match but, against Russia, we mixed it. Physically, I think we intimidated them a bit.

'But we had players who could play football. Ronnie could play. Kevin Sheedy could play. Under Jack, the defenders were told categorically, "You get the ball and you knock it." Our centre-backs weren't allowed to play.

'We got a name for being very direct so the quality of our play used to surprise teams when we got the ball down. Our passing and movement was as good as anybody's. That never gets enough credence.

'It's always been about what Jack did. Load of bollocks to be honest with you. Was it the system? No, it wasn't. It's always about players.'

The performance definitely had nothing to do with Jack. If it had, we wouldn't have played that sort of football. It was the best game I've ever seen Ireland play. That was a good Russian side and Ireland passed them off the park. The shame was that we didn't win it. Because, once Ronnie got the goal, they just capitulated.

I remember Tony Galvin had a chance, John Aldridge had

another. We were all over them. Everybody on that team sheet had genuine mental strength. Everybody would talk and shout and encourage. Bollock someone if they had to. The thought certainly struck me that this looked a pretty decent international side without me.

But our failure to win meant that we needed a result against Holland in our final group game. A little guiltily, I admit, I was restored to midfield at Kevin Sheedy's expense for that clash in Gelsenkirchen.

I spent the entire week sitting by the training pitch, a bag of ice on my knee. There was absolutely no way physically that I could have played against Russia and, realistically, the Dutch game should have been way beyond me too. But this was no ordinary game. No ordinary time for Irish football.

On the morning of the game, Mick Byrne put me through a fitness test beside the team hotel. All week, he had been unequivocal in his belief that I would make it. Sometimes Mick seemed just as gifted with his words as he was with his hands. Looking back, there was never much doubt about me playing against the Dutch.

I should have scored in the game. A straightforward header that any striker would have buried. But I knocked the ball against a post, it ricocheted off the back of a defender's head and was scrambled away to safety. Pretty much summed up our day too.

I can still see the Dutch goal in slow motion. Eighty-one minutes. Wim Kieft. Miles offside. The wicked spin of the ball. I knew after the first bounce that it was going to end up in our net. I was helpless. Speechless. It was like watching your own funeral. The whole stadium became a tangerine blaze. It was over.

We flew home on the Sunday to an astonishing welcome, Dublin airport jammed and an open-top bus waiting to take us down O'Connell Street and around into College Green where the throng was absolutely extraordinary and I got my first real taste of the 'Ooh Aah' chant . . . Beating England had sealed our legend. The madness had begun.

It is the spring of 1990 and I am in a recording studio with earphones on and a great deal of alcohol sloshing about my system. This is the famous building in Dublin's Barrow Street where U2 have recorded some of their greatest hits.

We are here to put the final touches to another melodic masterpiece. 'Give it a Lash Jack' is Ireland's anthem for Italia '90. We are all here, drinking as we rehearse. Pint glasses of Budweiser. I'm loving it. A girl keeps arriving with a tray and I'm taking two glasses at a time.

I've got the giggles. I'm telling anyone who cares to listen just how well we sound. I can hear voices in the headphones. They're talking technical stuff. I mimic the conversation. I'm the funniest man in Ireland, telling the lads, 'Few more takes and we'll be perfect.' I'm drunk as a lord.

Then my legs buckle and I know I've gone too far. I'm on the ground. I can hear the others saying to Mick Byrne, 'Mick, you'd better take him out.' But I'm indignant. I'm shouting. 'Look I'm fine, there's nothing wrong with me.'

Mick is being Mick though. He's getting me down the stairs and out into a car, all the time telling me he knows I'm fine. That everything's perfect. There's a girl driving and we're on the dual carriageway heading for the airport hotel. Mick's in the back seat with me, our arms linked. I'm getting agitated.

I know what I've done now. I reach for the handle, open the door and make a lunge for freedom. The girl screams. Mick yanks me back in a headlock. He pulls the door shut and locks it. Back at the hotel, he brings me in a back entrance and gets me to my room. He puts me to bed.

As I feel the blackness coming, I tell him I'm sorry.

Glimpses into the abyss.

Frank Stapleton: 'I remember we all went out in Dublin before one of the big Irish games. We were in a bar beside the Gresham Hotel. I always give up drink for Lent so I wasn't drinking this night. Paul was on the dry too, but I could see he was getting twitchy.

'The lads were all around, the place was buzzing. It was my twist, so I asked Paul what he was drinking.

'"Aah just a Diet Coke."

'I knew he was uneasy so I said to him, "You're not thinking of having a drink are you?"

'"I'm tempted."

'I had a car at the time. So I said, "Look, I'm going to go in a minute. I'm heading back to the hotel. Why don't you come with me?" I don't actually think a lot of the lads realised. Even now I sense people don't fully realise. They know he's got a problem but there's this attitude of one drink won't matter.

'It's ignorance. And that was kind of the attitude with some of the lads. "The big man's alright . . ." People just saw him as one of the lads. He got pissed with everyone else. He was the same as everybody else. But he wasn't the same.'

Kevin Moran: 'We were down in the Nuremore once and everyone was going out. But Paul wasn't allowed. For some reason, I said to the lads in the lobby, "Look, ye go on, I might see ye later . . ." I went back up to the room. I wanted to see how Paul was. And he was halfway out the window, trying to climb down a drain.

'He told he was going out to have "just one". So I said, "No way Paul," and just sat in with him for the rest of the night.'

Mick Byrne: 'One night in the Nuremore, I discovered this tray of drinks going up to a room. I asked who it was for and was told it was for Kevin. But Kevin was in the bar with Jack and the boys. So I went up with the order. There were four pints on the tray. Walked into the room and there's Paul in jeans and a leather jacket, ready for town. I asked him where he was going.

'"I'm getting out of here," he said. "I'm sick of it. Sick of football. I'm goin' . . ."

'I told him he was going nowhere. I said, "See this chin, stick one right there on me if you want, because that's the only way you're getting out of this room." Paul sat down on the bed and started crying. I felt so sorry for him. We'd been in the hotel for over a week and there's only so much time you can spend lying on a bed or playing cards.

'It's difficult when a man has a problem. I mean, sometimes, I'd go to Jack and say, "Why not let him go with the lads?" But we both knew the answer. Once Paul got the gargle on board, he wasn't in charge of himself. He wouldn't come back.'

Jack Charlton: 'He was such a likeable lad. Apart from the drinking, Paul did everything that he was told. He was a very, very good player who listened when you told him things. I tried to make him aware of the fact that the only reason he was with us was we liked him as a person when he was sober. We didn't like him as a person when he was drunk.

'It was only partly true, though, because you would just move mountains to have him in your team. You would tolerate all sorts of things that you wouldn't have tolerated from anyone else. I'm sure he knew that too.

'We kept things strictly in-house. We handled it the way we thought was right to handle it. We kept an eye on him. Paul used to come to me sometimes. "Can I go out with the lads?" He knew the answer. I always felt a little cruel.

'Brought him up a box of chocolates once I felt so bad about it.'

Just an endless cycle. I'd sit, watching the lads get ready. All the gear on, tidying themselves, combing the hair. The lot of them smelling like a bombed aftershave factory. 'Hope ye have a good night lads,' I'd lie.

Then I'd go back upstairs like a lifer returning to his cell and I'd be looking out the bedroom window, the little clusters of them down the front of the hotel, queuing for cabs. God, how I envied and resented them. What I'd have given to be part of that.

I'd sit on the bed thinking 'They're treating me like a child here.' And they were. But only because they had to. If I went out with them, I could have ended up anywhere. In another country even. I knew that. We all knew.

I didn't drink the normal way. I swallowed for oblivion. This was for my well-being, my safety.

But right at that moment, it would be 'Poor me, why am I so different?'

21

HELLO RON

Ron Atkinson's appointment as Aston Villa boss in May 1991 was just the news I wanted to hear.

My reasons, of course, were questionable. Nothing to do with the fact that, having done brilliantly in a spell at Sheffield Wednesday (winning the Rumbelows Cup and promotion), he was indisputably the right choice for Villa; no, Ron understood me.

In the increasingly strange world of Paul McGrath, that was the most important consideration.

After the rigid formality of the Venglos regime, I surmised Ron would restore a little wit and spontaneity to the Villa dressing room. He'd bin this obsession with sports science. He'd loosen the reins a little, let us breathe again. Ron, you see, brought fun to football. Yes, there were times when he blew off steam, but that was just his way of venting frustration. It never lingered. It was never personal.

Above all, there was a sense that with him on board, we'd never again have to endure the pressures of a relegation struggle. I was certainly determined that I was going to do well for him and well for Villa.

But if I'm honest, I was also pleased that we had a man in charge now who would indulge what I considered a manly attitude towards socialising.

Ron was actually in place even before we took our summer break, busying himself in feverish transfer dealings that would drag on deep into pre-season.

Dalian Atkinson and Kevin Richardson were signed from Spanish club Real Sociedad, Shaun Teale from Bournemouth, Earl Barrett arrived from Oldham and my Republic of Ireland teammate, Steve Staunton, came as a surprise £1.1 million bargain from Liverpool.

Going the other way were Tony Cascarino to Celtic and, most significantly, David Platt for a world record £5.5 million to Italian Serie A side, Bari. Platt's move involved lengthy negotiations and meant that Ron could not actually travel with us to our pre-season camp in Hamburg.

We were thus left in the hands of Andy Gray, now juggling his Sky Sports commitments with the role of Villa assistant manager.

Ron would literally fly in, take charge of training, then shoot straight back out again.

Ron Atkinson: 'I was commuting from Birmingham to Hamburg, flying over and back. Backwards and forwards. Mad stuff. Eight players would make debuts for Villa at the start of that season, so I was constantly trying to tie up deals.

'I remember the squad was based in this sort of mansion, about fifteen miles from Hamburg airport. I was nearly punch-drunk from travelling over and back. I mean I signed this left-sided midfielder, Paul Mortimer, from Charlton. Left him with my car at Birmingham airport. "Take my car and get your medical done," I told him, "I'm off to Germany . . ."

'Everything was fine until one evening, Andy Gray rang me. He said, "Boss I've got to tell you, the big man's gone over the top. But, don't worry, we're going to find him . . ."'

It's probably pointless even to attempt exploring my mindset. A drinker's motives don't have to be complex or profound anyway. True, insecurity would have been tugging away inside. I was slightly paranoid about any new defensive signings, always wondering 'Is he coming in to do my job?' Even full-backs carried an implicit threat.

But deep down I knew I was in a position of strength too. I had just been voted the supporters' Player of the Year for the second season running. I was an international regular.

Being honest, I didn't have an excuse for breaking out. What I *did* have was opportunity.

In Ron's absence, I took advantage. Andy was new to the job, and I knew he would be leaning heavily on Jim Walker for assistance. And Jim always picked up the pieces for me when I messed up. How risky could this be?

I was rooming with big Cyril Regis, a recent free transfer arrival from Coventry. A few years earlier, I had had a rather sobering introduction to Cyril's unique physical power. Having just broken into the United first team, we were playing West Brom at Old Trrafford.

A ball was hit down our right flank and I can still see Cyril running full pelt to collect it. I was in control, or so I thought. No one beat me for speed, you see. So I slid in nonchalantly, only to see the ball flicked past me just before the point of contact. Ended up tackling thin air.

Cyril made me look a total fool and taught me an important lesson. It was that I couldn't strut at this level. I couldn't play the peacock.

Off the field, people gravitated towards Cyril. He was just one of those people you wanted to know. We had developed a friendship long before we would become teammates at Villa, mind. Whenever he had a game in Manchester, we'd meet up for a night out. He was good friends with Bryan Robson too. There was a lot of mutual respect at play.

Cyril's arrival at Villa maybe just added to my complacency for that pre-season trip. We were mates. He knew how to keep a secret. And what harm would a quick visit to the bar bring?

Jim Walker: 'We're in the hotel and Gordon Cowans comes to me. "Jim, have you got a minute . . ." I walked over to him and he told me Paul's in the bar! Blimey. Here we are with a new manager, a new start and Paul's drinking. So I go in and just say, "C'mon Paul . . ." I get him up to his room. But he must have ordered more drink as soon as he got inside.

'We're training in the afternoon. Just a bit of head tennis on a concrete tennis court. Four teams. Everybody has to come down. So they all arrive down in their trainers. Paul's on time. But he's got studs on. So he's trying to play head tennis, wearing studs on a concrete floor.

'Eventually, Andy Gray turns to me and says, "Sort him out Jim . . ."

'"C'mon Paul," I said, "we'll go and get you changed into flats." Didn't make a big deal out of it. I brought him up and put him to bed.'

'Sid' Cowans: 'What actually happened was, we'd train in the morning, have the afternoon off, then train again around five in the evening. So, in between, a few of us were having this little walk down the town. Next thing, someone says, "Where's Macca?" Turns out we lost him for a couple of hours.

'We're walking back and then, in the far corner of this bar, we recognise this shape. And there's Paul, sitting on his own, surrounded by empty beer bottles. A whole tableful. He's well pissed. We go in and tell the barman not to serve him anymore. That he's needed elsewhere.

'So we get him back to the hotel. We're due to go training

241

that evening and we're telling Paul, "Just stay away from it, we'll cover for you, we'll sort it out . . ."

'And that was the head tennis. We're ready to start when, next thing, you can hear this "clack, clack, clack" as Paul arrives down in his boots. It was just so obvious that he was pissed, he was slipping all over the place. But typical Paul. He wanted to have a go.'

Once up and running, there was now no controlling me. I was returned to my room, parted from all my money and given the obligatory warning. But it was like trying to dissuade a hungry bear from eating. I was on a roll now. So, I pulled open the bedroom window and considered my options of escape. The drainpipe looked a good one.

Shaun Teale: 'I knew Paul was a world-class player. Everybody knew. But I had just joined Villa and my first memory of him would be seeing him shimmy down that drainpipe in Germany. He went straight into the restaurant and proceeded to put everything he drank on the club's bill. Which I thought was absolutely fantastic!'

It didn't take long before the bright lights of Hamburg, specifically the Reeperbahn, had drawn me into town again. I don't have any clear memory of the 'jailbreak'. All sense of responsibility had now well and truly fled.

This was familiar and dangerous territory. Just drink calling and obliterating all else from my brain. I had done it before and I'd do it again. Take myself off into a strange city, immune to the fact that I didn't even know the name of the hotel we were staying in. In other words, without being rescued, I'd be lost.

It was lethal really. My eyes would glaze over, my brain would sit in neutral. I might settle into the roughest bar in the roughest city and just accept whatever the night brought me. Somehow, someone always found me. I have a blurred image in my head of Peter Withe once pleading with me to return to the team hotel in some unknown town. And of me helpfully telling him to 'relax'.

That night in Hamburg, my memory is of Andy Gray and Jim Walker materialising almost magically in front of me.

Jim Walker: 'The players were allowed slip into town in the afternoons. There wasn't very much to do in the place we were staying in, so the instruction was that they had to be back at such a time. The next afternoon, Paul – of course – is nowhere to be seen.

'So Andy Gray and I walk down to the local taxi rank to ask if anyone had taken him into town. As luck would have it, the first person we ask is the one who has driven him in. "Take us to where you dropped him," we say. The journey was about twenty miles.

'So we get into the city centre, we're walking down this street and, next thing, there's Paul coming towards us, walking in the other direction. Before we could open our mouths, Paul sees us and says matter-of-factly, "Out for a night out lads?" And you're just thinking "Em, Paul . . ."

'Andy was very good. He understood the situation. So we just played it cool, had a couple of drinks with Paul and got him back in a taxi. There wasn't any trouble. And, bottom line, when we played a few games out there, who was our best player? That's right, Paul.'

Hamburg was just a variation on a theme. Pre-season and end of season trips invariably drew the worst from me. With pre-season, I'd put it down to nerves. End of season was just a matter for relief. Either way, I usually drank to cope with whatever energy was at play.

I have vague memories of going missing in cities like Kuala Lumpur and Hong Kong. Of teammates trying, vainly, to talk some sense into me. Always trying to protect me from the fallout. Always being loyal, virtually to a fault.

Shortly after we returned from Hamburg in 1991, we flew to Dublin for a pre-season game against Shelbourne at Tolka Park. I was given dispensation to travel early for some family commitment. By the time I linked up with my Villa colleagues just hours before kick-off at a hotel by Dublin airport, I wasn't exactly in the whole of my health.

Shaun Teale: 'When he had turned up at the hotel, he was paralytic. Poor Paul couldn't even see the ball.'

Jim Walker: 'I went to Ron before the game. "He's had a drink gaffer and he's not fit," I said. Ron said, "I don't care Jim, this is too daft now." He was starting to lose patience. I tried to argue against it.

'"Don't play him boss," I said. "He's not going to be right to play . . ."

'But Ron was adamant. "No, he's playing," he said. "In fact, I'm making him captain. We're in Ireland. Everybody's come to see him."

'And I remember thinking "Dear me . . ."

'Next thing Paul comes to me. He knows there's something up. "What's going on Jim?" And I said, "Well, you're playing, you're captain and I can't do anything about it Paul . . ."

'So the game is on about five minutes and we get a free kick in the centre circle. Now Paul never took free kicks. He did as little as possible in a game. But what he did was so effective. This time, though, he walks over to take the free kick. And he's never done that. Ever.

'A natural Villain', playing and posing
for Aston Villa.

'Pressure Game', no goals and no garlands from a 0-0 draw with Egypt in Palermo during 'Italia '90'.

'So Close…', ready to pounce as the Dutch goalkeeper, Hans van Breukelen, defies John Aldridge during the Euro finals, Gelsenkirchen, June '88.

'Stonewalled', the great Paolo Maldini cuts a lonely figure in Rome 1990, policed by Sheedy, Houghton, myself, Quinn, Townsend and McCarthy.

'Holy Father', a treasured visit to The Vatican prior to our World Cup quarter-final against Italy in 1990. (That's me looking cool in the shades.)

'Stalemate', clashing with the Spanish goalkeeper, Zubizaretta, during a scoreless World Cup qualifier in Seville, November '92.

'Jack's Army', that's me (second from right at the back) with the squad that changed the face of Irish football.

'Number One', probably the proudest day of my career, being presented with the
PFA 'Player of the Year' award in '93.

'Return of the Prodigal', scoring against Latvia in Riga, June '93, just two weeks after missing the trip to Albania.

'You're the boss Jack…', taking advice from Jack Charlton in Orlando during 'US '94'.

'Derby Days', a clash with my old friend, Ian Wright of Arsenal, during my last season in the top flight.

'High-kicking magpie', tussling with Newcastle's David Batty.

'Salute the Fans', standing behind a peace-loving Mark Bosnich as Andy Townsend lifts the League Cup after our 3-0 final win against Leeds in '96.

'He puts the ball down and walks back ten yards. Then another ten yards. I remember thinking "What's he doing?" Next thing, he's running at the ball as fast as he can and he's kicked the ground, hasn't he? And the ball's rolled maybe ten feet. Now the ground is absolutely packed, remember.

'Ron says to me, "Get him off!"'

Ron Atkinson: 'I'm looking at him and he's missing the ball by miles. So I call Gordon Cowans over. I say, "Tell him he's got a bad ankle and to go down . . ." So he goes down and we bring him off, supposedly injured.'

Jim Walker: 'So Paul's come off, and of course the press are now wondering if it's something to do with drink. Ron had devised this thing that, if it happened again, we'd say he was injured. The problem was it was always his knees. So I said to Paul, "If this happens again, say you're injured but it's not your knee . . . Don't make it your knee because that story is big enough already."

'So we fly back to England, train a couple of days and our next game is Worcester away, the Saturday before the season kicks off. Game starts and, next thing, Paul goes down injured in the box. I run in and he says, "My groin's gone . . ." And I'm thinking "Jeez, the season's kicking off on Saturday."

'So I get him off, take him straight to the changing room, put ice on it, get him in the shower and tell him I'll be back in at half-time to look at the injury. I go back out to the dugout and Ron just can't believe it.

'"What's wrong?"

'"His groin's gone!"

'"His bloody groin?"

'"Well gaffer, he's never had an injury since he's been here . . ."'

'About five minutes before the end of the first half, Paul comes walking down to the bench. He taps me on the elbow and winks. And I've gone, "Have you been drinking?" So he says to me, "Remember you said that if I've had a drink, no one's to know? That I'm to say I'm injured, but it's not to be my knee? Well, I've not got a groin problem!"'

You can probably gauge from this just how cavalier I had become in my drinking. For a new manager, I was a walking nightmare. Ron was already under significant pressure because of the nature of his departure from Sheffield. There was a sense among Wednesday fans that he had somehow reneged on a commitment to stay.

And as luck would have it, the fixtures computer had decreed that Villa go to Hillsborough on the opening day of the season. So Ron had a lot on his plate.

It was clear that he wanted to rebuild Villa completely and he wanted to do it quickly. I, of course, imagined I was assured of a pivotal role to play in the new Villa. Ron, though, was beginning to think differently.

When the team was named for Hillsborough, the two centre-backs were Shaun Teale and Derek Mountfield. I was named, effectively, at right-back. It was a team selection that didn't altogether surprise me.

Ron had already indicated a willingness to listen to offers. He had expressed his frustration with me in no uncertain terms. But we came from two goals down to beat Wednesday 3–2. Our season was up and running.

Ron Atkinson: 'Remember, I'm new at the club. I've got to make my mark. And I'm only starting to hear other stories about Paul. I'm not sure I like what I hear. So I'm beginning to think that maybe this has gone on for long enough now, that maybe I need to do something. I'm actually prepared to sell him.

'Liam Brady comes on to me from Celtic. He offers about £750,000 I think. If he goes to between £1 million and £1.5 million, I'll probably do the deal. My attitude is "Let him be somebody else's problem now." But you get lucky escapes in the game, don't you?'

Ron told me that Liam Brady wanted to talk to me and he'd given permission. So Liam comes to the house. He says he wants me at Parkhead and I'm absolutely electrified by the thought. To me, it's a dream move. For any child of Dublin, Celtic are as big a club as Manchester United.

Better still, Liam is offering a wage increase. I'm sitting there, looking at this Irish football legend, listening to him give me his sales pitch, and I want to travel back to Glasgow with him there and then. I try to be cool, but it's not working. 'Jesus, I'd love to play for Celtic . . .' I keep saying.

There is more drawing me to Scotland now than maybe meets the eye, though. Claire and I are going through a bad spell. My own infidelities are rumbling on relentlessly and there's a lot of anger between us.

A clean break – from the house in Manchester, from the commuting to Birmingham, from the fraying circle of friends – sounds like exactly what we need.

I have my heart set on a new beginning with the Bhoys. Then I go and mess it all up. By playing some of the best football of my life.

Ron Atkinson: 'We had something like six players making their debuts against Sheffield Wednesday. So I was trying to compensate. I asked Paul just to sit and play. He didn't look over-comfortable. I quickly decide "The centre's the only place for you big man . . ." Gradually, we start to progress and he starts coming onto his game.

'After a while, there is no doubt in my head that he is the main man. The fans are singing his name all the way through games. I decide he's going nowhere.

'I worked on the premise that if he produced on the field and wasn't a bad apple off it, he'd do for me. I mean, if the rest of the players had shown any resentment about his training arrangements, I'd have had to think about changing things.

'But every player to a man took the view that he was a special case because (a) I think they recognised he had a problem, (b) he was always a popular lad with them and (c) he was magnificent when he played.

'I mean I always remember "Sid" Cowans – a proper pro and a good lad – saying to me, "Gaffer, all we want is Macca playing. He's special."'

Being honest, I was gutted when I realised the Celtic move was off. I couldn't help thinking that I had sabotaged it myself. Had I put in a couple of nightmare performances, I've no doubt that Ron would happily have sold me. But I did the opposite. Perhaps energised by the thought of a new life up north, I played out of my skin, winning a few successive man-of-the-match awards.

As it happened, Ron decided upon one pretty radical course of action to keep me on the straight and narrow. He effectively booked me into a health club for the entire season. It was well known that my marriage was beginning to fall apart, so for the guts of eight months, I lived in the Ashby de la Zouch leisure club in Derbyshire.

The routine was that I would go back there after training, do a session of weights, maybe have a jacuzzi. I had my own room, and would generally eat alone at night unless the owner, Steve Perdue, was about.

The arrangement worked well. I usually got an extra day off after games, allowing me to stay with the kids in Manchester. But I couldn't help wonder what life might have been like for me in Glasgow.

My partnership with Shaun Teale really began to develop in a straight back four. Shaun was strong as an ox and unflinchingly honest. A definite trust developed between us. Often, Ron would issue instructions to us and we'd just exchange glances, knowing deep down that we'd do it our way on the field.

It's funny, but I was only reacquainted with Shaun in 2005 when my son Chris started playing for him at Chorley. At forty-two, Tealy was still going strong as player-manager. We had great fun revisiting old times and memories together, card-school stories, whatever, almost a decade and a half on.

Having won just two of our opening nine League games in that 1991–2 season, Villa found some real form, winning six of the next seven. I was playing well and enjoying the journey.

But one of the big disappointments for me that season was a decision taken, mid-campaign, to let 'Sid' Cowans leave for Blackburn. Sid was a real class act, a guy I related to in the dressing room and one of those I imagined that any rebuilding programme would have to involve centrally.

I always felt that Sid was a little like myself. Not in terms of problems, but in personality, in general outlook on life. I mean I would rate him second only to Bryan Robson as the best midfielder I played alongside. He was just a slip of a lad, but was two-footed and had astonishing skill.

Bear in mind, he played on the Villa team that won the European Cup in 1982. He was *that* good, yet there wasn't an ounce of conceit about him. He was so down to earth and unassuming. You'd never hear him blowing his own trumpet.

I felt we developed a special little understanding on the field. We were always connecting with little comments, little signals. We'd slag one another off if a mistake was made, just sidle up to the other's shoulder and murmur, 'Jaysus, what was that all about?'

That may give the impression of not taking the job seriously but I think we were both hugely competitive on the field. In a sense, that was what we shared. The point was we knew how to let our hair down when a game was over, albeit me on a slightly more manic level.

His departure announced to me loud and clear that Ron had his own ideas on how to build a winning team and how none of us could take it for granted that we would be part of it.

Our big problem that season was an inability to score goals. Dwight Yorke was beginning to come through strong, but big Cyril had slipped into the twilight of his career, was nursing a long-term ankle injury and, while often leading the line magnificently, he wasn't exactly banging goals in for fun.

In one appalling run of eleven League games, we scored just a solitary goal (a winner by Cyril at Oldham). Five goalless draws and five defeats was our sorry tally from late January to late March. Ron knew what was needed.

Mind you, I didn't exactly help matters in mid-April by going AWOL the day of a home game against Liverpool. We won the game, mercifully, through a Tony Daley goal, Ugo Ehiogu stepping in as a late replacement for me. I had been with the team right up to the pre-match meal then, for whatever reason, decided to avoid the coach to the ground.

Shaun Teale:'I remember that night I went to one of our regular haunts, the Barley's pub, for a drink. And who was sat on a stool at the end of the bar? Paul. He was paralytic. I remember him saying, "How the hell did you win without me?"'

We ended up finishing a respectable seventh in the League and being knocked out of the FA Cup in the sixth round by eventual winners Liverpool. Nothing spectacular, but certainly a significant improvement on the season with Dr Jo.

That summer I flew off to the US Cup with the Republic of Ireland, ducking down to Florida afterwards where I linked up with Claire. The tension between us must have been palpable now to anyone in the same building. We just weren't getting on, always rowing, sniping, arguing.

I remember Claire storming out of a club after one of what seemed an endless succession of rows. Needless to say, I didn't follow and just went missing for the night.

So I drank to blot out the anger. Despite the events of pre-season, I had done well for Ron. That was my consolation. Whilst all else was anger and recrimination, the football came easy to me. It was where I felt confident and safe.

And with the arrival of the new Premier League, I was ready to take my game to another level.

22

'93

Gordon Taylor is adamant.

'You *have* to be there Paul, now give me your word.' He's talking about the PFA awards dinner in London. It's black-tie business. Gordon knows what I'm like with these gigs. He knows I'd rather spend a day in the dentist's chair than walk into a crowded room.

'Em, I'll do my best Gordon . . .'

We've developed a kind of a relationship since the day Manchester United tried to persuade me that retirement and an insurance payout would be the answer to my prayers. Four years on, we're laughing at the absurdity of that memory. I'm on a shortlist for Footballer of the Year, you see.

'No, your best's not good enough Paul. You've got to be there. End of story.'

I detect from the urgency in his voice that something extraordinary may be about to happen to me. I don't say it, of course. How could I? I'm Paul McGrath. I've still got that voice in my head. '*You don't belong there.*' I still feel that I'm somehow hamming it in the company of real football people.

But I'm not stupid. I'm on a shortlist, and right now the Chief

Executive of the PFA seems remarkably insistent that I attend the dinner. My heart is pounding, but I can't ask because I know that he can't tell me. But it does sound suspiciously as if . . .

'Do I have your word, Paul?'

'Em . . .'

'Paul!'

'OK, I'll be there.'

The best season of my football career is an enduring mystery.

It evolved against a backdrop of utter chaos in my private life and arrived largely without warning. In some respects, maybe I had begun to take refuge in the game. All the turbulence in my world would abate at three o'clock on a Saturday afternoon. Then, and only then, I felt in control.

For me, football became a getaway. It wasn't that I would be immune to the unravelling of my marriage. Things got to me from time to time. Sometimes after games, I could sense people knew that, emotionally, I was in a pretty strange place. I could feel them looking at me, wondering 'Is he going to be around for the next game?'

To some degree I was leading a double life. The cracks were clearly showing. My marriage was falling down around my ears. My kids were suffering. Rarely now did I ever arrive home with a smile on my face.

But it wasn't something I would discuss with anyone in the dressing room. I didn't have that kind of relationship with any teammate. So I bottled it all up. In a peculiar way, the only thing I found that I could properly focus on was playing football. My drinking wasn't exactly out of control, but it was becoming an increasingly private activity.

With the dawn of the Premier League, Ron had been busy reshaping Villa into a side capable of challenging. Perhaps his shrewdest signing was that of another of my Republic of Ireland teammates, Ray Houghton, from Liverpool. Ray was a hugely clever player, capable of pickpocketing teams with smart runs and subtle passing. Exactly the kind of creative presence we lacked since 'Sid' Cowan's departure.

But Ray, too, was only now being brought up to speed on my lifestyle.

Ray Houghton: 'The thing was you weren't in his company all the time. Away from the game, Paul was very private really. He didn't come out with the lads very often. He just kept himself to himself. He was quite secretive I think from that point of view. His drinking was never in front of you.

'I know there were a couple of games with Villa where he had two or three pints before the match. You'd only hear about it afterwards. But he'd still put on a man-of-the-match performance. And you're thinking "Christ, how has he done this?"

'It was incredible. But it still wasn't right for him. I mean no one knew really how to talk about it, how to try and change him around. He was his own man. After training, he'd be gone straight back to Manchester. No one would see him.

'I think the fact that he was playing so well on a Saturday convinced people that whatever he was doing, it can't have been that bad. The few seasons I was there, he was getting man of the match nearly every week. He was just a very strong character, very single-minded.

'And he sort of had this attitude "I've done something daft, I've had a drink, so I've got to get myself out of this by playing well."'

The final piece in the new Villa jigsaw would also draw Ron to Anfield. We had already made an indifferent start to the season, winning just two of our opening seven, when Dean Saunders arrived as a much-needed partner for the now fit Dalian Atkinson in attack. Just after Dean arrived, Liverpool were the visitors to Villa Park and he scored twice in a spectacular 4–2 victory.

Immediately, you could sense something change within the fabric of the whole team.

In three games (and three victories) Dean would score six times. Playing alongside him, Dalian would notch three. Suddenly, Villa had an attack to be feared.

One significant back-room change was Andy Gray's departure as the practicalities of juggling life as a TV pundit with that of an assistant manager proved just too difficult to overcome. In response, Ron appointed Dave Sexton – the very man Ron himself had replaced as Manchester United manager in 1981.

Dave was a lovely, soft-spoken figure with an air of real authority about him. He took preparation extremely seriously, and was in many ways the perfect foil for Ron's spontaneity.

But to begin with, I think I scared him.

Ron Atkinson: 'I brought Dave in specifically to work with the young players. I think he's the best teacher I've ever seen. Just working with young players on technique and that. Absolutely brilliant. We went to Germany on another pre-season tour and Paul hadn't trained.

'He might have been on the bike for twenty minutes a day or something like that. But he hadn't really done any pounding like the rest of the boys had to do, 'cos to do that would have knackered his knees completely.

'So, while we're out there, we go and play this game against Dynamo Dresden. Now Dave's a very shrewd, all-seeing, all-watching type of guy. But he hasn't seen Paul play. First minute of the game, this ball is pumped down the channel towards this well known German international.

'He goes running to it and, boom, Paul just explodes past him. Cleans up. Few minutes later, their big centre-half goes up for a header, but big Paul launches himself almost a foot above him. Seconds later, boom, he does something else.

'Dave Sexton turns to me and says, "This is not possible. What McGrath is doing is just not possible with the amount of preparation that he's had . . ."

'And I say, "Dave, that's just what the big man does . . ."'

Most people wouldn't have seen it, but I certainly wasn't on my best behaviour during that pre-season. I remember we went training in some hills near Oxford and the lads were complaining that the runs involved were pretty brutal.

Ron spared me the worst of it. That was his way. I usually wanted to participate fully in those sessions because I understood the benefits to be gained from a good pre-season, but Ron was trying to balance that against any potential damage to my knees.

When the players went on a run, staff would follow on bikes. And Ron always included me among staff. 'Get on the bike Macca, you're not doing this . . .'

I used Oxford as a bit of a holiday camp though. At night, we'd have card games in the rooms and I was shameless in my consumption of wine during those card games. The other players seemed to grow indifferent to the sight of me downing bottles of vino on the basis that, by now, different rules applied to different people.

In my case, performing on a Saturday was the only yardstick that mattered.

From the moment Dalian and Dean linked up in attack, our season went into overdrive. We had a solid back four of Barrett, McGrath, Teale and Staunton, with Nigel Spink and – later – Mark Bosnich offering top-class cover in goal. Houghton brought real cleverness to a midfield where Richardson, Parker and Froggatt were now all strong players. In attack, Dwight Yorke was maturing into a pretty special option to the first-choice pair.

For two thirds of the season, we played football that seemed to have the whole country buzzing. I was loving it. Tealy and I could almost read what the other was thinking now. We covered for one another, even fought one another's fights.

Shaun Teale: 'Ron might tell us to push up ten yards towards the halfway line. We'd just exchange glances. Because Paul couldn't do that. His legs wouldn't allow him. So we had to defend deep. It suited us both. I covered Paul's arse as much as I could. He covered mine.

'It was quite strange for two people who didn't really socialise off the pitch that much to become so close.

'I remember one game especially. We were playing Sheffield Wednesday at Villa Park. Paul had gone up for a header with Mark Bright and been split open by Bright's elbow. He was absolutely ranting. I remember it so vividly because normally you never saw Paul get angry. But this time he was all but chasing Bright around the pitch. He was absolutely livid. It was real anger.

'About two minutes later, the ball comes down my side. Bright comes in to challenge, and now I've split his head wide open. So the pair of them have blood pouring down their faces. Nonetheless, they finish the game.

'Afterwards, I walk into Jim Walker's room and who's there, lying on the two beds? Paul and Bright. There's total silence between them. Not a word spoken. But Paul was still coiled. I think if Bright had said anything, Paul would have knocked him out there and then. He was seething for days after. Which was most unlike him.

'You see, Paul and me actually preferred playing against the likes of Fash [John Fashanu] because you knew what was coming. You knew you'd probably end up with blood coming out of somewhere. You'd have kicked him, he'd have kicked you. But you could accept that. That's the way it was.

257

'People like Vinnie Jones really were nothing people to us because they weren't hard by our standards. I mean Paul was like a piece of old teak. He was a very tough lad. I don't think people realised how hard he could be if riled.'

Ron never chose to complicate things in the dressing room. He was a breath of fresh air. 'Go out and entertain me!' he'd bellow to his front men. 'Do something that'll bring a smile to my face.' The team reflected his spirit. We were afraid of nobody.

But in mid-season, Dalian Atkinson sustained a long-term hamstring complaint that would sideline him for almost fifteen games. That injury almost certainly cost us the title.

Without it, I believe we would have been well clear of Manchester United coming down the home straight. Instead, we were neck and neck. And the season turned on a single afternoon in April.

That was the day we drew 0-0 at home to Coventry and United were rescued by two injury time Steve Bruce goals to beat Sheffield Wednesday 2-1 at Old Trafford. The length of injury time played in Manchester is still a matter of bitter debate among Villa fans.

Ron Atkinson: 'That was the moment when I realised we weren't going to win the League. I know we won the next two games (including a 3-1 victory over United at Villa Park), but it was all about that day. It was fated. You see, if United lost to Wednesday, they'd have crumbled I think. All the pressure was on them.

'Carlton Palmer told me afterwards that he went across after ninety minutes and asked the referee how long was left. He was told there'd be three minutes of injury time. Eight minutes later, they were still playing and Wednesday were still winning! Oh yeah?

'We were flying that season. Dalian and Deano were the best two in the League at the time. They had that little chemistry.

They were mates, very pally, always gibbing each other up. You'd be watching them and thinking "Christ almighty, we're on fire here."

'But once Dalian got that hamstring, he never got back to the same again. And we paid the price . . .'

The wheels came off badly in the end. You could say that we were psyched out of it. We lost our last three games of the season to Blackburn, Oldham and QPR. United won the title by a ten-point margin. It was an illusion of ease.

The Blackburn defeat (0–3) was particularly humiliating. They just battered us. It was a total embarrassment and, needless to say, my old mate 'Sid' Cowan played a stormer for them. That was one of those days when few words were exchanged between Tealy and me. We just communicated through facial expressions.

I loved my life as a footballer that season. I loved the sense of being part of a team that played with genuine verve and flair. Under Ron, a real sense of camaraderie developed in the dressing room. It was, I believe, reflected in how we played.

We had a lovely card school running on the coach to away games and around this time I became dealer and banker. The school was really just a means of killing time. A way of getting painlessly from A to B.

I always brought a wad of notes with me on those journeys in case anyone needed a loan. Sometimes Jim Walker would join in, and I always saw to it that he didn't end up in the red at journey's end. By now footballers' salaries had stretched a long way ahead of physios' and I just felt it would be immoral for Jim to be handing money over to people on six or seven grand a week.

The flip side was that he could win money and I always relished it when Jim was flush at the end of a session. It was, I felt, the least I owed him for all the care he was giving me.

We usually played Three-Card Brag where, essentially, you have three cards face down and bluff on their value. The resident 'lunatic' of that school was 'Bossy' (Mark Bosnich). Actually, he wouldn't even be playing when suddenly he'd march down to the back of the bus and announce, 'I'll go fifty quid blind!'

We'd be furious. 'It's a friendly game for fuck's sake Bossy!' Someone would take the bait eventually. Someone would get brave. So you'd throw your fifty in blind, at which point Bossy would announce, 'I'll go another fifty blind!'

We'd be fuming now. 'Look, we're not getting into this. We're not fucking Arsenal!'

Bossy would just blow in and end up wrecking the school, then blow out again just as fast. He'd invariably lose two hands in a row and be gone. But every now and then he'd win, and that would be the ultimate sickener.

I always considered myself quite an accomplished Brag player, but the truth was I couldn't resist the temptation of an extravagant gamble. I might have a shit hand but I'd keep on bluffing to the end, determined to break people. That was the ultimate buzz, when you'd wear everyone down, collect the pot, then reveal an absolutely crap hand.

That school was largely fun back then but, in time, spiralling salaries would change the whole dynamic of it and force me to wave a white flag.

I probably can't adequately explain the release I would feel getting on that bus in 1993. The one thing I knew I was doing well was playing football. I routinely picked up man-of-the-match awards. There was a sense of reassuring permanency around the team, certainly the defence.

That's not to say, mind, that I didn't have my blowouts. One of my worst days in football came on Boxing Day 1992 when Villa went to play Coventry in a Midlands derby at Highfield Road. My job that day was to mark the Coventry striker Mickey Quinn.

Now Quinn was a decent finisher but he was never the most

athletic of footballers, and opposition supporters would taunt him mercilessly about his rotund figure. Just the usual 'Who ate all the pies?' stuff.

From admittedly shaky memory, I think I had slipped into the spirit of the festive season by the time I got to Highfield Road. I certainly remember being affected by drink on the pitch that day. Anyway, Quinn banged in a hat-trick against me as Coventry stuffed us 3-0. I was hopeless, absolutely all over the place.

I have a vivid recall of Tealy looking across at me once and just muttering, 'Jesus Christ . . .' He couldn't believe what he was seeing. This was a classic case of me getting the balance wrong, drinking too close to a game and not doing my job properly.

Yet nobody bawled me out afterwards. To be fair, it didn't happen that often and I think people generally just felt that my good days far outnumbered the bad. And they did, too.

After all, I was ever-present that season, playing all forty-two League games. Beside me, Tealy missed just three. I was on good appearance money, you see, on top of my basic salary. It was in my interests to be in the team.

I remember heading the only goal in an important win away to Nottingham Forest at the beginning of April and all the handshakes and back-slaps that followed. On that journey back to Birmingham, I felt like royalty, loved and appreciated by management and team. A big player in a big team.

Ron Atkinson: 'How good was Macca in 1993? Immense. The best centre-half I've ever seen is John Charles. But I would say that, of that type of centre-half, McGrath is as good as any I've seen. I mean you look at superb players now like John Terry or, before him, Tony Adams.

'McGrath was better than either. He was so powerful and he could manipulate a ball.

'If I had a criticism of him, it was that I felt he should have been better with the ball. Just in terms of playing the more ambitious pass. Because he was a good ball-player. But, by and large, he just did his job.

'Sometimes you'd be watching him and thinking "Where's he going now, where's . . . oh, there's the ball, stuck to his foot!" He was a defender who always attracted the ball. Sometimes you'd think "Uh oh, he's gone too far past the near post", but the ball would just come to him. He seemed like a magnet to the ball.

'And he had such immense power.'

No one knew, of course, that by April 1993 I was heading home to a sundered family, Claire now in the Priory, the kids being looked after by friends. In a sense, I was leading a double life. Serene on the outside. Breaking down within.

I didn't really confide in people. One of the few colleagues who would have known the full extent of what was happening was Jim Walker. I always knew that I could speak to Jim in confidence. Over time, he pretty much became three parts physio, seven parts agony aunt with me.

When it eventually came to court and seeking custody of the boys, Jim was a huge support to me. Just a commonsense voice. A twenty-four-carat friend. It wasn't that he was taking sides. Quite the contrary. He'd routinely remind me that I couldn't have been the easiest person to live with.

He was there for me endlessly. I often use this expression of 'someone just looking over me' throughout my life. By that, I suppose I mean a supernatural presence. An angel of sorts. Probably Okune.

But in career terms, Jim Walker was that angel. The human force who, for the best eight years of my life as a footballer, kept me sane and healthy. If I was – as my fellow professionals voted – the best footballer in England in 1993, Jim was the most profound reason.

He was, in many ways, the star.

London was bizarre in a number of ways. Firstly, because I went to the function sober. Secondly, because I stayed that way. Thirdly, because I actually enjoyed the feeling.

Deep down, I suppose, we all have vanities and mine were nourished royally on the night. Ordinarily, I was allergic to this kind of attention. I usually dreaded walking up to collect a man-of-the-match award far more than I ever did facing down the most menacing strikers in English football.

The mere sight of a camera lens or microphone was sure to bring on a panic attack. Certain to reinvigorate that voice within. Old Beelzebub himself. *'You know they're going to see through you . . .'*

Naturally, I had weighed up the options of escape. I felt there was something absurd about me even being present at such a ceremony. But a no-show would have looked appalling if I won the award. It would have fed the stereotype.

I remember taking a deep breath the moment I stepped into the ballroom. Two of the first faces I saw were those of Kenny Dalglish and Liam Brady. Ryan Giggs was there to get the young player award. *'You're out of your depth here, you're just stealing this . . .'*

But somehow I held it together, and collected the trophy off Bobby Charlton that evening with more than a little pride. That same week, I remember one of the local Birmingham papers carried a front-page headline beside my picture, declaring 'Player of the Year, Every Year'.

I was now undeniably at the height of my powers as a footballer. But my confidence was strictly superficial.

When, at season's end, Villa brought all the players and their wives or girlfriends off to Mauritius as a thank-you gesture for their efforts, I made the trip alone.

I was on the run now from a life in virtual meltdown.

23

SINS OF THE FATHER

Easter 1993. Chickens coming home to roost.

The explosion came with a phone call that left everything as wreckage. A female friend called just as I was leaving Bodymoor Heath. She was selling her story.

My recklessness had finally caught up with me. She was a single mum, living in Didsbury. Her daughter had a famous, mystery dad. For a tabloid newspaper, that was £30,000 worth of scoop. Too bad if there was collateral damage.

In many ways it had been an accident waiting to happen. There was no relationship between us. Just an occasional dalliance running to no more than single figures over four years, by my estimation. It wasn't exactly romantic.

That time Jim Walker tracked me down to her house, I had spent the previous forty-eight hours lying in bed, drinking vodka and vomiting sporadically into a bucket on the floor. That was romantic me at the time. Rightly or wrongly, I felt a sense of entrapment about the whole business. Cameras always seemed to materialise at opportune moments when I found my way to her home in Didsbury. Evidence was being accumulated.

But yes, the contact had been adulterous. And yes, there was a chance I was the father of her little girl.

Maybe a year and a half had passed since she told me she was pregnant. On hearing that, I had submitted to reflex. I signed a cheque. I tried to flush the news right out of my consciousness.

Again, I was up in Birmingham that day. It began with, 'You're what?' Then, 'But I thought you were on the pill . . .' Had I asked? No. Did I even think of asking? No. Eventually, we came to what I considered to be some kind of resolution. I was a married man. I had three boys of my own. I needed closure.

We had met in a club in Hale, Norman, Robbo and I sitting at a table. A smile from across the way, 'tin-head' here left smitten. Four years later, my United days were in the past, but not my United baggage. 'Hi Paul, it's &%$£@ here . . .'

By and large, alcoholics are accomplished liars. We even lie to ourselves. Myth displaces fact. We have tales, sob stories and excuses almost on tap. If I had become a father out of wedlock, I carried on as if I just had an extra pair of shoes in my life. I said nothing, did nothing. I bottled it up. I still called around to that house in Didsbury occasionally, but only when under the weather.

Routinely, there were little rumours of a story breaking, and those rumours invariably triggered panic attacks. Panic attacks brought binges. And with the binges came bouts of utter chaos.

My infidelity was a matter of habit now. There was a girl I saw regularly in Birmingham. Maybe she was filling an emotional void in my life, as my marriage began to disintegrate. Tony Cascarino was my roommate for a year at Villa and he has always alluded to the fact that sharing with me was never, shall we say, boring.

Through all of this, I suppose there was an undercurrent of guilt. Claire knew about the girl in Birmingham, but she was trying to bring up three boys in as calm an environment as she could, and for that reason I think she was prepared to turn a blind eye.

Yet deep down she was hurting and, I suppose, lonely. I was

taking her for granted, and over time that loneliness led to her looking for emotional support elsewhere. When I discovered that she was having an affair with my best friend, I was absolutely devastated.

The friend in question was a police officer who I even paid for to come to Dublin a few times through 1990 and 1991 to keep Claire company while I was on international duty with the Irish team. It seemed normal to me. He'd regularly accompany Claire to Villa games because I didn't want her going on her own.

I do remember people like Frank Mullen expressing reservations about their closeness at the time, but I never even considered the possibility of anything happening.

When I discovered their affair, the sense of betrayal was seismic. If I was angry with Claire, it was nothing compared to the rage I felt towards my so-called best friend. I despised him for what he did. I will always despise him.

The atmosphere at home became sour and habitually hostile after that. We were, it seemed, on the road to nowhere.

Not long after Graham Taylor left Villa, I began to slip into a familiar place. I was drinking ridiculous quantities, taking terrible chances. One night, driving home from Birmingham, I was swigging from a brandy bottle. There was another bottle on the back seat, just in case I ran out.

For some reason, I chose to slip off the motorway and take a back road for the last few miles. By this point, I was very depressed and, worse, extremely drunk.

It was as if the church wall spoke to me the moment it came into view. I saw escape in it. All the energies building around me had become so negative, so draining. I remember thinking 'I'm tired of all this . . .' I hated everything I had become. The deceitful husband, the shallow father, the flaky teammate. I decided to check out of the black place I was in.

The church wall was the answer.

So I reversed my car back up the road into a narrow lane, undid my seat belt and reached back for a final, numbing swig of brandy. Then I checked that there was no other car coming, closed my eyes and slammed the throttle to the floor.

The next thing I remember is being at home and two policemen arriving at the front door. 'Mr McGrath, we have to give you a breath test.'

Claire. 'He had come home in an ambulance. I didn't realise the circumstances of what had happened. I mean I wasn't proud of myself having that affair. I don't think Paul ever got over it, mainly because of who it was with. Even though he had had plenty of affairs himself, he just felt such betrayal over it.

'But to me, that crash was just another unbelievably lucky escape. The policemen said he had hit a wall about five miles from home. He had a few cuts and bruises, but nothing serious.

'They seemed genuinely concerned for him but I was amazed when, after they breathalysed him, they said they weren't going to prosecute. I just couldn't understand how he hadn't failed the test.

'It was only after they'd gone that Paul said to me, "I just saw this brick wall and speeded up . . ."'

What astonishes me in hindsight is that all through this time I was playing probably the best football of my life. Maybe I was using the game as a release, channelling all my anxiety and aggression into Villa's push for honours. That 'accident' never did make it into the papers. It never even got through the door of the dressing room.

But I was living a double life now. The life of the duck, serene above the surface, flailing frantically underneath.

Claire and I were still living together, trying hard to paper over the cracks. The kids would have heard the rows and felt the anger.

It was almost a blessing that I spent most of the week in Birmingham. That way, the pretence of normality was sustainable. But it *was* a pretence. On the surface, we were putting things right between us, even trying for an addition to the family. In reality, we were probably just delaying the inevitable.

And that was the emotional climate in which I took that call at Easter 1993. Claire still yearned for a little daughter. I could hardly explain to her that I might already have one, so we had applied to adopt an orphan from Romania, a gorgeous little baby girl. Everything seemed to be going to plan. We were maybe just weeks away from welcoming her into the family.

Then, 'Hi Paul, it's &%$£ here . . .'

I drove home from Birmingham like a condemned man. I kept planning and replanning what I was going to say. Practising the tone. The look. Where would I break the news?

Claire: 'I remember it was lunchtime and he came in from training. He said, "I've got something to tell you, let's go for a meal." There was this little bistro we liked in Hale. Everything was relatively light-hearted to begin with. I even remember us joking with the waiter.

'Then he said it again. "I've got something to tell you and you're not going to like it." I'll never forget the feeling that came over me. My stomach just went tight. Then he spat it out. "I've got a baby with somebody else."'

Claire burst out crying at the table. She couldn't believe it. She started asking me questions about the circumstances, the time frame. Then she got up from the table and just rushed straight out the door. And I sat there, staring at the uneaten food, wondering how deep a hole I had just dug for myself this time.

I had already been in touch with a journalist friend, Peter Fitton of the *Sun*, asking him to run some of kind of sanitised version of the story and thereby, nip the scoop in the bud. I couldn't deny that the girl was mine. I wouldn't. But I wanted, if possible, to dilute the impact on the news-stands.

Peter did what he could. The storm, though, was on its way.

Claire: 'He came back that night and I said to him, "Can you not ring her and ask her not to do this?" The newspaper had put her up in a hotel in Manchester. So Paul rang. I actually took the phone from him and said to her "Why are you doing this?" Her answer was, "Well, he doesn't want anything to do with the child and it's not my fault." I just felt sorry for her really. But I was very angry with Paul.

'Anyway, he went training the next morning and I didn't see him for days. He just went missing. It was dreadful, the worst time of my life. It was the Easter weekend and the press were all camped at the bottom of the garden, knocking on the door, asking me how I felt.

'There were pictures of this beautiful baby girl in the papers. The spitting image of my own little Romanian baby, I thought. I was trying to hide that from the boys. My family had come around. All my friends were phoning up. Eventually, the police had to come and stand at the bottom of the path. I think it lasted for three days.

'Paul had just gone missing and I thought "I'm never going to forgive you for this, dumping this on me and not being able to face it yourself." And that was it. I just couldn't take it anymore. I ended up taking an overdose, which put me in the Priory.

'And I never went back to him after that.'

Maybe six weeks before all of this happened, I had met Caroline Lamb in a Liverpool bar. She was pretty, a computer operator based in London, who had come home to stay at her parents' for the weekend. We started seeing one another. I told her about Claire and the boys, but insisted that although we still lived under the same roof, we were effectively separated.

I suppose Claire's overdose facilitated me in taking on the role of victim. I now had three kids to look after, while my wife underwent counselling in the Priory. In many ways I took advantage of that situation. I played on people's sympathy. I was, to all intents and purposes, the injured party.

When Villa announced they were bringing the players and their partners on an end of season trip to Mauritius, I even went through the motions of asking Claire if she'd be able to travel. Her doctors were unequivocal, naturally. It would have amounted to reopening a raw wound.

So I travelled alone and came home early to be with the new woman in my life. I had become pretty shameless now. In late May, Caroline came with me to Cork where I was due to do a few days of coaching before linking up with the Irish squad for a World Cup qualifier in Albania.

Of course, I never did link up with the team and the infamy that followed is well documented later.

It didn't matter to me. I was moving on. I was in love. By August, Caroline had moved in with me and the boys, my separation from Claire now absolute. While in the Priory, she had met Matthew Schutt, a really decent bloke. There was now no question of a reconciliation between us. We were both getting on with our lives.

It was all remarkably civil compared to the bitterness and recrimination that would define the break-up of my second marriage ten years later.

The battle for custody was unpleasant, without being vicious. The media covered it in gruesome detail every day. Our marriage was just about put on a Petri dish. Claire's mother had to speak in court about seeing me under the influence of drink. I have a vivid memory of watching her, shaking in the dock and just being a little repulsed by what people were being put through.

I was still drinking, yet claiming to be on the dry. As ever, I wasn't quite absorbing the seriousness of what was happening. We were in court for three days, much of it taken up with Claire and a variety of witnesses speaking out about my alcoholic excesses.

In the end, it came to my turn to face a grilling and I just decided I couldn't take this any further. We agreed a compromise. Claire had now begun a four-year course in prosthetics and orthotics, so it suited her to have the boys for weekends and holidays. I would take them Monday to Friday.

Contrary to widespread belief, I didn't win custody. We agreed 'joint residency'. And the kids seemed to take it in their stride.

Christopher: 'I suppose I saw arguments and maybe stuff that I shouldn't have seen. But that happens. It's why people get divorced. And it all seemed to be over very quickly. Just a case of Mum moving into a new house and us going there at weekends, then back to Dad's for the week. It just seemed practical. We didn't love one person more than the other.'

Within twelve months, I was married to Caroline and Claire was happily settled down with Matthew. A sense of normality settled back upon us. Over the coming years, my one-time female friend would appear sporadically in the newspapers, selling another story about the heartless celebrity father of her daughter. Good luck to her. She was getting money for recycling old news.

The one sad part for me is that I never felt it possible, in these circumstances, to have a relationship with that little girl. She's beautiful, and yet another innocent victim, I suppose, of the dysfunction that can occur between consenting adults.

I just don't want anything to do with her mother now. And, as ever, a child has been caught up in the crossfire.

24

PAIN

If it's possible to befriend pain, I had commenced an intense courtship with it by the mid-nineties.

I felt I had explored every corner. I knew its shades, its rules, its extremities. We were intimate now. The morning after a game, I would come shuffling down the stairs like a withered pensioner trying to negotiate his way off an ice rink.

The boys would look at me from the breakfast table with a mixture of impatience and pity. They could see that I was fighting nature.

For all the gentility of my match preparation, the knees were a source of endless discomfort now. I routinely declared myself unfit for a game only for Jim Walker to give me that knowing smile of his and say gently, 'OK Paul, we'll see how it is at two o'clock with a little jog maybe.'

That 'little jog' invariably resulted in me playing. In hindsight, it was probably as much a test of mind as body.

The extraordinary thing is that I never once had surgery on my knees at Villa. Under Jim's supervision, the emphasis was always on recovery. The less I trained, the deeper it was felt I could dig on a Saturday afternoon. And the deeper I dug, the more people were probably fooled by appearances.

Jim Walker: 'When you have knee problems like Paul had, the pain is there all the time. I don't know how he managed to play with it really. Essentially, the cartilage that protects the bone ends is worn away. So it's bone on bone. It's pain every step that you take really.

'Paul just seemed to be able to play with it. I don't know how, but he did.'

Without cartilage there is no cushion, and without cushion there is no comfort. On bad days, I would get this horrible sensation in the knees. Just endless grating and grinding. The feeling of trying to force something that Mother Nature was telling you shouldn't be forced.

But pain? Bah, what was pain? I had a Masters degree in the stuff and felt sure that nothing it could ever throw at me would be too much. I was beginning to find ways of blotting out all unwelcome stuff. Physical and emotional. Pain could never weaken my resolve.

Silly me.

Join me for a night in London. It is 26 March 1994, the eve of Villa's Coca-Cola Cup final against Manchester United at Wembley.

Now I still have baggage with United. I have yet to be fully reconciled with their decision to offload me in 1989. The last pretence of communication between Alex Ferguson and me was a pretty risible, champagne-fuelled *News of the World* interview I did shortly after my departure from Old Trafford.

At the time, Alex was taking a bit of a kicking from a succession of former United players and I happily joined in, studs-first. The gist of my message was that Alex needed to lighten up, and maybe relax with a few drinks.

United were incensed by such temerity, and on their insistence I was hauled in front of the Football Association. The charge was that I had brought the game into disrepute. I was fined a whopping £8,500.

So my mindset wasn't exactly complex approaching that 1994 Cup final. This, finally, was my opportunity for redress. Sure, I had been part of League wins against United since my departure, but this was a chance to take a major trophy at Alex Ferguson's expense. This was a chance to make some kind of conclusive statement on what had gone on between us.

Villa's League form had dramatically dis-improved from the previous season, despite the acquisition of yet another Irish international teammate of mine, Andy Townsend, from Chelsea. United had gone green too, breaking the British transfer record in recruiting Roy Keane from Nottingham Forest. As good a player as Andy undoubtedly was, Keane would prove the signing of the decade.

United had already beaten us in both League games, and much of the previous season's momentum was now lost at Villa. But we genuinely believed we had the flair to hurt them at Wembley, especially with Tony Daley and Dalian Atkinson playing down the flanks.

You could see that Ron really fancied the challenge too. We all did.

That night, the butterflies were certainly kicking in as I popped my customary sleeping tablet and drifted off into a peaceful slumber. Next thing I remember is the pain. Absolutely shocking pain.

Jim Walker: 'I got a knock on my door at about two in the morning. It was Paul. His first words were, "Jim, I've not been drinking!" He said he'd got a terrible pain in his shoulder. At the time, he was almost living on Ibrufen. He'd already taken some, so I gave him a couple of paracetemol.

'The following morning he was still clearly in a lot of pain. So we do what we can but we're not quite sure what we're working with here. When we get to Wembley, we weren't sure whether he should play. So it was decided to give him some painkilling injections.

'I remember saying to him, "I've not done this before Paul, but if you're going to have this type of injection, the shoulder is probably a good place to have it." Because it's not weight-bearing. Much as you wouldn't want to do it, this was a Cup final. And it was against Manchester United. Everything added up.

'So he had three or four injections and another one at half-time to help him through it.'

I remember the buzzer was going in the dressing room as the last needle went in. I was getting a little flustered. The buzzer made me jump, ramming the needle into the socket. I screeched with the pain. By now, I just wanted to be out there, finding my bearings, dealing with that first ball.

I knew that the afternoon was never going to be gentle, given that Mark Hughes would be my direct opponent. Perhaps it was just as well too. In different circumstances, I might have been inclined to play percentages. Against 'Sparky', you just went to war.

Ron Atkinson: 'The thing with Macca was that you knew he'd get through anything once he'd got on the pitch. Once he got the adrenalin flowing. It was never a case of "Well, I wonder . . ." So, to me, the shoulder just wasn't an issue. I'll tell you how little concern it was to me.

'I didn't even put Ugo Ehiogu on the bench. I was actually more concerned about Stan [Steve Staunton] than Paul. Stan was just coming back after a hernia operation. So I put Cox on the bench as back-up. That meant, when Stan came off, I could put Earl Barrett at left-back on Kanchelskis and use Coxy at right-back.

'Macca? I'd just give him the dig in the stomach and say the usual. "Macca, c'mon, get out there and play. Cowboys don't cry!"'

Ray Houghton: 'I remember Paul being in absolute agony before the game. He was holding his arm above the waist. But that was his mental strength. He had to get his mind around that and go out and play. Once again, he was outstanding in that game.'

As it happened, we won the game comfortably. It still irks me a little when people suggest that it was an under-strength United team we beat. The truth is that they had everyone on duty that day except goalkeeper Peter Schmeichel. And he was replaced by one of our former Villa colleagues, Les Sealey. Hardly someone to be considered a weak link.

Dalian Atkinson put us in front midway through the first half; Dean Saunders added a second after the break, and though Hughes managed to lose me for a United goal in the eighty-third minute, Saunders got his second in the final moments with a late penalty after Andrei Kanchelskis handled on the goal line.

Poor Kanchelskis was ordered off for the offence, which hardly seemed necessary given that the game was now over.

Still, sympathy was in short supply among the claret and blue hordes. We had beaten the all-powerful United in a Cup final and the celebrations reflected the euphoria. It was Villa's first trophy of note since the 1982 European Cup.

But in the midst of it was a gesture that caught me entirely by surprise. Alex Ferguson stepped into the maelstrom with an outstretched hand. 'Well done big man,' he said. I was flabbergasted.

'Em, thanks Alex,' I replied, suddenly feeling a distinct affection for someone I had imagined to be a sworn enemy. It was a lovely, humbling moment. There and then, I just felt that all the angst between us was suddenly flushed away.

I returned to the dressing room grinning manically. Not a care in the world now. Except for that burning in my shoulder, now slowly beginning to tug at my attention again.

Jim Walker: 'We got him back up the next day to Birmingham and made a few enquiries. We needed to know what the condition was. Turns out it was a virus in his shoulder, something similar to Bell's palsy where it becomes almost paralysed. The symptoms include extreme pain in the first two or three weeks. And he certainly had that.

'I mean we headed down to Southampton right at the end of the season. Paul had missed the last six or seven games because of the shoulder. He was trying desperately to prove his fitness in time for the World Cup.

'I think it was the only time I can remember him having to come off in a game. But he was just in too much pain with the shoulder to continue. It was only after that game that we got the problem finally diagnosed. His shoulder was effectively paralysed.

'The advice was that, on average, it took six months for a person to get back to normal . . .'

That Southampton game was horrendous. I had to ask to be taken off. People were running past me as if I was a lamp post. I had no balance, no sharpness, no confidence. We got stuffed 4-1. Worse, it was our penultimate game of the season. I was running out of time.

The injury had become increasingly worrying and humiliating over time. After an initial two-week period, the pain level at least tapered off to something bearable, yet the discomfort was pretty constant. And the embarrassment. I couldn't even dress myself. With the World Cup on the horizon, I became panicked by the absence of much palpable progress. In effect, I started playing with my left hand hanging limp down by my side.

Our final League game of the season went some way towards redeeming me. I played reasonably well as we beat Liverpool 2-1 at Villa Park. It was 7 May. One month exactly before Ireland left for the World Cup.

Villa finished a deflating tenth in the Premier League, the shoulder injury having forced me to miss seven consecutive League games on the run-in. Otherwise, I had been largely ever-present through the season, except for a rather public FA Cup mishap in January.

We were due to travel to Exeter in the third round but, amidst growing newspaper speculation about the state of my private life, I had spent a couple of days taking solace in the bottle. As ever, my knees were hurting too. So I skipped the bus to the West Country and retired instead to the Barley's for a beer.

Shaun Teale: 'Earl Barrett ends up playing alongside me in Paul's place. We win 0-1. When we get back from Exeter, I pick the wife up from home and we head across to the Barley's. Walk into the pub and there's Paul fast asleep on the settee.'

Inevitably, the story hit the newspapers and there was speculation that I might even face the sack. Ron was absolutely furious. He hauled me over the coals the following Monday and ended up fining me £5,000. That money was put towards taking the team to Tenerife for a few days before our subsequent fourth round FA Cup tie at Grimsby.

Rather pointedly, Ron told me that while the lads were sunning themselves, I could stay back and train.

Otherwise, I was still doing a relatively decent job for Villa. The crowd seemed inclined to forgive me everything. Sometimes, when I'd be coming off a bender, they'd hold up these Guinness signs as if to offer moral support. Sometimes there'd be a placard declaring simply 'Welcome back Paul!'

For four successive seasons, they had voted me Player of the Year. It was as if I could do no wrong in their eyes.

I had also played the role of peacemaker during an extraordinary dressing room blow-up between Dalian Atkinson and Big Ron just a couple of weeks after the Exeter game.

This followed a 1-1 draw against Chelsea at Stamford Bridge. Dalian was one of the most physically powerful footballers I've ever come across. When he was 'up' for a game, he could look unstoppable. But he had other days where he would look slightly passive and disinterested.

This had been one of his, shall we say, more docile performances, and Ron was not amused. In the dressing room afterwards, he deliberately set about goading a reaction out of Dalian.

The gist of what he said was that no one could blame Dalian for missing chances, given that it was pretty difficult to come upon a chance when you haven't crossed the halfway line all day. Dalian began to bristle. One word led to another, and before we knew it they were swinging at one another. I dived in between them as they went tumbling into the showers and, with a bit of assistance from Andy Townsend and Jim Barron, managed to prise them apart.

Almost instantaneously, the BBC's John Motson arrived in the dressing room, looking for Ron to do the customary post-match interview. Little did he realise, he had just missed a major scoop by seconds.

Jack Charlton hedged his bets for a long time before bringing me to the World Cup that summer, my shoulder still far from rehabilitated. But the tournament was a qualified success for us (we made the knockout stages), and within a week of returning (to yet another heroes' welcome in Dublin), I had flown to Mauritius for my wedding to Caroline.

After that, I came home to embark upon what I imagined would be a new and utterly blissful phase in my life. In America, I had been dry from start to finish of the tournament. A new man, I imagined. But in Mauritius, I drank to soothe my wedding-day nerves. An old failing was returning to haunt me.

Villa started the new season unconvincingly, Ron now coming under fire from some shareholders who accused him of concentrating more on TV appearances than dressing-room business. Pressure began to build with poor results.

Unbelievably, between September and early November we took just one point from nine League games. A riveting UEFA Cup victory against Inter Milan was completely devalued by elimination in the next round against Turkish side Trabzonspor. The ninth of those League games brought us to Wimbledon midweek. Having led by two goals, we ended up having Andy Townsend sent off and losing 3-4 to a last-minute goal. It would be Ron's final game in charge.

His sacking left a lot of us feeling guilty. Me especially. On the field, I had always given Ron everything I'd got. Off it, I had become increasingly careless. I knew that Ron would do anything for his players, so long as they delivered on a Saturday. The general consensus was that I delivered.

To me, that was my only duty of loyalty.

Trouble was, I had begun leaning on people now. I was drinking too close to matches. I was taking tablets. I was trying to balance my intake against my responsibilities as a professional, and quite often failing. I would walk into the Villa dressing room and go straight to the guys I felt close to – Tealy, Yorky, Mark Bosnich, Dean Saunders – and tell them I'd need 'a bit of help today'.

It wasn't exactly a one-way thing. I think the players appreciated how much I gave on my good days. They knew that I would literally put my body on the line to protect them. But, being honest, I don't know how I'd have felt if the shoe was on the other foot. How would I have reacted if Shaun Teale was coming to me with his worries, having taken a few drinks on board before a game?

Shaun Teale: 'To be fair, I don't think there was ever an issue with any player. The hardest part was when Paul came in drunk to training. He'd go on the bike for ten minutes. And it was a case of trying to keep him a mile away from Ron. Except invariably Paul used to get the giggles when he was pissed.

'So what would he do? He'd go in the dining room and sit next to Ron. And we'd just cringe. You knew Ron would have sussed by then. And you knew Paul was going to start giggling. So it was like, get your food down quick and get the hell out of there before you got dragged into something.'

Maybe the problem was that I knew I could do it. I could actually play football under the influence. I remember once coming back from Dublin and playing a match against Everton while still drunk. It was surreal. I was named man of the match that same day. A friend who had travelled over with me was sitting in the stand and could not believe his eyes.

I just felt unbelievably confident out there. I attacked everything. I went for balls I wouldn't normally dream of going for. I felt impregnable. And that was dangerous. My survival was fuelling the illness.

Once, I remember having to have this shot of brandy in the dressing room just to get me through a game. The brandy would be kept in the skip for use on bitterly cold days.

Jim Walker: 'Players would have just a taste of it if the weather was particularly cold. From my point of view, I knew it wasn't right. It made people feel warm but had the opposite effect. It actually dilates the blood vessels, so you feel colder. But it was a thing from the old days. Give the players a sip to warm them up.'

Shaun Teale: 'I could never drink brandy. It just was never my cup of tea. But Ron had started this thing that if the day was freezing cold, lads could have a sip. Paul wouldn't be included. Ron would look over at him and say, "Macca, no chance. You're not having one!"

'Paul always sat beside me in the dressing room and this particular day, he said to me, "Just get me one for God's sake. I feel like shit!" So I got a brandy and walked back to my seat. Just put it down and turned around. Next thing, I looked again and it was gone. Paul knew I wouldn't say anything.'

Lads would protect me on the basis that, by and large, I'd die for them in battle. Whatever the flaws of my preparation, I never shirked a challenge on the pitch. And the lads knew that.

After a while, Ron even decided – quite sensibly in my opinion – to allow me to room alone, because I must have been one of the strangest human beings to room with. At times, it bordered on sharing with a lunatic. No one would know where an escapade was leading. I might end up laughing hysterically through the night. I might end up crying.

Alone, at least, I wouldn't interfere with anyone else's rest.

People like Steve Staunton and Tony Cascarino were good as gold to me. 'Stan' loved a pint himself. But he was rock solid. He knew when he'd had enough, when it was time to go. He'd invariably be one of the ones trying to get me into a cab at the end of a night out. 'C'mon Paul, time to go . . .'

Sometimes nobody could rein me in. I remember being in

Marbella once with Villa and Sheffield Wednesday were there at the same time. I ended up drinking down the harbour with Viv Anderson and David Hirst. It was absolutely idyllic.

Just one problem. I wanted to drink quicker than the others. Everything was too slow. So I got up from the table, announcing that I was going to buy some sunglasses. The next thing I remember is waking up about ten o'clock the following morning, lying face down in a lane maybe 150 yards from the hotel.

For all anyone knew, I could have been a corpse.

So I just staggered to my feet and walked back to the hotel, utterly confused as to where the night had taken me. Viv told me later that I had, indeed, arrived back at some point wearing these ridiculous glasses, only to promptly disappear again.

In my own mind, all of this was happening under the illusion of normality.

There were a couple of times with Villa when I'd be sitting in the dressing room before a game, fighting the jitters. I'd be asking the lads for a dig-out. It was an horrendous way to live as a sportsman, surviving on the edge all the time, pushing my luck (and Ron's patience) to the limit.

Ray Houghton: 'People talk about Paul's physical strength, but there was this mental strength too. I mean I personally don't know how you can go out and play football if you've had a drink. And I'm not talking about the night before. I'm talking about the day of the game itself. It would be just about impossible for most people.

'But Paul did it and it didn't really seem to affect his performance level. Which was incredible.'

It wasn't a constant condition by any stretch. Far from it. In my time with Villa, I'd say there were maybe eight or ten games when I sailed too close to the wind. Maybe four games when I was drunk as a lord. The problem was that even one game would have been unacceptable. And I drank regularly before training.

Villa were endlessly trying to keep me on the straight and narrow. They knew the dangers of Dublin especially. They'd fly me home from international games almost as soon as the whistle blew.

Ron Atkinson: 'I remember there'd be a 6.10 flight back to Birmingham from Dublin. We'd always try to get him on that. I used to organise to have a car ready outside Slattery's pub near Lansdowne. I used to say to Jim, "Soon as the game's over, man-mark him! Don't let any of the hangers-on get to him. Just get him in that car and have him on that 6.10 flight back to Birmingham. And, if you don't, you're sacked!"

'Ah no, Jim was good as gold. He would mark my card. He sort of sensed the cycles.'

Jim Walker: 'But later on it did get out of hand. Paul would be the first one to admit that. The amazing thing about it all is that the press, by and large, didn't find out things. Nobody knew at all. The players were excellent in that regard. They just had so much respect for him, you see.

'I used to take a chance with Paul really. I always knew if he had been drinking or if his knee was sore. I knew, within reason, how Paul worked. He trusted me and I trusted him. Sometimes, I might have my doubts, but I'd say that he was OK.

'I'd be sitting there at five to three, fingers crossed really. After quarter of an hour, he'd have paid his way though. He just seemed to change for ninety minutes. Out there, he was exceptional, you see.

'It was the other stuff he didn't like. He was quiet in the dressing room. I remember one day he let out this shout in the dressing room. "C'mon lads, let's go beat these ..." Something like that. And everyone stopped and stared. The first reaction was "Has he been drinking?" Because he was so quiet.

'He was a different person on the football field. Maybe that was the real Paul out there. He could lose his temper out there. Very few people argued with him. When he was right, he was a perfect lad really. The best player, the centre of everything.

'Mind you, he just seemed to have that knack of, no matter what he'd been up to during the week, he was there on a Saturday, walking off the pitch at quarter to five as man of the match. And everyone just forgot about the other stuff.'

When Ron was fired, I felt I was left hanging in a certain limbo again. We were a good team under his stewardship. We passed the ball. We entertained. I think most of us had assumed that our form would come back again if people were patient. That the defeats were just a blip.

Ron wasn't the kind of manager to transmit pressure to his players. His temperament seemed bombproof.

I remember sitting in the canteen at Bodymoor Heath two days before that fateful game against Wimbledon and he was just his usual, effervescent self. 'Macca, when are you going to bring us some of your Irish luck?' he shouted.

'Jesus, yeah, we could do with some boss,' I answered.

'It'll all be different Macca on Wednesday when we're coming back on that coach after giving Wimbledon a good tanking. We'll hit Wimbledon more than McEnroe ever did.' That was his personality. Always up for the fight. Always bullish. To my mind, a masterful man-manager. A people's person.

There was this public perception that Ron was endlessly fining me. In actual fact, he rarely did. Ron could forgive a player anything so long as they performed for him in battle. He certainly had no inkling of the unseen depth of my troubles.

But I was getting worse. I was getting more careless. By the time Ron got the bullet, I think I was pretty much lost in a private world of escapism, denial and pain. Endless pain.

And from pain came insecurity. After a game, most of the others might have two or three pints in the players' lounge. I'd be having eight. Then just out the door as if it was the most normal behaviour imaginable. I was covering up. Running away.

Shaun Teale: 'Sometimes I felt Paul drank to get rid of his pain. Because you could see that he was in a lot of pain at times. I honestly believe that later in his career the pain in his knees was pushing him towards drink. Because he wanted to keep playing. He was desperate to keep playing football.

'Because he knew that football was his lifeblood and, once it finished, he could really have a problem. He was terrified of finishing.'

Jim Walker: 'If you looked at an X-ray, you could see the arthritic changes around Paul's knees. Lots of players today would have similar problems. But if you're training continuously, you don't get a chance to recover. The point is that with an arthritic knee, the more you train, the worse you're going to make that knee.

'In the end, Villa got eight years out of Paul. I mean I'm a physiotherapist and I've always felt that one of the problems in football is this belief that when you've had surgery, that's the end of you problems. Because, oft times, it's just the start.

'Paul was a one-off, no mistake. But I think if he had trained every day, he probably would have played just a quarter of the games he played. By not training, I honestly believe that he added another three or four years to his career.'

There was a kind of surreal dimension to Ron's departure. It was clear that despite results, he still had the general backing of supporters. The gates of Villa Park were locked as news of his sacking hit the headlines and Villa's commercial manager, Abdul Rashid, read out a prepared statement to the media.

There was almost an atmosphere of guilt on the club's behalf. Ron had presided over the worst run of results in the club's history, yet for players and supporters alike he was still the right man for the job.

For me, perhaps the only man.

25

LITTLE

For Brian Little and me, there were early signs of impending strife. He became Villa's new manager in November 1994. I started just three of his first eight League games in charge. His preference was to partner Ugo Ehiogu with Shaun Teale in the centre of defence. I resented it, but I couldn't exactly argue with the reasoning.

Little was ambitious and modern in his thinking. A former Villa player, he had just had managerial success at Darlington and Leicester City, guiding the latter into the Premiership just six months before his appointment as Ron Atkinson's successor.

He clearly wanted to put his stamp on the club quickly and to clear anything he perceived as dead wood from the dressing room.

I may not quite have been considered in that category just yet, but it was clear he wasn't exactly bowled over by my long-term prospects. Put it this way, if I was a second-hand car for sale, I imagine he'd have placed the rider 'needs some attention' in any small ad.

After all, I was now closing in on my thirty-fifth birthday, I didn't train very much, my knees were five years older than the

288

pair Manchester United had tossed towards the wrecker's yard and – the absolute *coup de grâce*, of course – I was a renowned boozer.

It was nothing personal, I knew that. It never is in football.

To be fair, Little wasn't a bullshit merchant. He was straight with me. He reckoned I had so much mileage on the clock (football and otherwise) that it wasn't practical to try rebuilding a team around me. The challenge was for me to prove him wrong, of course. Which is exactly what I did.

It took a little time (mid-January to be precise) but I became a permanent fixture in the team for the second half of that season. Just one problem. It was a season that ended with Villa dangling precariously above the relegation zone in eighteenth position, our Premiership status only secured by a 1-1 draw at Norwich on the last day of the season.

Worse, our cup form had been abysmal too, dumped unceremoniously (as defending champions) from the League Cup by Crystal Palace (1-4) just days after Little's arrival, and then ejected from the FA Cup by Manchester City in January.

It was clear that change was needed.

Brazen summer efforts to recruit the likes of Dennis Bergkamp and Paul Gascoigne came to nothing, but Little suddenly broke the club transfer record twice within a week by signing Gareth Southgate from Crystal Palace for £2.5 million, and then the largely unknown Serbian, Savo Milosevic, from Partizan Belgrade for £3.5 million.

Unfortunately, going the other way were Dalian Atkinson (to Fenerbache) and one of my best mates in the Villa squad, Dean Saunders (to Galatasaray).

Approaching the 1995–6 season, it would be fair to say that we had an apprehensive dressing room. It was just a little difficult to see how the new faces would gel. Being honest, none of the signings had palpable star quality. If anything, there was a sense that maybe we were a little top-heavy now with journeymen.

But Little produced two tactical masterstrokes that would completely energise our season.

The first was switching Southgate, previously a midfielder, to play in a three man central defence alongside Ugo Ehiogu and yours truly. The second was turning Dwight Yorke into an out and out strike partner for Milosevic.

I remember being a little puzzled at the time of Southgate's arrival. I just couldn't see where he was going to play. We already had Andy Townsend and Ian Taylor as midfielders, while Little's summer spending spree had concluded with the £3 million capture of Mark Draper from Leicester City.

Little did I know that Southgate would develop into one of the best centre-halves in the Premiership.

Actually, I came to love playing alongside him and Ugo in that Villa back line. We just lived on one another's calls, covering one another's asses. You could say we played in each other's slipstreams. It felt effortless.

Just as Graham Taylor had mastered that system with a Nielsen-McGrath-Mountfield triumvirate, Little now found real defensive stability in a Southgate-McGrath-Ehiogu coalition. I was ecstatic. There was so much security in the system that we cruised through games. It was unquestionably the most comfortable football I played in my time as a professional footballer.

Southgate and Ehiogu prolonged my career, no question. I say that because it was clear that Brian Little had arrived harbouring serious reservations about Villa's ageing Irish centre-back. With good reason, he doubted my long-term value to the club. He also questioned my preparation.

Jim Walker: 'When Brian Little came in, he decided – quite rightly as a manager coming to a top club – that he wanted things done his way. And he wanted Paul training. He went along with the special arrangements we made for Paul up to a point, but he wanted to be able to see people on the training ground too.

'My advice to Brian was, "Look, this has worked. So why not keep it going?" And he was OK with that suggestion for a while . . .'

Our first game of the season brought Manchester United to Villa Park and it set the upbeat tempo for the campaign. By half-time we led 3-0, Taylor, Draper and Yorke (a penalty) getting the goals. It felt as if the whole stadium rose in acclamation as we went in for tea.

United got a goal back in the second half but our 3-1 victory was widely lauded, and when we followed up with a 0-1 victory away to Spurs, expectation began to soar for the reconstructed Villa. As it happened, we were never out of the top six all season, but without ever quite launching a title challenge.

The Championship proved a two-horse race between United and Newcastle, Alex Ferguson famously out-psyching Kevin Keegan on the run-in.

But Villa were back on the ascent again. We finished fourth in the table, while still reserving some of our best football for the cup competitions. Though Liverpool thumped us in the FA Cup semi-final, we went all the way in the League Cup, beating Leeds United 3-0 in a one-sided Wembley final.

I have few vivid memories of that final, apart from an absolute belter of a goal from Savo to give us the lead.

I do remember that Leeds played a distinctly odd formation which played right into Villa's hands. I was marking Tony Yeboah, a tough Ghanaian with a penchant for explosive shooting. We had a bit of a physical battle but, to be fair, he got no service, and therefore carried no threat.

Winning the Cup meant that the season was seen as a resounding success for Little, and having started twenty-nine League games, I suppose I had reason to feel very much part and parcel of the new Villa.

Yet there was a different sense of hierarchy in the dressing room now, and in many ways that new hierarchy was reflected in the dynamic of the card school.

Bear in mind that around this time, players' wages were just beginning to go through the roof. Some of the younger lads especially were on a weekly salary of £25–30,000. Suddenly the 'pot' became ridiculously large.

I remember a couple of trips where one particular individual lost close to £45,000. It was at this point that I chose to leave the card school. It had ceased to be fun. One thing to lose a few hundred on your way down to London for a big game. Quite another to be betting (and losing) fortunes.

In retrospect, it had been drifting that way for some time. I remember Jo Venglos coming down the bus one day protesting that people were wagering far too much money. At the time, £2,000 would have been considered a very big win.

Needless to say, Dr Venglos was given pretty short shrift by the sharks at the back.

'Aah no, it's no problem Jo.' Then under our breaths, 'Go on, piss off . . .'

We were a closed community, you see. We didn't want outside interference. Jo walked back to the front of the bus that day shaking his head like a man who knew that the school was headed for trouble.

Every season, the betting just went higher. By 1996, you might have a kid earning £30,000 a week who's at the table thinking 'If I bet £5,000 here, no one's going to say anything. And if I lose, well it's not the end of the world . . .'

Now I wasn't exactly Mr Sensible, but I didn't like what I was seeing. It got to a stage where it was no longer fun. The stake was just beginning to build and build. It was out of control almost.

And you were trying to put yourself in the shoes of the guy who loses big.

Imagine stepping off the coach outside Highbury, say, knowing that you now owed a teammate £40,000. Your mindset for the upcoming game couldn't exactly be great, could it? You had to be thinking 'Fuck, I've had a bad day here. I'm forty grand down!' Your head couldn't possibly be right. How were you going to break the news when you got home?

So I bailed out of the school when I felt it was getting scary.

And that wasn't easy. Because playing cards is such a convenient way to pass a three hour bus journey. But the energy was different now. People were different. No one got a kick out of winning hundreds anymore.

There are probably a lot of different layers to an old pro's gradual alienation from the game he plays, but maybe the main one is a sense of social discomfort.

Suddenly you find yourself slightly adrift of the banter. You eavesdrop on mischief that you once manipulated. You pretend to sleep, because that way you become invisible.

My departure from the Villa card school probably reflected something deeper. It hinted at a fall down the dressing room pecking order, a growing unease about my status within the group.

Approaching pre-season in late summer 1996, I certainly knew I had a fight on my hands to stay in the Villa first team. I was now hurtling towards my thirty-seventh birthday. The game seemed to be getting faster all the time.

I decided that to survive, I needed to be fitter.

So I threw myself into pre-season like a teenager keen to impress. For the first time in years, I participated fully. I knew I was on borrowed time and my plan was to give Villa a final, glorious season to be remembered by.

And I surprised myself. I stopped drinking. I wasn't taking

sleeping tablets, painkillers or tranquilisers of any sort. My system was clean and it reflected in my performance.

I did everything: cross-country runs, sit-ups, press-ups, sprints. For a month, I was a model pupil. I was to the front of every drill, I carried people up and down hills. I ate sensibly, drank only water. Approaching the start of the season, I felt absolutely invigorated. Sheffield Wednesday away was our opening game. I couldn't wait.

Then Brian Little named his team and I wasn't in it.

I vividly remember sitting there in the medical room, this sense of disbelief washing over me. Hadn't he seen my pre-season? Didn't he understand the enormity of what I'd put in? Did he not know I was in the best shape of my life?

This was a once-only deal. A single season of Paul McGrath playing by the book.

Little's decision left me utterly shattered. I couldn't leave it at that. So I knocked on his door.

The conversation was civil and businesslike. I might have felt like having a rant, but it just wasn't my style. I tried, instead, to be rational. 'No disrespect,' I said, 'but I don't want to be a sub. Can you honestly see me coming on with ten minutes left to chase a goal or even try to hold onto a lead? Especially with my knees, if I'm not warmed up properly? Look, I'm more likely to give away a goal in those circumstances. I respect your decision. But the way I am I have to start games. If I'm terrible, you take me off.'

Little was polite but absolutely unwavering. 'Well, this is the way we want to go for now . . .' he said.

I was incredulous. Twenty minutes earlier I had been sitting in that medical room, thinking 'I'm in the team . . .' Now I was being told that I wasn't even in the manager's general plans for the season. The shock of the announcement had been pretty brutal. Waiting there with maybe twenty other lads, hearing this voice say to me 'Paul, you'll be on the bench . . .'

With the benefit of time, I can just about see his reasoning. I was on a big salary. I was closing in on thirty-seven. In Steve Staunton, he already had an international player more than capable of filling in beside Gareth and Ugo. In other words, I was cover. And I needed to get over it.

I suspect that Little thought I would be appeased by the financial end. By the fact that, as a substitute, I'd still qualify for all bonuses. But the money didn't mean anything to me now. I just wanted to play football.

I've no doubt that my age was the pivotal factor in his decision. It made me an easy scapegoat. I had even sensed it the season before. If I mistimed a header or someone threatened to run by me, the hook would be out immediately. 'Alright Paul, take a breather big man . . .'

The bottom line, I suppose, is that all of sport is fundamentally ageist. It's probably inescapable. When an athlete arrives at a certain juncture in their lives, they are judged differently. Their mistakes are interpreted as evidence of unavoidable decline. There is no longer any margin for error.

Villa lost that opening game 2-1 at Hillsborough, but then won three on the trot without conceding a goal. I didn't figure for a single second of those games. The decision had been made for me.

I asked for a transfer. And the request was granted.

Jim Walker: 'Everyone was genuinely saddened when Paul left. I remember we got on the bus to travel to the first away game after his move to Derby and they had a minute's silence in the card school to mark his departure. It was funny. For years, he had been the banker. He kept the money. Everything was written on his notepad, everything right down to the last fiver. Nobody ever did him on money.

'Personally, I was glad he was going to Derby. I had started my own career there. I knew the club and I knew that Jim Smith would look after him. And it was probably time. We'd had a long time together. He'd been hard work really. Hard work, but different class too. I said that to Jim Smith. I said, "This is what he's like, but he'll be your best player."'

To this day, I maintain that had Brian Little given me the chance that season, I would have repaid him with some of the best football of my entire career. Even though I was getting on in years, I was starting to enjoy my football more. I'm convinced that the older you get, the easier it becomes for a defender to read a game. You just get calmer. You become less inclined to overcommit.

The key factor is that you must still have that spring in your legs. And I still had it approaching the winter of 1996. More than that, I even had a desire to play things by the book. To stay sober. To be the best that I possibly could be.

Maybe for the first time in my life, I was being utterly professional as a footballer.

And that was when my career began to die.

26

PRODIGAL SON

In October 1997, I was the subject of a tribute programme on Ireland's most popular television chat show, the *Late Late Show* on RTE.

It amounted to two of the most excruciating, if deeply flattering, hours of my life. I was effectively duped into appearing. With my international testimonial looming the following summer, the arrangement was that I would pop into Studio Four for 'a five-minute chat' with host Gay Byrne.

I never suspected a thing until we were literally shaking hands and the whole studio suddenly erupted with the 'Ooh Aah' chant. It was then I spotted Big Jack sitting next to Caroline on the stage. *Uh oh . . .*

A powerful impulse to run was overcome by the rationale that this was live television, with cameras already rolling. Right through my career, television always filled me with a sense of dread. So I settled into my chair next to a man known across Ireland as 'Uncle Gaybo' and listened sheepishly as a wide variety of people proceeded to pay the kind of tributes that ordinarily only tend to get paid posthumously.

It was actually quite humbling. The Taoiseach (Ireland's prime minister) came on the phone from somewhere near Buncrana and joked that I had 'come a long way' from my days working as a security guard in the city. People like Alan Hansen, Ian Rush and the then world snooker champion, Ken Doherty, sent lovely messages of support.

Frances Black and Christy Moore sang songs and there was a link to the airport hotel where Mick McCarthy and the Irish team were chilling out on the eve of a World Cup qualifier against Romania.

Needless to say, the players – looking about as comfortable as children forced to sing for a distant aunt – rounded off their tributes with, yep, a resounding rendition of 'Ooh Aah' . . .

I was mortified. Only one thing could ever have made me comfortable in that environment and it was the one thing I couldn't have. At the time, I was still clinging to the remnants of my career, having signed a contract with Sheffield United. My knees were problematic, but in every other way I was healthy.

The programme was a lovely tribute with many of my former teammates speckled throughout the 200-strong audience, sitting shoulder to shoulder with old Dalkey pals like Gramps, Marti and Gilly.

Needless to say, the drink flowed into the early hours afterwards. Even during the programme itself, some of the lads were dipping in and out of hospitality, storing the pints at their feet whenever the camera came their way. Someone even brought Jack a pint of Guinness on the stage. Everything was light-hearted and normal and quintessentially Irish.

In many ways, drink becomes a social impulse in Ireland. It's everywhere. Funerals, weddings, birthdays, christenings. Drink is normal.

Some would probably find it odd that a programme dedicated to an alcoholic could be so flippant in its attitude to drink. I didn't.

I've always wanted people to behave 'normally' around me. The last thing I need is someone sipping mineral water just to be sensitive towards my illness.

That night, I was delighted to see so many old friends genuinely enjoy themselves. But it was also a bit like old times. I was also a little distracted by just about every drink glass in the building.

After Ireland played in the 1990 World Cup finals, I was voted our Player of the Tournament. We had reached the quarter-finals, losing out eventually to hosts Italy, and a Toto Schillachi goal in Rome's Olympic Stadium.

Every game we played in that tournament is pretty much embedded in Irish sporting folklore. We drew 1-1 with England in the thunder and lightning of Cagliari, then 0-0 with Egypt and 1-1 with Holland, both games in Palermo. We went to Genoa and, after a 0-0 stalemate, beat Romania on penalties to reach the last eight.

There is no real point in recycling the detail, other than to say that – despite not actually winning a single game at those finals – we became gods at home.

In the aftermath to every game, RTE would supply us with pictures of the celebrations in Ireland, and after a while most of us were wishing we were fans at home rather than players in the belly of the story. I played well in that tournament. After some early teething issues, I had completely come to terms with the role that Jack wanted me to fulfill. I revelled in it. Playing against the likes of Robson, Gullit or Hagi held no fears for me (though I must admit that the little Romanian was unbelievable during our game in Genoa).

Maybe more than anything, I had regained a fair degree of self-confidence after moving to Aston Villa and encountering in Graham Taylor a nurturing, compassionate manager. After my initial breakdown – universally recorded as 'injury problems' by a largely unsuspecting media – I had recovered sufficiently to be voted Villa's Player of the Season by their supporters.

Even my knee troubles seemed to have eased. Life was relatively tranquil. And I will bring to the grave the sense of astonishment that swept through our plane as we flew into Dublin, the pilot circling the airport so that we could absorb the sheer scale of the welcome awaiting us.

Footballers don't often do emotion, but as we banked high above Dublin that day, most of us choked up a little. The airport itself was submerged with people, but it was the road into the city that really stole the breath. Every inch of it lined five or six deep on either side with supporters waving scarves and flags.

I still look at photographs taken of the open-top bus, snaking painstakingly through the throng – every one of us terrified a kid might slip under the wheels – on its way to another dubious coronation in College Green. I look at the slightly glazed expression on my face as I wave like a pope from the balcony of St Peter's Square.

There's a beer in my hand. I am, it goes without saying, 'Ooh Aah' up there. And I can almost read the workings of my own mind . . . *'What could ever go wrong in my world again?'*

Kevin Moran: 'Even though we always roomed together with Ireland, Paul and I never really discussed any personal problems. It was a big group and everyone got on so well.

There were no little cliques. So there was never any real deep stuff to the conversations. I suppose it was always more or less superficial talk.

'Back then, there was never a day I would have looked at Paul and thought "Bloody hell, this guy has a major problem." Everybody was just out. That certainly would have been the case with the Irish set-up. Like United under Ron, it was very much founded on lads going out and enjoying themselves. To the extent that it was just amazing how well we did.

'Because when I look back now, it was almost ridiculous. To think that you could go out on a Sunday night till all hours before a game on a Wednesday. And all hours was all hours.

'A lot of the players could drink a huge amount. Because you're working it off then in training. So you could go on a long, long time.'

The knees provided the first inkling of trouble. Villa were due to play a Rumbelows Cup game against Barnsley that October. I didn't want to play as there was just too much pain coming from one of the joints. Under Graham Taylor, I feel certain I wouldn't have had to. But Graham was now manager of England.

I tried to convince Jo Venglos of my predicament. But Dr Venglos was new to the dressing room and, more pertinently, new to the strange quirks of my training arrangements. He insisted that I take a fitness test on the pitch. It was clear that he wanted me to play.

Jim Walker: 'I remember being out on the pitch with Paul. Josef asked me, "How is he?" My answer was, "Well, he's not normally as bad as this so I can't say for definite that he'll play." I stayed out with Paul right up to the team sheet going in.

'I'm saying to him, "C'mon, let me take you for a little jog, then see how it feels." And Paul's saying, "No Jim, my knee's too sore today." But I'm pushing. "C'mon Paul, let's go out and try . . ." I encouraged him, rightly or wrongly. And he ended up playing.

'Best player on the pitch as usual.'

The story of what followed has never properly been told before, largely because I was an unreliable witness. Let's just say there was a blank fixture list in England for the following weekend, so – naturally – I started drinking. I did so comfortable in the knowledge that I could lump the blame for any chaos that followed on an insensitive new regime at Villa.

One week after the Barnsley game, Ireland were due to commence their European Championship qualifying campaign against Turkey at Lansdowne Road. I was already in the grip of a serious bender by the time I landed in Dublin, five days early. There was, you see, business to be done.

My 'music career' now in full swing, I was due at a recording studio on Sir John Rogerson's Quay to recite a few lines of rap against a backing track. Not so much Fifty Cents as Fifty Pence, you might say. I had been persuaded to do it by Eamonn Carr, the former drummer of one of my all-time favourite Irish bands, Horslips.

They were still setting up the studio when I got there so I suggested to the two female backing singers that we might just pop out for 'a loosener'. Once in the pub, I performed my usual stunt, sneaking double vodkas in between every pint. Every effort they made to move, I countered with, 'We'll just have one more . . .'

Needless to say, the rest is a blur. Back in the studio, I did every-thing bar say my lines. Worse, it had been agreed that a camera crew would film the recording. So I'm standing there, earphones on, laughing like a complete simpleton at the most inane things. One of the lines I've got to say is 'To be the best, you've got to be committed' . . .

I'm practically on the floor every time we come round to it. 'I should be committed,' I'm whimpering now, tears all but rolling down my cheeks. Everyone else is being sincere and businesslike, but I'm Jimmy Tarbuck at the Palladium. The minutes slip by and minutes are expensive in a recording studio.

Eventually it's done and everyone politely thanks me for my 'efforts'. Mercifully, the video shots never actually make it to television. Someone with a conscience decides to bin them.

Deep down, of course, I know I've fucked up again. I've let people down. And letting people down is like pulling a trigger. As of now, I'm running away. That night I slip into whatever company I can find. I drink everything, smoke everything, take everything that's offered.

My head is all over the place. There's too much going on in my life. Too much secrecy and lies. The game? It's an eternity away. I don't care what's coming. The truth is I don't even care about the consequences of falling out with Jack. Drink is the gaffer now.

I'm 'on one'.

Mick Byrne: 'By the Monday night, Paul hasn't shown. But we're hearing of sightings. There's a network of people that we go through. Barmen, doormen, the Special Branch even. Eventually, we get the name of a girl he had apparently met in the Burlington Hotel and track down a number for her mother. It leads nowhere though.

'So I head out in a car searching. I'm being driven by one of our sponsors, Opel's PR person, Trevor O'Rourke. We're liaising with Paddy Daly in the Westbury Hotel. Paddy was a Garda, based in the detective branch in Mountjoy at the time. But he was one of the country's top referees too.

'This night, he's working as international liaison officer for the FAI [Football Association of Ireland], looking after the referees in the Westbury. So he's making calls for us as well, trying to track Paul down. We're going to all the familiar haunts. Up to Crumlin where his mother lives. Around by Leeson Street. Down to Rumours in O'Connell Street. Not a glimpse.

'It's quarter-past midnight now and we're running out of guesses. Then Trevor takes a call. Someone wants to speak to me. It's an unfamiliar voice.

'"Paul McGrath is fine, he's with us, we have him in the car."

'I say I want to speak to Paul. He comes on the line. Typical Paul. "Ah Mick, how are things?" Usual laid-back way. I ask him if he's OK.

'"I'm grand," he says. "Just with a few friends . . ."

'So I lose the cool a little. "Fuck's sake, get yourself together Paul. You've got to come back in. Don't let me down, you've got to come in."

'He doesn't answer, but hands the phone back. I am back talking to a complete stranger. I'm giving it socks now, telling this guy that there'll be hell to pay if Paul isn't brought back to the team hotel immediately. A deal is struck. It's agreed that we're to drive out to the Mulhuddart Inn, pull into the car park and wait. A car will drive past the entrance with its lights off and we're to follow.

'Now this is like something out of a gangster movie. We don't know who or what we're dealing with here. Trevor's getting nervous. "This doesn't look very clever, Mick," he says. I tell him I'll do it on my own if I have to.

'Anyway, we park in the car park and wait. It's now half-one in the morning. The whole thing sounds like a wind-up. Then this car comes up the road, flashes its lights, turns them off and drives on by. We sweep out behind them. They travel up a few hundred yards then veer into a housing estate. They come to a standstill. Trevor pulls up alongside.

'Paul's sitting in the back seat. There's a girl beside him and two lads in the front. I get out to talk. Directly across the road, someone's having a party. The front door is open. One of them recognises me and shouts, "Hey Mick, c'mon in, we're having a party. They have no idea . . ."

'Paul won't budge for me. "No, I'm with me friends . . ."' The two guys in the front are getting stroppy. I'm getting nowhere. Next thing I just grab Paul, pull him from the car and throw him across the back seat of Trevor's. I dive on top of him and scream at Trevor to drive.

'Trevor throws the car into gear and we go flying up the road, Paul and me sprawled across the back seat, our legs sticking out the door. And I'm thinking "Is this really happening?"'

They brought me into the hotel through a fire entrance and straight down to Jack's room. Mick just knocked on the door. 'Here he is boss,' then left me to face the storm. Jack began to shout, but quickly saw the pointlessness of it. I was in a daze that no raised voice could penetrate.

Truth is, I wasn't afraid of Jack's anger. I was never afraid of it. Because I knew he'd always soften. You see, Jack could read me the riot act for ten minutes, spitting fire with every word. Then it would end with him putting his arm around me. He'd know the only place for me was bed.

Jack Charlton: 'It was pointless to rant at Paul. He wouldn't look at you. He would look down or look away. You'd be trying to bollock him, but you couldn't. He'd just sit there, wouldn't say anything and shake his head. And you sort of thought "Well, I'm not getting through to him that way . . ."'

The nightmare began the next morning. I got up, took a long, lingering look in the bathroom mirror and wanted to die. Kevin, as ever, stayed diplomatic. 'Get yourself some fresh air, you'll be fine.' That sort of thing. But I wasn't going to be fine. What I was looking at in the mirror was a wrecked shell of a human being.

I had been drinking non-stop for a week, yet all I wanted now was another one. Something to blur things. To numb the sense of shame.

Kevin Moran: 'I'm trying to get Paul right. "C'mon big man, you can do it, you'll be fine."

'And he's saying, "Kevin, I can't play, I can't do it."

'"You can, you've got another day to recover. C'mon, get yourself thinking about it that you're going to play. We need you." I'm giving him all the usual stuff . . .'

Mick Byrne: 'The night before the game, Jack told me to sleep outside his door. So we got a kind of camp bed and a few blankets. I didn't sleep a wink. But if Paul came out the door, he'd have fallen over me.'

The morning of the game, I'm still in the horrors. I'm nauseous, shaking. My nerves are gone. I'm gripped with fear, but no one's listening.

Jim Walker: 'Jack was ever so good with me. He'd let me sit in on team meetings, travel on the coach. He made me very welcome. So this day, the players are getting on the coach to go to Lansdowne Road. Paul is the last one. As he's about to get on, he comes over to me and says, "Jim, I can't play, I've had too much to drink."

'I tell him to just nip to the toilet and have a think about what he was saying. But when he comes back, there's no change. "I can't play Jim." We get on the bus together. He's shaking. We arrive at the ground maybe an hour and a half before kick-off. Paul won't get off the bus.

'It's not a problem to begin with. I stay sitting with him. Trying to talk him round. But then it's starting to get later and later . . .'

Kevin Moran: 'For whatever reason, I've got off the coach thinking that Paul is just behind me. We're all into the dressing room. Everything's normal. The usual banter. Then, with about fifty minutes to go to kick-off, someone pipes up, "Hey, where's Paul?" And so it starts . . .'

Ray Houghton: 'We knew there was no way he could play. I mean we knew when Paul was on a bender, what that bender meant. It would have been non-stop. Sleep, wake, drink again. But I think Jack just thought that, having had a night's sleep, he'd be alright.

'But Paul had the shakes. I remember being really surprised when his name went on the team sheet.'

I had walked on a football pitch in the horrors many times, relying on other players to bail me out. But this was impossible. I knew that I could not physically get myself to the dressing room, never mind play a game of football. Sometimes you can get through a game on simple instinct. A kind of automatic pilot. But nothing was working now. If I walked into that dressing room, I knew I would make a holy show of myself and, worse, my country. I was ill.

Jim Walker: 'With half an hour to go to kick-off, Jack wants to put the team sheet in. He comes on the bus, a little agitated.'

Jack Charlton: 'Actually, I just wanted him to come in and watch the game with us. I'm telling him he just needs, literally, to walk to the dressing room. To come in and sit down, because all the lads know that he's not well now. But he wouldn't budge . . .'

Jack's angry and I don't blame him. He's laying it on the line. He says, 'If you don't come into that dressing room now, you'll never play for Ireland again!' It means nothing. 'Well then I'll never play for Ireland again,' I tell him. A few of the lads come out. Kevin tries to talk me round. They're wasting their time.

In the end, Mick tells them to leave me be. He can see the trouble I'm in here. Eventually, Eddie Corcoran, our logistics manager, is dispatched to take me back to the hotel. So I'm walking out through the car park with Eddie, out through the crowd now pouring in. It's the most surreal feeling I've known in my entire life.

I'm supposed to be playing in this game and here I am being led out to a taxi. People are shouting. 'What's up Paul?' I'm not even acknowledging them because I'm in a zone now.

Eddie gets me into the hotel and straight up to the room. I collapse under the covers, shivering and sweating at the same time. By now the game will have started, but I don't bother with the telly. I'm too sick to look. And I'm afraid, too. Afraid that things won't work out.

Kevin Moran: 'We win the game 5-0. Bit of a cruise. Afterwards, we come back to the hotel and I head up to the room. Paul's kind of half sitting, half lying in the bed. He looks uneasy.

"'Hey, it worked out fine," I tell him. "We won five nothing." He's telling me how sorry he is. But I sense something's not quite right. I smell something's going on here. So I walk around the side of the bed and there's six bottles of Heineken, partially hidden, two or three of them empty.

'And, for me, that's when the penny drops. That's the moment that slams it home to me. To think that, after all that's happened this day, the thing he's turned to is another drink. It may seem ridiculous having been his roommate for so long. But that's the moment I realise the extent of Paul's problem . . .'

Things are out of control now. Getting scary. Apart from the recording, I've also done a gig for a friend, Krish Nadoo, who owns Rumours nightclub, a favourite haunt of the players. He pays me in cash, yet by the time Mick and Trevor pick me up, I've blown all the money I've earned.

It ends, of course, with a flight back to Birmingham and a disappearance trick. And the need for Jim to find me.

Sometimes I think about the sleepless nights I must have given Jim Walker and Mick Byrne over the years. Nights when no one knew where I was or what I was doing. When the media buzzed with suspicion, and Jim and Mick were always left to pick up the pieces.

In Ireland, the papers were largely decent and non-judgemental. A lot of the journalists would have known what was going on. They could have written scoops but invariably decided not to. Some of them would even join Mick Byrne in the search. They'd drive him round, dipping in to all the usual watering holes, looking for the 'missing' person.

It seemed as if every doorman in Dublin was some kind of secret agent, feeding back information about my whereabouts to the Irish team hotel. Cab drivers too. Even the Garda Special Branch unit became a part of the network.

So many people looking out for my interests, yet at the time I was practically oblivious to their efforts. When finally located, I would return to base in a pretty dishevelled state, walk in to Jack, bearing a well-practised expression of remorse and just let the storm blow itself out.

Jim and Mick were the primary firefighters. To me, they are two very similar people. Technically, they were employed as physios, but in the environment of the dressing room, everything went through them. And I mean everything. Any problem the players had – a kid might be sick, the wife might be in bad form, a horse might have come in last – would be channelled directly through the 'physio'.

For me, they became absolutely vital support systems. Both of them got to understand my moods better than anyone else in football. Some people just couldn't read me. Some people would look at me as if – like the song said – I needed to be committed. On occasion, they might even have been right.

Jim and Mick knew instinctively what approach to take. They were fully aware of my problems and treated me accordingly.

In the Irish set-up, some of the lads would try to fight my corner. Again, I'd be kind of manipulating them emotionally. I'd go down to Mick and say, 'Jaysus Mick, everyone else is going out. Just a couple of pints . . .' The lads would see this and take pity. They'd be saying, 'Look, we'll look after him . . .' I remember Andy Townsend especially volunteering to look after me

But it was never that simple. Because drink took me down a loner's road. I might have seen it as a way of bonding, but ultimately it took me away from them. We'd be in a bar somewhere, I'd nip to the loo and suddenly I'd be flying solo. I'd be out the door and gone before they'd notice.

This happened a few times. The problem was that I never actually drank to be sociable. I would drink basically until I hit the wall. I drank for oblivion. I would see it coming and I didn't really care. There were no friendships in the place I went to. Just glasses and bottles and ice cubes.

Mick Byrne: 'In fairness, the lads would look after him to the best of their ability. But after a while they'd maybe stop concentrating on him, and next thing he'd be gone. So eventually we just realised we couldn't let him go with them.

'I mean other players had their problems too. A few of

them would even have had the same problem as Paul. But they handled it better. The "cuties" I used to call them. Paul wasn't cute. No matter what hour of the morning it was, the others would always find their way home. But Paul would maybe get one too many and fall asleep somewhere. That was his downfall. So he was the one you had to be protective of. You had to protect him from himself. I mean there was never a time when I could say that Paul McGrath stepped out of line in any other way. His problem was an open problem.

'There were times he'd be in such a state in the hotel that I almost felt like bringing him a drink myself, because I understood what he was going through. But my job was to have him right for the game. That was the promise I made to Jack. Jack would say to me, "You're the boss inside, I'm the boss outside . . ."

'He was such a clever man. Jack understood players. He could be brutal if need be. If someone stepped out of line, he'd cut the legs off them. But he would never go outside the door to confront a player.

'I mean I eyeballed him a few times over Paul. Towards the end especially, he'd be getting the hump. I remember one time he was absolutely furious. "Where the fuck is he? That's fucking it, I've had enough . . ."

'And I said, "Look, we're his family. We've got to look after him. Now either you do that or them wolves out fucking there will get him . . ." And I walked out, slammed the door. About ten minutes later, Jack came down, put his arm around me. Never said a word. And walked out again.'

Jack Charlton: 'Everyone loved him you see. The players loved him. It was sad some of the time, but it was good most of the time. Because when he was good, he was very good.

'But I said to Paul many times, "While you're a player and you're good, people will look after you. But the moment you stop being a good player, they'll get rid of you as quick as they can." He knew that and accepted it.'

We didn't make it to the Euro '92 finals, despite twice drawing 1-1 with England, now managed by my old friend, Graham Taylor. The game in Dublin was a tough, hard-hitting battle maybe best remembered for Graham's decision not to name Paul Gascoigne in his starting line-up.

Graham's view was clearly that more seasoned pros like Steve McMahon and 'Sid' Cowans would be better suited to coping with our physicality. He looked like he'd be proved right, too, until a late Tony Cascarino goal cancelled out David Platt's opener for England.

That game was almost exactly one month after my Turkey aberration, and for that period Villa booked me back into the Woodbourne in Edgbaston, where I was put through a serious detoxification programme. As part of the treatment, I was given tablets that would make me physically ill if I consumed as much as a mouthful of alcohol.

Villa chairman Doug Ellis picked up the tab and I was certainly a far healthier specimen reporting to Dublin to face England. At least I got off the bus this time!

The following March, there was a sense of the Irish team really maturing when we absolutely dominated the return game at Wembley, but just couldn't kill it off. I delivered the cross for Niall Quinn to score, but Ray Houghton spurned a late opportunity for a winner.

I didn't get a chance to talk to Graham after either England game. He was already taking some serious flak in the media, and would in time be exposed to the most vicious coverage I suspect any international manager has ever faced. I was appalled by the depths some journalists sank to.

The wheels came off our campaign in two games against Poland, a 0-0 draw at Lansdowne Road and a 3-3 stalemate in Poznan, where we actually led 1-3. We completed the campaign with a 1-3 victory over Turkey in Istanbul, but it was not enough, Gary Lineker's strike giving England victory in Poland that same evening.

And here's the strange paradox. I was now playing the best football of my career, yet my life was teetering on the edge of chaos. My marriage was falling asunder. I was drinking for fun. When we went to the US Cup in 1992, I didn't exactly cover myself in glory. The tournament was a kind of consolation prize whenever Ireland failed to qualify for major finals.

It was essentially three friendlies played in a week, usually in hot conditions against teams better equipped than us for competing under a burning sun. I always looked on the trip as a jolly, a time to unwind after the stresses of the season.

To be fair, Jack allowed us quite an amount of freedom too. There was no real pretence of the games being anything other than obligations to be met. But some of us met those obligations a little less purposefully than others. In 1992 I took to having drinks sent up to the room. It meant that when we did head out as a group for a beer, I was invariably a little the worse for wear.

Ray Houghton: 'Paul would be just sitting in his room. You'd see bottles of Budweiser going up on a tray and you're thinking "Hang on a minute, I know it's only friendlies, but that's not quite right . . ."

'But you just didn't know how to stop it. You're thinking "Well, he's only having a couple of beers, he won't be bad," blah, blah, blah. You never really take it on yourself. You never really know for sure exactly what's going on.

'I mean there are stories out there with other lads who've seen him drink a minibar dry after a game. You hear that and you think "Christ, that's pretty serious!" I mean, we all went for a few beers after a game. But none of the lads were coming in after the beers and going to the minibar to finish it off.'

My consumption, naturally, led to certain incidents that – miraculously – never became public knowledge.

Our first port of call in 1992 was Washington for a game against the USA. The day we arrived, a reception was held in the team's honour at the Irish embassy. I got so drunk I had to be carried down the stairs by Mick Byrne and Mick McCarthy and put onto the coach for my own safety.

Mick McCarthy: 'I kind of wedged Paul into a seat on the coach so that he couldn't go anywhere. I'll always remember, the US assistant coach – Steve Sampson – arrived alongside the coach. I was manager of Millwall at the time and I had a couple of the US players.

'We started talking through a window. But Paul was a bit pissed off at being stuck on the bus, so he wasn't too complimentary to either of us. Just one of those days, unfortunately, that got on top of him.'

I played all three games in that tournament, without ever quite reining in my drinking. Actually, in the second game – a 0–2 defeat to Italy in Boston – I was sailing a little too close to the wind.

Jack Charlton: 'I was sitting in the dugout next to Kevin Moran and Paul was out on the pitch in our back four. And he was ridiculous. Absolutely ridiculous. I said to Kevin, "What's up with Paul?" And he said, "Nah, he's OK Jack, he's fine."

'I mean he got away with murder to be honest. But when you'd got the ability he had . . .'

My next big challenge to Jack's authority came in May 1993. Our World Cup qualifying campaign had got off to a reasonably bright start with easy Dublin victories against Albania, Latvia and Northern Ireland as well as hard-earned scoreless draws against Spain in Seville and Denmark in Copenhagen.

The Danes were reigning European champions and we were relatively unperturbed to draw 1-1 with them at Lansdowne that April. Exactly one month later, we were due at the Qemal Stafa Stadium in Tirana for the first of three difficult games in Eastern Europe within the space of three weeks.

It was at this time that I was named the PFA Player of the Year and Villa took the first team squad (with wives and girlfriends) off to Mauritius as a kind of thank you for our efforts in finishing runners-up in the league. With Claire now in the Priory, I travelled alone.

There was a game organised against Everton out there, but I didn't play. In fact, I flew home early, keen to link up with Caroline and fly over to Cork where I had agreed to take a coaching session in Crosshaven for my former St Patrick's Athletic teammate, Joey Malone.

We fulfilled that obligation on the Friday, and the arrangement was that I would link up with the Irish squad in Dublin on Sunday lunchtime, as usual. But the drink was flowing and, with it, the denial.

We went greyhound racing on the Saturday night instead of an awards dinner I was committed to attending. On Sunday, I decided to alter the itinerary further. We would fly up on Monday morning. Of course, that flight was by passed too, and by Tuesday, my absence from the Irish squad was prime-time news.

We were staying in the Silver Springs Hotel, and as we strolled down to a nearby petrol station to get a newspaper that Tuesday morning, I suddenly spotted my picture on a giant billboard in the forecourt. There were five words in bold print underneath the picture: HAVE YOU SEEN THIS MAN?

Sometimes things have happened in my life that make me think it's all just a video that I'm watching. This was one of those occasions. It didn't feel real. No doubt the volume of alcohol in my system compounded that feeling. But this was truly off-the-wall.

In the petrol station, I flicked through a few of the newspapers and I was everywhere. I *was* the news. McGrath missing! Suddenly I could sense people beginning to stare. We went scampering back to the hotel, like pickpockets retreating off a busy street. I needed to plan an escape here.

It was at that point, brave man that I was, that I got Caroline to ring the team hotel and tell them that my knees were sore and I wouldn't be able to make it.

What followed bore a hint of pantomime. I was now a convict on the run. That's how it felt, at least. I was certainly reneging on all responsibilities. The three boys were staying at a friend's in Manchester, but I had little intention of flying home to collect them. I was in that escapist's bubble again. Running scared.

The hotel staff were extremely helpful, spiriting us to the airport in the back of one of their vans. But it was hard to be inconspicuous, and in the terminal I was accosted by a number of journalists seeking an explanation for my absence from the Irish squad.

I did what was coming naturally now. I lied. Knees. Pain. Usual guff.

The flight to Birmingham was now closing, and as Caroline and I hurried across the tarmac, an RTE camera crew intercepted us. There was a chap with a microphone. 'Paul, how do you explain . . .'

I marched on, eyes down, lips buttoned. I felt like a caged animal. He matched me stride for stride. Every now and then, I muttered the equivalent of a voice recording. Knees. Pain. Jack knows. Blahdi-blah. He was unbowed and unimpressed. 'But Paul . . .'

I finally bounded up the steps of the airplane, boarding card in hand, relieved to be out of the witness box. The stewardess smiled. 'I'm sorry Mr McGrath, this is an Aer Lingus flight to Heathrow. Your flight is to Birmingham.'

Down the steps again. More questions. Another sprint, another pursuit, all of it to be filmed on that evening's main television news bulletin. It wasn't just rumour any longer. Paul McGrath *was* on the run.

From Birmingham we flew to Israel, settling into the resort of Eilat where – in time – a photographer materialised, looking for a picture. Again we bolted, this time to Tel Aviv. By now, I realised I couldn't keep running. I needed to come home.

Mick Byrne: 'We actually found out what hotel he was in, even the room number, from Interpol. It was amazing. We had tracked him down even before he got in touch with us. We were actually waiting for him to make the call.

'I remember being at an FAI dinner in the Burlington when my wife Breda phoned. Paul had been on and left a number. So when I got back to their airport hotel, I rang him. He was in bits. Told me he just wanted to come home. I assured him everything would be OK, that he should just get himself on a plane.'

It was at this point that Jack decided to teach me how to fish. It helped his mood that Ireland had won in Tirana, Tony Cascarino's goal settling a hard-fought battle. Had the result been different, I'm not so sure I'd have been welcomed so unequivocally back to the Nuremore.

As it happened, everyone just moved on as if nothing untoward had occurred. A few days after being repatriated with the squad, we flew to Riga where I would score in a 0-2 victory against

Latvia. The handshakes and bear hugs that greeted the goal confirmed that the prodigal son had been forgiven once more.

In the end, that qualifying campaign would take us to Belfast on a sour November night when the island of Ireland seemed almost to rupture with hatred over a game of international football.

I've endured hostility in my time, but this truly bordered on the surreal. I was called everything under the sun from 'nigger' to 'Fenian bastard' to 'mercenary'.

It seemed a little bizarre running that gauntlet of hatred in Windsor Park, knowing that one of my best friends in football, Norman Whiteside, grew up on the nearby Shankill Road. Norman is, of course, a Protestant. To me, that never meant anything.

I, after all, spent most of my own childhood being brought up in the Protestant faith. I was born in England. I was black. What did any of it matter?

It has always seemed to me that certain people are only too happy to use religion as a cover for some deep-seated bigotry that has nothing to do with where or how people pray. Just ask them to explain the difference between the two faiths and you're likely to get a glazed expression.

Here's a funny thing. When living in Manchester, Kevin Moran and I once brought Norman to a Wolfe Tones concert. Now the Wolfe Tones are often derided for their choice of music, a pretty rabble-rousing brand of nationalist ballads that do, I must confess, carry some dubious lyrics.

But Norman was big enough and bold enough to engage in some fairly sparky banter that night in the company of some rabid Wolfe Tones supporters without feeling remotely threatened or offended. He just gave as good as he got. And he went home laughing.

Put it this way, a good few years ago, I went to a Bernard Manning show in Manchester. Made the mistake of sitting near the front row. And Manning absolutely slaughtered me. 'Holy fuck, a black, Irish Catholic, you've been done, haven't you . . .' I'm sitting there and he's hitting me with these one-liners. Bang, bang, bang.

Now some of the stuff is pretty hard core, pretty shocking. But he keeps coming with it, hitting me between the eyes. 'Fuck, I know we've all got crosses to bear, but you poor . . .' And I sat there laughing. I actually didn't mind. It didn't bother me. Because these things don't actually matter.

Colour, religion, nationality. They're just words. Unless, that is, people choose to hijack them and disfigure them. Which happens all too often.

Alan McLoughlin's goal rescued us from a pretty fraught situation that night at Windsor Park, and I suppose the vitriol of the occasion was well sedated in our memories by the time we arrived at the 1994 World Cup finals. But it would return with pretty shocking echoes the day we opened our campaign against Italy in the Giants Stadium.

Members of the Ulster Volunteer Force burst into a bar in Loughinisland – a tiny village in mid-Down – and shot dead six innocent people who were watching the game on television.

We were already en route to Orlando, celebrating a momentous victory, when the news came through. It fell on the mood of the plane like a heavy blanket on a fire. Everything just went quiet. Heads went down into books and magazines. Walkmans were switched on. Some players just closed their eyes and chased the escape of sleep. No one spoke. No one.

We were bound for Florida now, flying ever further away from the mixed up little island we called home.

27

END OF THE ROAD

I played eighty-three times for my country, despite the handicap of starting late as an international footballer.

That period – from the mid-eighties to mid-nineties – brought extraordinary energy to Ireland through the catalyst of its football team. Three times we came home from major tournaments to receptions that would scarcely dull by comparison to what Italy encountered when parading the World Cup through the Circus Maximus in Rome in July 2006.

We were superstars, footballers elevated onto an impractical level of celebrity by a sports-mad country that, prior to 1988, had never even seen its soccer team compete at a major finals. In a sense, reality was suspended. This was the '*Ole*' generation.

The dynamic of what happened was something you could never adequately explain to club mates back in England. It wasn't rational. How could an English colleague possibly relate to 100,000 people piling into a public park to welcome home a team that had lost two and drawn one of four games played?

That was what we were met by in Dublin's Phoenix Park after being evicted from the 1994 World Cup finals. Embarrassing? Yes.

Surprising? No. The Irish supporters had a connection with that team far beyond normal boundaries. They took pride in our competitiveness. We took pride in their behaviour.

On both levels, there was this intense drive to put Ireland on the map. The team was credible on football's highest stage. The supporters represented a vast, humorous and famously civilised back-up army. Together, we took on the world.

I sometimes look back at videos of that time. Not so much the games, but the footage of the people. The deserted streets when we were playing. The carnivals when we won. The mix of old and young, male and female, everyone just caught up helplessly in the surging, feel-good wave.

I'm not sure that Ireland will ever see its like again. Not because the next generation of players isn't capable of getting us back to that level – I'm sure they are – but because so much of the innocence is gone now. Our team was seen as groundbreaking. We took the story of Ireland and its people somewhere it had never been before.

I roomed, as ever, with Kevin Moran during Italia '90. For much of the time, we moaned. The rooms were generally cramped and claustrophobic. In Rome, prior to our quarter-final against the hosts, the situation bordered on the farcical. We were effectively in a single room with two camp beds. There wasn't enough space to open the door of the wardrobe.

We fumed. We were accustomed to better with our clubs. Rumour did the rounds that the guys in suits, the FAI officials, all had fine, big double rooms. For a time it was easy to forget where we were going and obsess instead on trivial stuff like bed sizes and dodgy air-conditioning.

Then one evening, someone from RTE brought in a video of the scenes at home after our penalty shoot-out win against Romania. The effect was extraordinary. We sat there, lumps in our throats, grown men trying to rub the moistness from their eyes without anyone noticing.

And that was the last time we ever spoke about the shit rooms.

I treasure those memories. Actually, I feel privileged to have been part of them. US '94 was one of the happiest experiences of my life. The three eldest boys came out to the tournament with Caroline. It felt as if we were a proper family.

Getting there had been a struggle. Jack Charlton harboured serious doubts about my injured shoulder, doubts that never quite lifted until a week before our departure for America when we went to Hanover and shocked Germany 0-2 in a friendly. That was the game that nailed my partnership with Phil Babb in the centre of the Irish defence.

Jack was mischievous and shrewd. He liked to spin the illusion that he was an old school football man who just sent his teams out to clatter into the opposition and pour ball after ball over their heads. Actually, Jack was incredibly thorough. Most of the time he could almost tell you how the opposition tied their bootlaces.

My relationship with him was unorthodox, to say the least. He saw the best and worst of me. At times, we almost fenced with one another, Jack trying to second-guess what strategy I might have in place to get an illicit drink.

Jack Charlton: 'When Paul moved to Aston Villa, he would sometimes get a flight in from Manchester, which we wouldn't know about. Sometimes he'd get a flight in from East Midlands. He was deliberately trying to confuse us so we wouldn't know when he was coming in.

'Aer Lingus were very helpful to us. They eventually started getting us the information, telling us exactly what flight he was coming on. That way, we could send Mick Byrne down to meet him off the plane. Sometimes we'd even have a car on the tarmac to make sure he didn't slip between our fingers.'

We didn't have a particularly good or bad US '94, but I think it was clear to most of us that Jack wasn't especially enjoying it. He obsessed about the heat. He was drawn into a seemingly endless argument with officials about getting water to his players on the pitch. Two of our games brought us to the hothouse of Orlando's Citrus Bowl for midday kick-offs. Both ended in defeat. To some degree, maybe we allowed ourselves become a little sidetracked by the soaring temperatures.

The heat had been high on our agenda from the outset. We set up base at the Seminole Training Camp in Orlando for ten days of acclimatisation, yet nothing quite prepared you for the reality of playing competitive football when the mercury was all but bubbling. The day we beat Italy in New Jersey, we all lay on the floor of the dressing room at half-time, trying to soak up the coolness of the concrete.

Some of the fairer-skinned players, like Stan (Steve Staunton), Denis Irwin and Tommy Coyne were like steaks on a griddle in that tournament. In fact, Tommy became quite dangerously dehydrated after that Italy game and had to lie in the aisle of the plane that evening as we flew to Orlando.

Not for the first time, the World Cup proved just another example of money and TV schedules taking priority over the footballers themselves.

Beating Italy was the high point of our tournament. We didn't win another game or, for that matter, produce another compelling performance. All in all, it seemed a mediocre return, given that our build-up to the tournament had featured victories in away friendlies against both Holland and Germany.

One of the more colourful events of US '94 from an Irish perspective was a training-ground spat between Jack's assistant, Maurice Setters, and, well, just about the entire squad.

For whatever reason, Jack was missing on the day in question and it was Maurice's way to try to assert his authority whenever the opportunity arose.

He tended to shout a lot and look busy. His training sessions were lacklustre and uninspiring. Most of the team were playing for big clubs and were, by now, well versed in sophisticated training drills. My own preparations may not always have been textbook but I at least knew how proper sessions were conducted. Maurice seemed to make it up as he went along.

Overall, I reckon he didn't contribute a great deal. During games, his instructions from the touchline would have us completely baffled. He was constantly sending signals.

One minute he's tapping his chest, the next he's tapping his shoulder. Then you'd look across and he seemed to be waving his hand in circles. You'd be on the pitch looking over, wondering what on earth he was saying, trying to decode it. We'd try to figure it out between us. He looked as if he was trying to direct a plane to its gate.

'Phil, what's Maurice saying?'

'Not got a clue!'

'Stan?'

'Search me.'

'Andy?'

'Nope, not an iota.'

'Cheers Maurice.'

We'd just give him the thumbs-up and carry on regardless.

This particular day in America, Maurice pretty much lost the run of himself. The sun was all but burning holes in the ground, yet he ran us pitilessly. Then, with everyone on the point of collapse, Maurice announced that we would have an eleven-a-side practice game on the full pitch.

It was a bridge too far. Most footballers are actually reasonably intelligent people. They sense when training is good for them and they *know* when it's bad. This was diabolical.

Andy Townsend went to him as captain and said that the players had had enough. Maurice wouldn't listen. So Andy walked off the training pitch and, one by one, the rest of us followed. In the end, Maurice was left ranting at an empty field.

For some reason, a story broke in the Irish media that the row had been between Setters and Roy Keane. So a kind of peace summit was stage-managed whereby Roy and Maurice were paraded shoulder to shoulder at an Orlando press conference, reiterating the fact that there had been no row between them. It was bizarre and just a little comical.

On reflection, the magic of the Charlton era was on the wane by then. I believe that we came home from America a slightly tired team. A little of the old ferocity had left us. Jack himself didn't quite have the hold on our attentions that he once had. The chemistry felt jaded.

Our efforts to qualify for Euro '96 died, technically, with a 0-2 play-off defeat to Holland at Anfield in December 1995. But, being honest, the Harry Ramsden Challenge (where we dipped into a chippy for dinner on the eve of a vital qualifier against Austria) had marked the end three months earlier. We were gone as a competitive force. And Jack walked before he was pushed.

It was a sad, even vaguely brutal end. I didn't phone him when I heard the news. I doubt many of the lads did. In football, people are always taking bullets. You become anaesthetised to pity. No one cares about yesterday. Tomorrow, the bullet might be yours.

I was pleased to hear of Mick McCarthy's appointment as Jack's successor. Not out of any personal ambition. I was thirty-six now. An old footballer with a lot more than just high mileage on the clock. I wasn't the future.

Mick played me in his first two games, friendly defeats against Russia and the Czech Republic. Then he phoned me one day in Manchester. Typical Mick, he was straight up. 'Paul, I'm trying to build a new team here, so I probably won't be needing you. I've got to go with the young lads.'

The conversation was extremely cordial. I respected his honesty. 'Mick, I've no problem with that,' I said. 'Fair play to you for being straight. I hope everything goes well for you.'

Of course I was disappointed. Who wouldn't be? But he hadn't bullshitted me. The last thing I needed was being patronised by an old teammate trying to avoid the issue. If I was finished, well and good. I had eighty-two caps. Not bad for someone who made his international debut at the age of twenty-five.

Mick McCarthy: 'Paul was probably the best player I ever played with. I've always said that it was fantastic for me that Jack chose to play him in midfield for so long, because that made life so much easier for me and Kevin Moran at the back. He made it all look so bloody easy. He was quick as anybody, yet he was always so unhurried. He never looked under any pressure at all.

'But by the time I became manager of Ireland, he was certainly past his best. Unfortunately, a number of the players were. And I, having played with them, now had to do the dirty deed of not picking them. Some went with good grace, some didn't.'

I was then off the international scene for Mick's next six games. Results were mediocre, something to be expected as he tried to blood new talent. Then, at the end of August, I was included in an extended panel of thirty-three to convene before the World Cup qualifier against Liechtenstein in Eschen.

I had been told there was some pressure beginning to brew at home for my recall.

Gareth Farrelly, a young Irish player at Villa, was also in the thirty-three. I loved Gareth. I used to look out for him a bit in Birmingham. We knew that Mick would be reducing the squad to twenty before departure and Gareth was absolutely convinced that he'd be among those going home. He was in my ear constantly. 'I know I'm going home Paul, it's obvious . . .'

So I spent the next couple of days playing the old sage (and a bit of a sports psychologist) with Gareth. 'Listen, just do your best. Get on the ball. Be confident. You just never know . . .'

We were getting off the bus after a training session when Mick called me aside. 'Paul, we won't be needing you. I'm letting you go home,' he told me. I couldn't believe it. Just seconds earlier, I had been trying to console young Gareth, never thinking for a second that I would be sent packing. How bloody ironic.

The decision completely stumped me. I couldn't understand it. Why bring me over to Dublin if he hadn't intended using me? I remember sitting on the plane back to Manchester that evening feeling seriously pissed off. I hadn't been drinking or misbehaving. I felt I had actually trained quite well. And suddenly, bang. I was surplus to requirements.

It occurred to me that perhaps Mick had used me to convey a message to his younger players. In other words, to get them thinking that if he was strong enough to send Paul McGrath home, he was strong enough to take on any player. He had to be under pressure at the time. In his first eight games, Ireland had lost five and drawn two.

I felt disappointed, maybe even slightly used. I genuinely loved Mick McCarthy. I admired his courage as a player, his manliness. I enjoyed the deadpan humour with which he could cut someone in two. To me, he was one of the main reasons for the great Irish football stories of 1988 and 1990. He stoked the fire in the rest of us. He kept us honest.

Ireland won that game in Liechtenstein 0-5 and followed up with a 3-0 defeat of Macedonia at Lansdowne Road. By now I had joined Derby and was resigned to my status as an ex-international footballer. Mick was clearly doing just fine without me.

But that November, he took a gamble that blew up in his face.

For a home game against Iceland, he picked Roy Keane at centre-half. Ireland looked toothless without Roy in midfield and ended up drawing the game 0-0. Mick was absolutely pilloried by the Irish press afterwards.

Three months later, I was recalled to the squad, winning my eighty-third cap in a nondescript 0-0 draw with Wales in a friendly at the Cardiff Arms Park, the game played out in a virtual monsoon. Pitted against the brawn of John Hartson and my old United mate, 'Sparky' Hughes, I cruised through the game relatively unfussed.

Though I was now thirty-seven, my form in the Premiership was pretty sound and there wouldn't have been any great surprise that April when Mick called me up for the World Cup qualifier against Macedonia in Skopje. In fact, most assumed that I was a virtually certain starter. And that was the beginning of the end.

I could tell that Mick didn't entirely trust me. He seemed edgy in my company. Frank Mullen and his wife Ellen called out to our base in the airport hotel on the Saturday night and we had dinner together. Unfortunately we neglected to tell Mick that I wouldn't be dining with the team and, spotting my absence, he not unnaturally jumped to the conclusion that I had gone missing.

Vaulting across the lobby in a panic, he spotted Frank, Ellen and me in the main dining room. Mick was apoplectic. 'Thanks for fucking telling me,' he roared.

Seconds later, he was full of apologies for his outburst. Ordinarily, Mick would never have used such language in front of Ellen. Manners mattered to him. It was one of the things I always liked about Mick McCarthy. He had standards.

And given my history, he was entitled to think the worst as he sat down to dinner with his team only to discover that there was no sign of Mr Ooh Aah.

The following night, I was up in the room, lying on my bed when a knock came on the door. There was a Bryan Adams concert in the Point Depot that evening and a lot of the younger players were keen to go. Mick had decided that if one went, we all went. The group psychology I suppose. We would do everything as a team.

But I didn't want to go to the concert. I just wanted to have a good sleep that evening and keep myself healthy. There were a few things going on in my head. Jim Smith had just announced that, despite me doing a good job for Derby, he wouldn't be offering me another contract. Some journalists were chasing my reaction.

I could see the logic of Jim's decision. I would be thirty-eight midway through the next Premiership season. The day was surely closing in when my legs would no longer carry me. Yet I had been playing decent football. So the news came as a bit of a sickener.

A rock concert was the last thing I needed now. Mick Byrne had been despatched to get us all down to the lobby and I argued with him. 'Look Mick,' I said 'with respect, I'm not even a Bryan Adams fan. I don't want this. I just want a good night's kip.'

But Mick had been given his instructions. One in, all in. So I got up off the bed with a bit of an attitude. I just felt that this wasn't the way to treat adults. To insist that they do something they patently didn't want to do. And without consciously taking the decision, I knew deep down that I was going to drink that night. Because drink was the only way that I could cope with that kind of outing.

I imagine Mick McCarthy's view was that it was better to have Paul McGrath where he could be seen than where he couldn't. Just one problem. I was an absolute master of deception.

The memories of what followed are pretty incoherent and frag-mented. I do remember standing at a wall in the Point that night, lads like Roy (Keane) and Andy (Townsend) coming across to check what I was drinking. They were looking out for me. They were also wasting their time. I was a master at this game.

Gramps: 'I remember being in the Wanderer's bar at Lansdowne Road with Paul at the players' reception after an international game. He said to me, "Go up and get six vodkas and Coke in a pint glass and get a pint of Coke as well." The deal was I'd give him the pint of Coke and keep the one with vodka in my hand.

'Every now and then, he'd say, "Quick, swap . . ." he'd guzzle a load of vodka, then hand it straight back to me. Jack [Charlton] would come over checking. He'd take the glass out of Paul's hand and taste it. "That's alright then . . ."'

I knew how to get drink and how to conceal it. No matter how attentive the other players tried to be, they couldn't concentrate for sixty minutes of every hour. By the time Bryan Adams had done his thing, I was grinning from ear to ear. Feeling no pain. The night ended for me in the Burlington Hotel, Andy and Cas (Tony Cascarino) trying to talk me into heading home. Eventually they succeeded, but the damage had been done.

I was rooming with Stan, and that morning I effectively invited him to hear my confession. I was still drunk as a lord. 'Stan, I've had enough of football,' I told him. 'I'm just so knackered with it all. I can't be doing this any longer. I'm finished.'

The room was pitching and rolling. I felt hopelessly tired. Lying on the bed, I might as well have been on a dinghy in the ocean. Then, it seems, I got up and went missing for half an hour. Where did I go? Who knows. Probably just to a toilet somewhere to swallow a few tranquilisers. Almost certainly somewhere for a top-up.

Mick Byrne: 'We were all ready to go when Stan comes across to me. "Mick," he says "Paul's gone!" I went up to the rooms to look around. There wasn't a sign. Came back down. About half an hour passed. Next thing, Stan calls me again. "He's back Mick!"

'I went up to the room and Paul was there, totally out of

it. And I mean totally. Just lying on the bed. He couldn't speak.
I lifted his hand and let go. It just flopped back down again.'

I remember Mick McCarthy coming into the room. He was angry.
'Right, that's it!' he said. My response was, 'Grand!' I was too far
gone. Stan was trying frantically to straighten me out. He was
reasoning that if they just got me on the plane, I could maybe
sleep the stuff out of my system.

But this time there was nothing left to straighten. I wouldn't be
travelling to Macedonia. I wouldn't be playing for Ireland again.
My international career was over.

I remember Frank Mullen sitting on the end of the bed. It
would be his job to get me back to England discreetly. Frank knew
the chief of the airport police. There would be no public humiliation at check-in. I would be put on a plane before boarding even
started. Frank would travel with me. I slept for the whole of the
journey.

Officially, it was announced that I had a 'calf strain'. To the very
end, I was being protected.

Mick McCarthy: 'I've never spoken about that incident and I
don't really want to now. Let me just say that Paul McGrath
didn't let me down intentionally, did he? A lot of things have
been said about different incidents and that was one that doesn't
rest easy with me. Because, in some quarters, people tried to
suggest that I was to blame for it. Which was complete nonsense.

'That's not Paul's fault. It was other people's perceptions.
Actually, I would defend Paul to the hilt. I think you'll find
that over the years, myself and Jack covered up for a lot of
people for a lot of things. Not just Paul McGrath. We did it
because they were the best players in the squad. And consis-
tently. Jack over nearly ten years and me over nearly seven.

'Because that's what it's about. Managing people. Everybody

loved Paul as a person. And, face it, we all maybe change a little when we have a few beers. Maybe we metamorphosise into something we're really not. When Paul was well, he was just a straightforward, honest, genuine, quiet, sensitive bloke.

'And he's a national icon, isn't he? He got me about forty caps playing at centre-half!'

I know that when I criticised Mick for his handling of the Saipan affair in 2002, he might have imagined I had some kind of personal agenda drifting back to 1997. Nothing could have been further from the truth. I believed then and I believe now that he was wrong in how he dealt with Roy Keane.

But my abiding memory of Mick McCarthy is of a big man. As I lay on that bed in 1997, different players arriving to say their farewells, I remember Mick walking across and grabbing my hand. And I remember the gist of what he said.

'Look Paul, try to get yourself well. I hope everything works out for you.'

Drunk as I was, that didn't escape me. I had let him down, yet he had the decency to say those few words. My days in the game were numbered now and he probably could see that.

Best to let a dying man go gently.

28

ADDICTION

'Room service!'

'Hi, I'd like a drink sent up to my room.'

'Certainly sir.'

'Em, vodka.'

'Of course sir, a vodka and . . .'

'No, no mixer.'

'Just a vodka, sir?'

'Em, maybe four . . .'

'Four vodkas?'

'Large.'

I am in a room in Dublin's Berkeley Court Hotel, pacing frantically from window to door and back again. Over and back, like a clockwork toy. The television blares, but all I hear is my heart trying to thump a way out of my ribcage. I'm about to 'slip'. That's what we call it when we circle the chairs.

Any second now, there'll be a knock on the door and I'll play the charade. I'll place the four glasses on a table and start talking the talk. Good angel, bad angel stuff. I'll remind myself of the big, gaping hole that I'm teetering towards. The chaos looming. But then I'll recycle the lie. 'It'll be different this time Paul, you won't lose it . . .'

The lie always wins.

It takes me maybe twenty minutes to dispense with the prelim-inaries. Pace the room. Recite the prayers. Mouth the slogans and commandments. Think of all the talking done during recurring visits to the Priory, the Rutland, St Pat's, all the old safe houses. Think of the boys.

And that's the depth of it. You can actually be thinking of your kids and it still won't drag you back. The only thing certain at that moment is that you're going to drink again. You're going to 'slip'.

The tray arrives and there's a feigned breeziness in the exchange. I tip the girl a fiver, as if generosity somehow moderates the sin. I scribble my signature. She knows and I know. This isn't a good thing.

There is always the sink, of course. I could always press the abort button and just pour away this dangerous, clear liquid that now has my rapt attention. But I won't. I have a desire to be numbed, a need to feel safe in the warm glow. Four large vodkas. The key to being normal.

I swallow them down, giddy and guilty and definitely scared. As of now, the night ahead is a great, black mystery. Where will it take me? Who will pick up the pieces? Will I come through alive? I step into the bathroom, brush my teeth, dab on a little aftershave and observe the reflection of weakness in the mirror. I say a quick prayer. 'Sweet Jesus I place all my trust . . .'

And I resolve that this will be the last time . . .

The 2002 World Cup ended my second marriage. Or maybe, more honestly, it hastened the end. I had signed up with BBC televi-sion to be a part of their coverage from the Far East. Money for old rope, you might think. Sit in a studio and have some unfail-ingly pleasant chap like Gary Lineker direct you through the analysis of a football game.

How hard could it be?

I vividly remember the night we agreed the deal. A Dublin restaurant. Caroline and my agent, Pat Egan, batting on my behalf. Everything cordial. Everyone laid-back and upbeat.

'You'll be a natural Paul.'

'You'll love it mate.'

'This could be the making of you.'

'Think of the spin-offs . . .'

I sat there, knowing it was too much. My ego wanted it, no question. So much money and prestige on offer. Caroline and Pat were absolutely right in everything they said, too. The deal *was* good. It offered the path to a new career. To the beginning of the rest of my life.

But the moment we agreed, my stomach tightened like a clench fist. I had already done a little TV work on RTE and just about got through it with John Giles all but holding my hand. The consensus was that I had already walked the tightrope. I hadn't. That night in that Dublin restaurant with the man from the BBC telling me how good I'd be, I knew I needed help to get through the World Cup.

And I knew exactly where I'd go to find it.

I should have been man enough to cry 'Stop'. But it just seemed easier to play along, to humour people. To feign sharing the sense of excitement others had for my 'good fortune'. Deep down, I knew where it was taking me. But the coward never speaks.

Let me tell you a story about that coward.

In the summer of 1998, with my testimonial out of the way and the full impact of retirement hitting home, I dived into a haze of alcohol and denial. I wasn't coping. Without the outlet of football, I felt lost. By July, things had spiralled out of control and I ended up back in Dublin. Back in St Pat's Hospital.

Someone got word of my fall to Christy Moore.

Christy is one of Ireland's best-loved musicians and a man with personal experience of the road I was trying to travel. He made a phone call. I don't have any vivid recollection of the first time Dr Patrick Nugent came to visit me, but his impact on my life over the next twelve months would be nothing short of a brilliant sunburst.

Patrick was the most amazing human. Technically, he was just a general practitioner. In reality, I suspect he was a saint.

He came from Limerick and had a strangely powerful insight into the mind of an addict. I have always used the expression that talking to Patrick was like 'having my brain massaged'. It wasn't that he'd indulge me. Quite the contrary. Sometimes I might be moaning about the bum hand that life had dealt me and Patrick would just cut me short. 'I suppose none of this is your own fault, then,' he'd say.

It was as if he got inside my skull and started rearranging the furniture. Of all the counselling I've undergone across the years – and much of it has come from some pretty eminent people – none of it came close to penetrating as deep as Patrick Nugent's words.

I had never met someone so willing to give up his time for people fighting addictions, people – frankly – who test the patience of the medical profession. He had a genuine care for addicts and alcoholics. Sometimes he'd pick me up from Dublin airport and we'd stop off along the way at someone's house where a doomed addict might be in his or her last hours.

'Just want to see the parents,' he'd say, removing himself to some awful, godforsaken scene inside.

We'd walk for miles together, always talking, laughing, connecting. Painstakingly, he worked on my low self-esteem, dismantling the orphanage days and the debilitating legacy of a childhood spent feeling largely abandoned and unwanted. I would ring him from Manchester, knowing that the mere sound of his voice could turn a simple conversation into therapy.

He had the gentlest way of scolding. Of tugging at your conscience. Of coming at truth from unorthodox angles.

One night that November, I was chatting to Patrick and his wife, Sybilla, over a pot of tea in their Powerscourt home when he said that I reminded him of someone. Someone that he couldn't place. Someone who should have had an abundance of courage, but just couldn't locate it when most needed.

Then, it was as if a bulb went on in his head. 'I've got it,' he said. 'I know who you remind me of. You remind me of that lion in *The Wizard of Oz*. Remember? Cowardly Lion!'

Patrick got me well. Our relationship went beyond the formalities of doctor-patient. We became good friends. When Ellis was born in the spring of 1999, Patrick and Sybilla became his godparents. It really was as if someone had shone a torch into my past and the glow made sense of everything. He simplified my condition. Maybe, more than anything, he made me take responsibility for my choices.

Patrick understood how drink is always in the subconscious of the alcoholic. But he dealt in reasons, not excuses. If you lapsed, there was a need to address exactly why you lapsed. Everything could be broken down. Explained.

Then, suddenly, in the summer of 1999, Patrick took ill. He was diagnosed with cancer and the disease attacked him with terrible aggression. Yet even when he was dying, he kept counselling, as if on impulse. 'Don't let your guard slip Paul . . .'

I remember thinking that the only fitting tribute I could pay to his memory was to stay well. That would be the truest expression of gratitude.

He was gone before the onset of winter. I couldn't believe it. I felt cut adrift. It was as if everything I thought I knew was now open to conjecture again. The panic attacks returned. I was slipping . . .

It would be easy and pretty trite to say that Patrick's death caused me to relapse again. I wouldn't offend his memory by suggesting that. He always saw straight through excuses, anyway.

But I'm not sure alcoholism is explainable to people unaffected by it. It *is* a choice thing. But maybe not in the way that most imagine. When the time comes to drink, there's not much that can draw you back from it. The following sounds terribly callous, I know, but it's the bluntest expression I can put on it.

If you put a bottle of vodka in one hand and your kids in the other – horrible as it is to say – the alcoholic will probably go for the vodka. It's a decision you regret after the very first sip.

There's this endless cycle of regret and resignation. It's difficult to articulate what drags you back to something you know is hell. I'm sure people who drink normally would be disdainful of that description. How exactly does a bellyful of booze qualify as hell? The difference is that people who drink normally have a fair idea where any given night is going to take them, by and large. They're not playing Russian roulette.

Hand on heart, when I'm 'on one' as I call it, I'm genuinely frightened that I won't come out the far side alive. Because my drinking always leads to blackout. To the obliteration of any ability to rationalise or see danger. Thankfully, I've never fallen into the trap of hard drugs (my poison has always been prescription), but given the company I was in, I'm sure there have been nights when I must have come close to injecting myself.

I mean the snapshots of chaos are endless. One night in Dublin, I was picked up by the Gardai, slumped in a narrow, syringe-filled alley with drunks and down-and-outs, swigging from a bottle of cheap sherry. Another time, I woke up alone in a caravan on a beach somewhere north of Dublin. Where or how I got to either place has never been explained.

Dublin actually became a dangerous town for me. I'd fly in for some promotional work and treat it as an escape of sorts. The bad angel would be on my shoulder before I even stepped into departures. 'You're just drinking the wrong things Paul. Have a few white wines. That way you'll drink normally.'

You know where the voice is taking you and it's really then, right at that moment, that you need to be sitting at an AA meeting.

The worst thing afterwards is just not knowing where you've been, who you've been with, what it is you were doing. You try to piece the jigsaw together. You dread the phone call . . . 'Jaysus you were in some state last night . . .'

One of my most public and least forgiveable benders came in June 2003 at the Opening Ceremony for the Special Olympics in Dublin. It was the first time the Games were held outside the US and virtually all of Ireland's best known sports people had been invited to Croke Park to carry the flags of the competing nations.

I've since seen glimpses of the ceremony on television and it was utterly spectacular. Nelson Mandela, one of my all-time heroes, was among the guests of honour, and my favourite rock band, U2, played a couple of songs that – even listening to them three years later – just put the hair standing on the back of my neck. It was, arguably, Ireland's finest hour. And I spent it in a stupor.

My memories of the night are pretty brief. I took a taxi to the stadium alone, knowing in my heart that I was going to mess up. Roy Keane was virtually the first person I met on arrival and I've always enjoyed Roy's company. But I clearly didn't linger long to talk to my old teammate because there's just no way he would have tolerated what was coming.

From what I can gather, it became clear pretty quickly to the organisers that I was in no condition to walk around the stadium, let alone carry a national flag. Suffice to say, I remember nothing. I have since heard that most people just kept a wide berth when they saw how drunk I was.

The next I remember is waking up on a chair at the house of Roddy Collins, brother of former super-middleweight world boxing champion, Steve. Apparently, Steve and ex-Republic of Ireland soccer manager Brian Kerr were two of the few people to take an interest in getting this very public drunk out of harm's way and – more particularly – out of the stadium.

Roddy just happened to be having a party in his house, with a marquee in the garden. So Steve rang him and asked if he could bring me up there to sleep off my excesses. I recall waking up, asking for a beer, then wandering around this marquee, utterly oblivious to my latest crime. I suspect that at some point I might even have challenged Steve to a little spar which, mercifully, he declined.

The guilt, of course, kicked in ferociously afterwards. I felt ashamed to have let down so many people. So many children. But guilt is routine in the addict's world. It never seems powerful enough to overcome the next temptation.

I mean my own children have seen me in shocking circumstances. I used to try to reassure myself that they hadn't seen the worst of it. That my blackest excesses were invariably in Ireland, out of view of family. It was a convenient illusion I would spin to soften my own feelings of remorse.

But the truth is they've seen things that kids should never see. Christopher especially. I sometimes try to imagine the emotional scars that he must carry. Quite apart from the wrist-cutting episode of 1989, he's had a front-row seat for a depressing array of his dad's falls from grace.

I would estimate that I've ruined at least five family holidays in my time. Holidays where I became a total mess. Where I ended up spending days in bed simply because I couldn't control my drinking. Imagine sitting to dinner and seeing your father quite literally slumped in his food?

Of course, I might think that I was being clever.

'Cokes all-round?' I'd say, sauntering up to the pool bar. I'd always position myself at an angle where I could down a few large vodkas without being seen. Then back up to the room and the minibar . . . I especially remember one holiday in Cyprus where I kept ringing down to reception to restock the fridge. Thought I was being very clever and strategic. No one would notice.

At the end of the week, when we went to pay our bill, the minibar tab came to £1,300! Considering I was drinking down at the bar itself too, that tells you something about the level of my consumption. I also returned regularly to the other old reliable of planting bottles of vodka in different locations around the apartment.

The good holidays were wonderful. The holidays where I drank nothing stronger than water and played with the kids in the pool or on the tennis court, they're the memories I treasure.

We had one amazing holiday in '98, Christopher, Mitchell, Jordan, Paul jnr., Ellis, Caroline and me. All told, we were away for the guts of a month and I stayed sober for its entirety. We started off with a trip to Canada that, from memory, entailed about five separate flights, the size of the planes seeming to dwindle with each one.

Given my fear of flying, it should have been a nightmare. It wasn't. I enjoyed every second of the adventure, interacting with the kids in the way of a proper, healthy father. From Canada, we went to Florida – taking in Disneyland of course – and the holiday ended with a glorious week down in Clearwater.

Ellis was tiny at the time and I used to take him away for long walks, leaving the others to play by the pool and Caroline to sunbathe.

You know through all the wildness and deceit, simple images like that are what I treasure. The greatest serenity I've ever felt in my life was to have each of my five boys, as babies, fall asleep while lying on my chest. I adored that feeling. Just lying there watching them breathe, smelling their breaths.

That was the most beautiful thing.

Caroline and I certainly have our differences now, but I loved the experience of the 1994 World Cup, where the whole family came out. The kids had a whale of a time and I distinctly remember getting on the flight home with a feeling that I had really accomplished something.

Looking back, I routinely wish I could rewind time. I wish I could take all of those holidays again and never touch a drop of alcohol, because the good days with the boys were exhilarating. Playing tennis with Christopher. Messing in the pool. Just feeling the rush of being a loving, responsible dad.

Caroline has chosen to sell details of my worst excesses to the tabloids, and while I've sometimes been tempted to reciprocate, the temptation just isn't strong enough to draw me in. Whatever I think of her (and I do still have serious issues), she is the mother of my two youngest boys. Their well-being is more important to me than any personal spites or recriminations. And I know that Caroline is a good mother.

That said, in April 2005 she provided a major interview, running over two weeks, to *Ireland on Sunday* that pretty much reefed me from start to finish. It was, she claimed, in response to an article I had done with the *Irish Times*, in which I proclaimed my support for the action group, Father for Justice.

I don't know how much Caroline got for the story, but she certainly didn't leave much to the imagination. The morning the first extract appeared, I was on my way to play in a charity soccer game at Tolka Park for former Boyzone member, Keith Duffy. I was mortified when I saw it.

Momentarily, I actually considered turning back. When I got to the ground Norman Whiteside, who was also playing, had a copy of the paper. He was absolutely merciless. Just walked around the dressing room, waving it like a bad school report. 'Whooooaa, look at this,' he roared.

In a sense, I was grateful to him. He lightened the atmosphere. And I have to say that, on the day, the crowd couldn't have been more supportive. The moment I stepped on the field, an 'Ooh Aah' chant went ringing around the pitch. I've seldom been happier to hear it.

Yes, I did – as Caroline outlined – once fall down my own stairs naked. I had been on an extended bender and for some reason the front door had been locked from the inside. I came downstairs to let Caroline in, and while trying to sprint back up again, just completely lost my co-ordination and tumbled backwards in a heap.

To be perfectly honest, I was in no condition to know whether the kids were standing there to see it all or were sitting outside in the car. Suffice to say, it wasn't clever and it wasn't dignified. Just another lurid entry in the Paul McGrath CV of mishaps.

The big difficulty, by then, was the mix of stuff I was taking. Sometimes I envy the alcoholic who just glues himself to a bar stool, day in, day out. Who becomes nothing worse than tedious. Who, to all intent and purposes, still functions, still interacts, still retains some kind of coherence in how he lives his life.

My addictions amount to a one-way street to oblivion. And on the eve of leaving for my big assignment at the 2002 World Cup finals, they kicked in with a vengeance.

I had largely masked my apprehension by sticking to tranquilisers in the build-up. Without the smell of alcohol on your breath, an addict's capacity for deception soars. Caroline, of course, could tell if I overdid it. But one or two? I felt in control.

The deal was that I'd fly to Dublin from Manchester and then travel to Japan on a flight carrying the wives of the Irish players. By now, of course, the story of Roy Keane and Saipan had the whole of Ireland convulsing. Roy was home in Manchester after a bust-up with Mick McCarthy that everyone, including the Irish Prime Minister, Bertie Ahern, seemed to be frantically trying to repair.

I have always considered Roy one of my better friends in football. At the time, we regularly went out to dinner as a foursome – Roy and Theresa, Caroline and me – and I was tickled by this English media depiction of him as some kind of wild, unbalanced

Irishman. Our nights out together were always filled with laughter and the kind of self-deprecating banter the red-top scribes just would not countenance.

To this day, Roy and I still exchange texts. I like the man, maybe because of the very straightness to his personality that others find difficult to accept. We travelled a road together for a while and I regard him as someone of serious integrity.

Anyway, I felt for him at the time of Saipan. There were battalions of media now parked 24/7 at the bottom of his drive in Hale. His daily walks with his dog, Triggs, had become a recurring lead story on Sky News broadcasts. There was a frenzy surrounding him that had long since shed all sanity.

So Roy had both my sympathy and support as the tournament loomed. But little did I realise that I was about to create my own piece of World Cup infamy.

I remember taking two Zimovane at Machester Airport just to soothe my nerves. I had the tablets stashed in the lining of my jacket, just so I could source them discreetly in case of panic. Looking back, it was pathetic and reckless.

On arrival in Dublin, the entire airport terminal was a sea of green. Irish supporters everywhere, queuing for flights to the Far East. I was recognised instantly and soon the chant took hold. 'Ooh Aah . . .' Heart racing, I dived into the nearest toilet and into a cubicle. The scale of my deception began to shudder through me.

I was going to the World Cup finals to work for the BBC on the basis that I was clean. Sober, in other words. I was a fraud. There were maybe thirty tablets in the lining of the jacket and, taking out a handful, I just swallowed them down, craving some kind of calmness. Some kind of bolt-hole from the pressure.

It's a strange sensation that overtakes you when you realise you've overdone the tablets. You've slipped over the line from being warm and self-confident to knowing that you're slightly inebriated. You have these farcical conversations in your head.

'Shit, I've taken too many . . .'

'Told you you would.'

'Christ, those last six . . . I only intended taking two, but six came out of the lining. Now what do I do?'

'Shut up, that's what.'

'I can't be rude.'

'You're a drunk, the rude thing is to speak.'

'Maybe a little red wine might settle me.'

'Yeah maybe . . .'

'I'll just get two small bottles and see how I feel . . .'

'Three might be better.'

'Yeah, that's what I'll do. It'll be grand . . .'

So the Zimovane got topped up with red wine and God knows what else, and en route to Japan I chose to fight the war for my old friend Roy. Can't say I remember the details. Most of my knowledge of what happened is anecdotal. It seems that at some point I presented myself to the players' wives and observed sarcastically (and repetitively) that they ought to be 'proud' of their husbands' role in betraying their captain.

Some wives were more upset than others. Some knew me well enough just to smile and turn the other cheek. 'Go back to your seat Paul, have a sleep.'

I do remember drinking with a few Irish supporters on the plane. Nice lads. A bottle of duty-free was opened and one of them poured me a mug of neat vodka. 'Want anything with that Paul?' he asked. 'Nah' I scoffed. 'It's grand as it is.' Macho man. Downed it in one gulp.

After a while, I could sense people becoming uncomfortable around me. Just expressions on their faces. I was getting a bit loud. Maybe becoming a pest. In the end, I just fell into a deep sleep. Borderline coma, I imagine.

I didn't come to until we were on the tarmac, maybe six or seven hours later. You might imagine that I was instantly overcome with remorse. I wasn't. I felt nothing. Actually, that's not entirely true. I felt relief. Huge relief that the pretence was over.

Someone collected me at the airport and drove me straight to an accreditation centre. The guy was pleasant and hugely polite, though − presumably − he could see that I wasn't in the best of shape. Clearly, news of my outburst had arrived virtually in advance of me.

I was barely settled in my hotel room when a chap from the BBC made contact. 'Paul, I have to ask you, have you been drinking . . . ?'

There and then, the arc lights dimmed, the cameras switched off. My career in television was stillborn. BBC. Big Bad Coward.

So they sent me home and I dealt with the indignity in the only way I knew. I went missing. I was flown to London where I left my baggage on the carousel. There I met this girl. Spun my usual web. 'I'm in such trouble, nowhere left to go, everything's crowding in on me . . .' I was looking for a bolt-hole.

Her name was Helen and she was kind enough to help me out. For two weeks, we effectively hid in a hotel in Ireland. Then we took off to Marbella, all the time trying to pretend that I was some kind of free agent, unburdened by any family ties.

It wasn't smart and it certainly wasn't very brave. I just couldn't face up to the consequences of what I'd done (or more pertinently failed to do). I couldn't face Caroline. Eventually Helen went back home and I ended up in a hotel room at Dublin airport, surrounded by dead soldiers (empties in alcoholic-speak) and wondering what the hell my next move would be.

It ended with Claire arriving to do the firefighting after another typically desperate cry for help.

She had been staying with my mum at the time, having arrived with the boys for a little holiday. So Claire smuggled me down a backstairs of the hotel, drove me across to my mother's house in Crumlin where she left Betty with the strict instruction that I wasn't to be given alcohol 'under any circumstances'. Much to my dismay, Betty adhered to that instruction.

On the far side of the planet, Ireland were still going strong at the World Cup . . .

For my marriage, that was the beginning of the end. It set in train a chain of rows and breakdowns that led to me being barred from my own home and, ultimately, facing a second divorce. I can't pretend things had exactly been perfect between Caroline and me up to the World Cup bender. They weren't.

The incessant arguments and shouting matches had already driven Christopher out, my eldest son moving back to live with his natural mother the moment he turned sixteen. Christopher and Caroline had never really clicked, and to this day he is never mentioned in any correspondence from her to the older boys.

It is as if he has been airbrushed from existence.

How did the wheels begin to come off? Well, from the outset, let me say that I must have been an absolute nightmare to live with. I was neither dependable, faithful nor attentive. For example, I spent that Christmas of 2002 with Helen and her family, my wife and children left to fend for themselves. In some respects it was probably a relief to them that I wasn't around to spoil the day. But it did emphasise how utterly detached I was becoming from reality.

But there were times I felt as if I was going to burst with anger. One night, I have to confess, I literally lifted Caroline out of the bed and pushed her against the wall. It must have been absolutely frightening for her and I do regret that. The police were called and I admitted what I had done.

There can never be any defence for a man raising his hand to a woman and the memory of that incident doesn't exactly make me proud. But, like I said, I still have issues with a lot of what was going on during the latter years of my marriage to Caroline (and she will know precisely what they are).

Let me just say that the problems in the relationship weren't entirely down to me, though I have to hold my hand up and accept the blame for most of them.

There were some shocking episodes, no question. Some scarcely believable ones even. And they dated back quite some way. On Christmas Eve 1997, I walked to the pub at the bottom of the road and proceeded to drink myself into a stupor (Christmas, you may gather, wasn't one of my strong points). Eventually, Caroline rang Frank Stapleton and it was he who got me back to the house.

Frank and his wife, Chris, were fantastic friends to us. Just solid, honest people who would instinctively always look out for the kids whenever I was in trouble.

A terrible storm was blowing through Manchester on the night in question, and as luck would have it, the wind sent a massive oak tree crashing onto the roof of the house. Needless to say, I wasn't of much assistance. Frank actually went up into the attic to check for structural damage. There was rain coming through, so we had to call out the fire brigade to make the house safe. Their biggest job, I suspect, was trying to keep me out of the way.

The following year, just four weeks or so after Ellis was born, I took an overdose.

This one was potentially lethal. I was in the house alone and proceeded to swallow small piles of assorted sleeping tablets. Again, it all felt quite rational, quite calm. I remember lying back on little Paul's bed and closing my eyes, wondering if I would ever open them again. Waiting to see what would happen.

Will I just go to sleep? Will I vomit? Will I die? I actually didn't care.

The next thing I remember is Frank Stapleton in the room. Shaking me.

Frank Stapleton:'Caroline had phoned me. There was an empty tablet box on the floor. I remember her saying, "I don't know what he's taken . . ." I got him up on his feet, tried to walk him around the room. We were getting him to drink coffee. I wanted to find out what he'd taken.

'"Just a couple of tablets . . ." he was mumbling.

'"How many?"

'All I'd get was a shrug. I remember feeling quite annoyed with him. There were tablets sprinkled across the floor, so I knew he hadn't taken them all. Again, maybe, it was just a cry for help. We had the same doctor in Hale Barnes. From Scotland, a great guy. Dr Kelman. So I rang his office. Asked him to come around and try to sort Paul out. We had him drinking coffee while we were waiting for the GP. As soon as he came, I just said, "I'm going now, it's not for me to be here . . ." I just felt it was a private thing.'

I was rushed to hospital and had my stomach pumped yet again. The memory of that episode still frightens me because it could have been fatal. I genuinely did not know what the outcome was going to be. The day I cut my wrists, I honestly don't believe that I wanted to die. In a sense, I was just crying out for help.

This was different. This was blacker. It could have gone either way.

Towards the end of our marriage, Caroline and I were essentially leading separate lives. One night I was absolutely desperate for a drink, but there was nothing in the house. I raided every single cupboard. It's difficult to explain the desperation that kicks in when the craving hits. You end up needing something to give you blackout. Anything.

So I took out a pint glass and filled it with Domestos. Maybe this gives an idea of just how skewed your reasoning becomes.

What I was thinking, I haven't got a clue, but everything was quite deliberate. I remember screwing the top back on the container, then looking at the glass. Knowing that I was now about to play Russian roulette with my life.

Then I did it. Took the glass and downed the Domestos in one go. Quite calmly, I then went upstairs, lay on the bed and waited. My chest was absolutely on fire. It was as if somebody was running a hot iron from one armpit to the other. And I'm lying there, thinking 'This time, you've done it. This one's going to kill you. You're now in the process of melting your insides.'

It was as if an alarm suddenly went off in my head. I jumped out of bed, ran downstairs and started swallowing pints of water. I was frantic now, trying to put out a fire I had just started. Imagining my intestines turn to sludge. Wondering if I was, maybe, seconds away from a heart attack, convulsions, whatever.

It's a sign of the distance between Caroline and me that I didn't even say anything to her until the following morning. She was asleep in another room. I just stood at a sink in the kitchen, guzzling water until I literally couldn't swallow anymore. Eventually, the burning began to ease. I went back to bed and I lay there, eyes wide open, fearing that if I closed them, it might be for the final time.

The following morning I rang the hospital, told them I'd been to a stag do and there'd been a bit of high jinks. A few silly dares. The girl on the line was unequivocal. 'Get yourself in here immediately.'

They checked me out and my main organs had come through relatively unscathed. I had gotten away with it. Maybe survival gave me a sense of invincibility.

Some time later, I repeated the trick in Claire's house. Just picked up a bottle of bleach and started swallowing it by the neck. This time, my body just wouldn't countenance it. As soon as I began to swallow, it was as if these red shutters snapped down over my eyes. Just a red flash. And everything in my stomach came up, spraying the room. I think Chris and Lucy heard the commotion and came sprinting up the stairs. Another lovely picture for the scrapbook.

About six weeks after the 2002 World Cup, I was in a dreadful state. Caroline had gone on holiday with Paul junior and Ellis, while Mitchell and Jordan were now with Chris under Claire's roof for the holidays.

I rang Claire. 'Please come and get me,' I pleaded. Naturally, she was reluctant to interfere. I told her I thought I was dying.

I went to live under Claire's roof but, unknown to her, I was still taking tranquillisers. Still getting my regular supply from a 'friend' who called by on a daily basis. Claire was absolutely incensed when she became aware of what was happening and stopped it immediately.

Eventually I got reasonably well again and moved back into our beautiful house in Lower Peover, near Knutsford, prompting Caroline to move straight out. The marriage was irretrievable now, but I was stubborn. My career had paid for this home. I had no intention of moving.

Then one day I was working in the garden when this chap arrived and handed me an envelope containing a barring order from my own home. He was all apologies. 'Sorry to be the one doing this Paul . . .' I was being evicted.

It was now war between us, I accept that. Being forced out of my own home filled me with deep resentment. Once, I turned up at the house quite drunk (why I don't know) and frightened the life out of the au pair by walking around the side and peering in the back windows. She didn't know me, so it must have been quite frightening for her. Soon enough, the local constabulary had been called. I left the scene in handcuffs.

The divorce case just deepened the divide. We communicated only through solicitors and what we did communicate was predominantly hostile. It just ran interminably. The only people getting anywhere were the legal representatives who just seemed to me like vultures profiting from the misfortune of others.

I didn't exactly conceal my frustration well. A couple of times, I turned up in court a little under the weather and lost my temper. Let myself down badly. Started shouting abuse at Caroline across the courtroom. I'm sure people were looking at me, thinking 'My God, just look what that poor woman has had to put up with . . .'

One barrister, especially, got right up my nose. The bills were suffocating, the progress miniscule.

In the end, I became sick and tired of the ritual. Manchester Crown Court. McGrath v McGrath. Barristers' fees. Bitterness. One morning, it was announced at short notice that a new judge had been appointed to hear the case. I stared across at the thick wad of files and felt my blood boil. 'How the hell is a new judge going to adjudicate when he knows absolutely nothing about us?' I asked the barrister.

'He'll speed read the files,' she answered.

By then, I just couldn't take anymore. It seemed that this was no longer about hearts being broken or even an alcoholic trying to pick up the pieces of his broken life. It had become a legal maze. And I was tired of walking it. Eventually, I decided to just retreat from the fight. Wave the white flag.

The final indignity of the break-up came with the division of possessions. A list had been drawn up, but as luck would have it, both removal vans turned up at precisely the same time.

By all accounts it wasn't an especially civil arrangement. At one point, someone's boot just happened to go through the canvas of a framed portrait that – it had been agreed – would stay with me. By now I was back in the Priory, getting bulletins from Chris on his mobile and becoming more and more incensed with each one.

It was an horrendous scene. So much so that, in the end, Chris decided to call the police as matters were becoming more and more heated. I was proud of how he handled himself. He showed more restraint than I would have in the circumstances.

Caroline and I don't communicate now. We were married for eleven years, some of it good, a lot of it not so good. No doubt she sees very few redeeming qualities today in the man she wed back in 1994. I can't pretend that things only began to unravel between us after the 2002 World Cup. We weren't exactly getting on for a long time before that. The truth is I didn't mean for any of the bad stuff to happen, but that, I'm sure, is the protest of every lonely addict.

We just fight a battle that wears out love. And we spend our lives regretting.

29

ONE DAY AT A TIME

I feel tired of the repetition now. Tired without the comfort of sleep.

It's tempting to lie about my future, but lies are what keep bringing me down. Truth is, there is no rainbow on the horizon. I'm still losing this fight, still slipping in and out of sobriety. Sometimes, I feel that there's a wire around my head and it just keeps tightening.

Even on the good days, I need a crutch. Usually, a handful of Benzodiazepine. Sometimes Zopiclone. Anything to dull the fear. I walk a six-mile loop through the countryside around my home. I do three-hour shifts in the gym. I watch Sky News until I know the bulletins by heart.

The bad days? Here's what I've become. Last April, Jordan came to stay for a week. Three days in, I began to waver. He was out on a quad bike with a few local kids when I opened the first bottle of vodka and began to drink. Just sips at first. Then clumsy gulps.

By the time he came back, a taxi was pulling into the drive. I could see the panic on Jordan's face. "Just nipping out" I told him. And that was when my sixteen-year-old son began to plead. First, to me. Then, to the taxi driver. "Please don't go. Please don't take my dad…"

And I just looked him in the eye and lied. I said that I'd be back in a few hours. I promised him. And Jordan knew the value of my promises.

He was gone when I returned the following day and, naturally, I felt a monster. So I drank. Bottles of neat vodka. Every swig of it making me wince, but dragging me closer to the peace of oblivion. What kind of father does that to a son? What kind of man?

Christopher, Mitchell and Jordan. They've seen things that they shouldn't have seen. Yet one factor never changes. They still give me support and love. They still help me pick up the pieces. When I'm well, I try to explain away the guilt. I give them the familiar sob stories, but I sense these bore them now.

Sometimes I can almost read their minds. "Yeah dad, whatever . . .'

I'm so proud of them. Christopher's ambition of a life in professional football hasn't come to pass. He was centre-half on a Liverpool under-17 team that went unbeaten through an entire season. He got capped for Ireland youths. The portents promised everything, but guaranteed nothing. Liverpool let him go in 2003. He works in security now and plays football part-time.

Mitchell has just started with the marines. He plays rugby for Sale and, once, had a month-long soccer trial with Liverpool, though nothing came of it. Jordan? He's the least sporty, but maybe the most creative of the three. Looks like woodwork might be his thing.

My three eldest boys. They are three phenomenal human beings.

When I'm sober and un-medicated, the fun we share can bring me out in goosebumps. I love being able to love them. It really is that simple. I treasure the way that they drag me from my shell. I mean I'm terrified of flying but, shortly after I moved back to live in Ireland, Mitchell and Jordan came to visit. We brought them to

Leixlip for flying lessons and I ended up going up in a Cessna with Mitchell at the controls.

Talk about kids peeling away the negatives.

The problem is, these days, no-one ever quite knows what they're going to get from me. No-one can relax. It's an endless guessing game. Will he be well when we see him? Will he stay well? I break almost as many promises as I make. And people just tire of the routine. The perpetual deceit. The weakness.

In 2003, after the collapse of my second marriage, I went for counseling with the Sporting Chance clinic set up by former Arsenal defender, Tony Adams. My spell there coincided with the making of a BBC documentary on the clinic, called Premiership Priory.

Against my better judgement, I agreed to participate in the documentary. It was broadcast in June of that year and a gala dinner was held in London to tie in with the broadcast. I drove down to the dinner alone and, with TV cameras rolling, began to drink.

It wasn't exactly the endorsement of their work that the clinic would have hoped for.

In February of 2004, I got my first proper job since packing it in as a professional footballer. I was appointed 'Director of Football and Development' with Waterford United in the Irish Premier Division. The club, essentially, created the role to give me a new life in football.

I wasn't quite sure what my job description entailed, yet I dived into it full of enthusiasm and innocence. I was going to change the world.

Apparently, I asked Jim Walker to come over for a week of coaching that summer. Jim cancelled the second week of a family holiday already booked in America to fit me in, yet I never got back in contact. I rang Graham Taylor to enquire about any available young talent in England, despite the fact that Graham was now out of the game.

To all intents and purposes, I was making it up as I went along. The club were fantastic. They had a bright, young player-manager in Alan Reynolds, who encouraged me to chat one-to-one with his players in the dressing room. They had a chairman, Ger O'Brien, who couldn't have been more supportive.

And yet it ended as it was always fated to. In failure. I went missing, eventually being tracked down at a wedding in Roscommon (don't ask). Waterford immediately booked me into the Edmundsbury Clinic in Lucan on the outskirts of Dublin and the story never leaked to the press, miraculously. After four weeks there, I signed myself out and continued drinking.

Waterford picked up the bill. They never saw me again.

Looking back, it was just too much too soon. I wasn't ready for a job so big or so public. When I'd turn up at Waterford's games, the crowd invariably responded with the 'Ooh Aah' chant. And I'd feel guilty about that. It almost ceased to be about the team. I was the celebrity. The star. A parallel story.

Don't get me wrong. I still have great spells in my life. Spells when I can go for months without a drink, when I can feel healthy and even athletic again. When I feel good about myself. Shortly after that time in the Edmundsbury, I went seven months on the dry. It felt glorious. I was living in an apartment in Dun Laoghaire, secure again near my roots you could say. There was a gym in the basement. Vanity brought me there on an almost daily basis. I looked well and felt well. There were no rain clouds.

Then I bought this beautiful house in Wexford, deciding that the privacy of a rural life was for me. And it was as if the deed triggered an old impulse to panic. I ended up in St Patrick's Hospital.

I hate that side of Paul McGrath. I hate this thing of being frightened of living and frightened of dying. Of existing on a constant edge. While in St Pat's, I pleaded with a doctor to give me something, anything that might make me feel more comfortable in public. 'Just give me a tablet,' I pleaded. 'I don't ever want to drink again.' I was agitated, shouting at him.

And he looked at me with the weary resignation of a man who'd had this conversation ten thousand times before. 'Paul,' he sighed, 'if we give you tablets, you'll abuse them.' He was right, of course. I would have. I do.

When I look at myself in the mirror, I sometimes see a desperately old man. And I think, 'My God, I've beaten this body to a pulp. How much more can it possibly take?' By rights, maybe, I shouldn't even be alive today. Juanita, a truly special friend, is the main reason I still am. She's the order, discipline and sanity in my world. The reason I still function. For much of the last four years, she's been the one trying hardest to build an honest, clean future for Paul McGrath.

We met, by chance, about eight years ago. I was in Dublin, on my way to the Camden Street offices of the humanitarian agency, CONCERN, for a press conference. Unable to find a parking space, I swung down into an underground car-park at the top of Harcourt Street. And there she was. Leaning against a car, smoking a cigarette. This vision of serenity.

I explained my predicament and Juanita took pity, telling me that I could park there until 6pm. I made sure to be back by 5.50pm, popping into her office to express my gratitude. I was immediately struck by her self-possession. Her sense of calm.

A friendship grew, but it was only when I came back to live in Ireland as an ex-footballer of 'no fixed abode' that she took a pivotal role in my existence. As luck would have it, I eventually moved into a house in Bray, about three minutes drive from Juanita's home. I stayed there for about six months, the last three of which carried more drunk than sober hours. Juanita would call every day with food, trying in vain to get me well. To all intents and purposes, she became my carer.

I can't bluff her. She has no patience for the charades of the alcoholic. If she sees me make an effort, she will fight my corner against anyone. But, if she detects a hint of fecklessness in my voice, the phone goes dead.

Juanita, essentially, keeps my world turning now. She knows how to reach beyond the superficial. Once, when I was living in beautiful woodland in Kippure, Co. Wicklow, I wasn't contactable for a few days. She drove out with Ronnie, a lifelong friend of mine, and – between them – they managed to scale a balcony to my apartment, no doubt fearful of what they'd find. As it happened, the place was empty. But the evidence of my condition was packed tight into almost every drawer in the apartment. Empty wine and spirits bottles. Dozens of them.

Juanita's response was typical. She sat down and wrote me a letter. Left it on the table for me to find. You see, she knew the horror I was now facing. The cold turkey. The strange faces staring out of concrete walls. The imaginary rats running at me. The terror and the self-disgust.

Her words weren't scolding because a scolding was the last thing that I needed. I still have that letter. It's a reminder of what her friendship brings to my life even if, mostly, her efforts get thrown back in her face.

You see, I drink. I gamble. I fall down. I drink again. It's a pitiful cycle. A lethal one. Sometimes, I go to an amusement arcade and sit for hours at the slot machines, pouring coins in as if by staying long enough something magical might occur. It never does.

I don't do this for a buzz. It's just the feeding of a compulsion. In many ways, I'm a mug gambler. I remember Tony Cascarino's exasperation with me during US '94. We'd be playing cards and Cas had all his little angles. He'd be counting cards, analysing expressions, working percentages.

Me? I'd just blunder through. I'd gamble blind. Cas would be spitting teeth. 'You can't fucking do that Paul ...' I'd do it. Sometimes

I'd even win and he'd turn apoplectic. He'd throw his cards on the table, complaining to the others that I hadn't got a clue. He was right. I hadn't.

Cas is a professional gambler today. I'm still chancing my arm.

That's what I need to change. I need to start earning again. I need to support my children. I need to stop panicking over simple things. Sometimes I wonder where my lack of self-confidence comes from. It's like a fear of fear itself. Just standing in a queue at a supermarket checkout brings me out in a cold sweat.

I reckon it's connected to my childhood, but I wouldn't blame anyone who reads that line and thinks, 'Get over it for God's sake, get on with your life.'

Trouble is, how do you reinvent your personality? How do you stop drifting back to your past when it holds so many mysteries? I mean I'm about to turn forty-seven and only now, only through this book, have I started asking questions about who I actually am and where I came from.

Looking for those answers hasn't upset me. The truth is I genuinely couldn't give two hoots about the identity of my father. He means nothing to me. But it upsets other people. And that's why, up to now, I haven't gone there. Why maybe I won't again.

I know I was a pretty decent footballer. I know that, despite my worst excesses, I can still be a pretty decent father. I just need to stop running. You know I live in a beautiful place now. I wake every morning to country sounds. I have neighbours who are fiercely protective, even though most of them hardly know me.

The first time Fr Aidan, my oldest friend from my days working in security, came to visit, he called into the local shop looking for directions. The owners, Mike and Alice, were slow to volunteer information. My house is just 300 yards from their place, but they had established what Aidan's business was before giving him a pointer.

I'm blessed in that way. Blessed by having good people in my life. Of course, sometimes, I can't see it. Sometimes, I find myself awash with self-pity. I side-step an AA meeting on the basis that I may be an alcoholic but, in Ireland at least, the one thing I can never be is anonymous. Some places are more comfortable than others. Some groups.

It's a get-out clause of a kind. My name is Paul, but I can't come to your meeting because people are staring. Not my fault, you see. And, so, the spiral begins again.

I've had a bad year in that respect. Too many 'slips', too few meetings. Yet, for all the lost days and broken promises, my life is incredibly rich too. I have three children I genuinely adore and three others that I pray – in time – will know me as a decent human. I have a mother I love, I have some extraordinary friends. Maybe I need to remind myself of that more often. To remember to count my blessings. To get up in the morning and think about what it is I can do as distinct from what it is I can't.

The past is unchangeable. It's time to stop looking behind.

Paul McGrath, 10 August, 2006

Tributes

LAST WORD

Sir Alex Ferguson 'It was incredible that he could play to the level he played at, given what was going on in his life. He had an athleticism that was musical, if you know what I mean. There was a rhythm about Paul running, this change of pace he had. You'd see him do it and be thinking "Jeeez, can he run . . ."

'I can understand why he's still so popular. It's the George Best thing again. People like flawed geniuses, because they see something of themselves. I personally believe that most people who go to a football game are inclined to say, "I could have been a great player . . ." I used to say that to my players. I'd say, "Don't ever be sitting in a pub ten years from now saying you could have been a great player . . ."

'Because the world is full of those people. And that's why players like George Best and Paul McGrath are always sort of revered in a way. Because they're *them*. They're ordinary people who did become great. They're reflecting the lives that ordinary people lead.

'Roy Keane is similar. The lad in the street sees the problems and relates to them. He says, "I could have been a Roy Keane," or, "I could have been a Paul McGrath." That's the reason. And, of course, you're talking about tremendously gifted players.'

Jack Charlton: 'He's one of the best players I ever had under me. Whatever clubs I managed, if I could have had Paul, I'd have had him. Even though he did have the problems. I would have probably had to look after him there as well, but I would willingly have done that. I think most managers who have had him would say that.'

Jim Walker: 'It's amazing how, for ninety minutes, he was – despite all his problems – the bravest footballer. But for the rest of the week, for the other 166½ hours, he could be a child really.'

'Just one funny story. It's his testimonial dinner and I'm sat at the main table with my wife, Susan. Paul is about four seats down and directly opposite him is Bertie Ahern. There are two body-guards at the table. Susan makes some observation about the body-guards and this chap says, "They're just here to make sure that things don't get out of hand . . ."

'And we're thinking "Fair enough, he is the Prime Minister, isn't he." Next thing, Bertie Ahern gets up to go to the toilet. The two bodyguards stay where they are. I look at Susan. She looks at me.

'So we say to this fella, "Why aren't they going with Bertie?" And he says, "No, no, the bodyguards are for Paul. Just so he can have his meal in peace without people pestering him . . ." And I just thought "Not bad, when you're bigger at home than your own Prime Minister . . ."'

Norman Whiteside 'Nobody could try to annoy Paul before a game. He'd just sit down. He knew what he had to do. I was the same. We'd just be focused. We weren't into talking about what we were going to do, tactics or anything like that. Big Paul would just put his kit on and sit there. Other people were all wound up, walking around, bouncing into lads, kicking doors. But Paul couldn't be bothered with any of that.'

Ron Atkinson: 'Paul was different. Shy, basically. I've always said that you could tell him he was playing against Signori, Maradona, Ian Rush, any of them. It's not a problem. Shearer? "Ah, grand boss ..."

'But I remember we asked him to go to a junior school once, just to present these medals, because he was a god at Villa then. Everyone wanted him. Everyone loved him. We're telling him, "All you've got to do is say 'Well done' and shake their hands." But he was adamant. "Can't do it boss." And he couldn't. He reckoned he'd panic. So he never went to the school.'

Victor Boyhan: 'He was a genius with a football. Everyone could see that. But it wouldn't be true or fair to say that the orphanage nurtured it. It's not as simple as the little black boy, hungry, came in, got clothes, got boots, got a ball and they pushed him up. It all came from himself. It was an obsession that took over him. He allowed it to. He wanted it. The relationship between a ball and a boy and how everything just rotated around it.

'I mean, he wasn't the easiest to like. I'm not going to paint him into something that he wasn't. He didn't like not getting his own way. But his needs were few. Food, money, football. So you very much knew where you stood with him.

'If he was a little black boy, brought up working class with two parents, he'd be a remarkable story. But the fact is that he was always disadvantaged, all these odds were against him – colour, racism, the narrow minds of sixties' Ireland. And he was very insecure. He had no particular academic qualification, but he did have one thing. It may sound a little strange to say that a child set out to be great, but I actually think that Paul McGrath did. He was just so single-minded. He drove his own destiny. Nothing, but nothing, was going to stop him.'

Graham Taylor: 'If you ranted at Paul, he didn't listen. So we didn't ever go over the top with him at team meetings. The only thing I could really remember saying is, "He plays there, Paul you look after him . . ." And I'd move on. You might go to other players and be saying, "You gotta get tight, you gotta push him this way, etc, etc." But all you ever said to Paul was, "Just look after him." That was enough.

'But I was always concerned that Paul would end up in the gutter. That was always my worry for him. So every time he's on the end of a phone line and speaking well, it's a relief. Because you hear now and again that things aren't so good. And you think about the gutter. But there's no way you can stop anybody drinking unless you're with them twenty-four hours a day, literally holding them down.

'He's got to be in the top three buys of my management career. He's got to be up there with John Barnes and Dwight Yorke. I mean I got Barnes for a set of shirts. Think I paid £10,000 for Yorke and sold him for £12.6 million. I'd put Paul right up there with them.'

Kevin Moran: 'Nine times out of ten, Paul would have the meal in the room. Why? I had no idea. Even if it was an evening meal, he'd try to have it on room service. As much as I roomed with Paul, there wasn't huge interaction in terms of finding out about his life. He was never one, I think, for looking at property or that type of thing. Never one for looking at the future.

'I would never try to talk him into coming down for meals. I'd just leave him. Like I say, you only realised the problems much later on. If you knew then what you know now, you might have changed so much. You'd have been more proactive. But at the time you don't see it. You really don't see it at all.

'It's unbelievable that, for a guy United basically told "Take the money and leave" he then went and was Villa's Player of the Year four seasons running. That's incredible. Bear in mind, he would have been up against someone like David Platt, who was England's captain at the time. Paul was still head and shoulders their best player. How awesome is that? It shows the extent of what this guy could do.'

Frank Stapleton: 'People tolerated what Paul did only because they were getting something out of him. A lot of them turned a blind eye to it, which in many ways was the wrong thing to do. Maybe the problem was that he was too good a player. He probably was.

'But Fergie didn't let him get away with it. I'm sure Paul looks back now and thinks "Fergie was right . . ." You can be a little bit bitter at the time, but you overcome that. Initially, you get angry. It's like the break-up of a marriage. Anger is natural. Then it clears and you start to see things in a different context.

'I suppose what Paul needed was twenty-four-hour guidance. But even that, after a while, is going to stop working. Because you feel like you're in prison. And that's probably no way to lead your life either.'

Claire: 'I've never seen him as a monster. Obviously there have been times when we've been really angry with him as a family. We've had words and told him to butt out until he's well again. But throughout it all, we've always been able to remain friends. If I needed Paul, I know he would help me. I know he's done some stupid things in his life, but it's always been under the influence of drink. He's never done it spitefully.

'But sometimes I think he's not happy. He's not happy at all. If he was handed a million tomorrow, he'd blow it. It wouldn't matter to him. I think he's done himself a lot of damage. When he's sober, he's quite void of emotion. But he's also got this knack of making everyone feel special and welcome. I think that's why people like him so much.'

'Sid' Cowans: 'He's the best defender I've ever played with. Without doubt. Absolutely world class. I mean he was probably only playing at seventy-five to eighty per cent of his ability. So taking that into consideration, he was absolutely awesome. Paul seemed to know where a ball was going before it was even kicked. It's just a gift that you're born with. And that's what he was. A natural-born footballer.

'And can I just say one other thing. He was an absolute gentleman with it. I mean we can all be idiots when we're pissed. But Paul was just a lovely, lovely person as well.'

Charlie Walker: 'I found him such a lovely lad and it saddens me that he got relatively little out of the game. When I see all the Beckhams of this world with their millions, these fellas on £100,000 a week, it just doesn't seem right.'

Gramps: 'I've never lectured Paul and I never will. I'd never say, "You fucking eejit, what do you think you're doing?" I might be tempted to, but I wouldn't. Maybe it's because so many other people are doing it. If he wants a lecture, he can go to anyone. I just want him to be able to think that he can ring me. I mean, if I thought falling out with Paul would sort him out, I'd fall out with him tomorrow. But I know it wouldn't.'

Mick McCarthy: 'I don't think anyone else could have played the role he played for Ireland with the same style and grace. But Paul never said a dickie on the field. He just did his job. And he was magnificent. I mean he got picked in the best eleven of the 1990 World Cup despite effectively being a centre-back asked to play midfield. That told you how good a player he was.'

Mick Byrne: 'Paul has great love. He has tremendous love when he is OK. But it was a constant game of cat and mouse with him. It often struck me that people watching Paul on match day would just see this fantastic player. And you're thinking "Bloody hell, how does he do it?" I think that's one of the great mysteries to everyone. Sometimes, I'd be watching *Match of the Day* and I'd know by looking at Paul exactly how he was.

'To this day, I know how he is when I see him on the telly, because Paul changes physically when he gets the few into him. His expression changes. There was never a confrontation between us. It's Paul's nature to be mannerly. You could have a thousand kids at training and he'd sign autographs for them all. He'd never do what some of the others did, sign four or five and just blow off.

'But we were a family. Everyone looked after everyone. I mean, when we met up, it was like brothers. Everyone had their problems, but Paul was the one that you had to be protective of. From himself more than anyone else.'

Christopher: 'I know he feels guilty about us. He thinks that he's put us through Hell and back. But we're fine. We deal with it in our own sort of way. He's got the love from all of us. He knows that. We just want him to have a happy life, to be obviously teetotal. Above anything, to be well. Because when he's well, we're all well.'

Mitchell: 'We just hope that he keeps being Dad, because we wouldn't change him for anyone. I've always been dead proud of him. I mean, he's never left us wanting for anything.'

Jordan: 'He shouldn't carry any guilt over what we've been through. Because we don't carry any burdens. He's a good dad. It's still a really, really proud feeling just to be walking down the street with him.'

PAUL McGRATH'S REPUBLIC OF IRELAND RECORD

Cap	Date	Opposition	Venue	Comp.	Result (Irish score first)
1	05-02-85	Italy	Dublin	Fr.	1-2
2	27-02-85	Israel	Tel Aviv	Fr.	0-0
3	26-03-85	England	Wembley	Fr.	1-2
4	01-05-85	Norway	Dublin	Fr.	0-0
5	02-06-85	Switzerland	Dublin	W. Cup	3-0
6	11-09-85	Switzerland	Bern	W. Cup	0-0
7	13-11-85	Denmark	Dublin	W. Cup	1-4
8	26-03-86	Wales	Dublin	Fr.	0-1
9	25-05-86	Iceland	Reykjavik	Tour.	2-1 G1
10	27-05-86	Czechoslovakia	Reykjavik	Tour.	1-0
11	10-09-86	Belgium	Brussels	Euro.	2-2
12	15-10-86	Scotland	Dublin	Euro.	0-0
13	12-11-86	Poland	Warsaw	Fr.	0-1
14	18-02-87	Scotland	Hampden	Euro.	2-0
15	01-04-87	Bulgaria	Sofia	Euro.	1-2

16	29-04-87	Belgium	Dublin	Euro.	0-0
17	23-05-87	Brazil	Dublin	Fr.	1-0
18	28-05-87	Luxembourg	Luxembourg	Euro.	2-0
19	09-09-87	Luxembourg	Dublin	Euro.	2-1 G1
20	14-10-87	Bulgaria	Dublin	Euro.	2-0 G1
21	27-04-88	Yugoslavia	Dublin	Fr.	2-0
22	22-05-88	Poland	Dublin	Fr.	3-1
23	01-06-88	Norway	Oslo	Fr	0-0
24	12-06-88	England	Stuttgart	Euro.	1-0
25	18-06-88	Holland	Gelsenkirchen	Euro.	0-1
26	14-09-88	N. Ireland	Belfast	W. Cup	0-0
27	07-02-89	France	Dublin	Fr.	0-0
28	08-03-89	Hungary	Budapest	W. Cup	0-0
29	26-04-89	Spain	Dublin	W. Cup	1-0
30	28-05-89	Malta	Dublin	W. Cup	2-0
31	04-06-89	Hungary	Dublin	W. Cup	2-0 G1
32	06-09-89	W. Germany	Dublin	Fr.	1-1
33	15-11-89	Malta	Valletta	W. Cup	2-0
34	25-04-90	USSR	Dublin	Fr.	1-0
35	16-05-90	Finland	Dublin	Fr.	1-1
36	27-05-90	Turkey	Izmir	Fr.	0-0
37	11-06-90	England	Cagliari	W. Cup	1-1
38	17-06-90	Egypt	Palermo	W. Cup	0-0
39	21-06-90	Holland	Palermo	W. Cup	1-1
40	25-06-90	Romania	Genoa	W. Cup	0-0
41	30-06-90	Italy	Rome	W. Cup	0-1
42	14-11-90	England	Dublin	Euro.	1-1
43	06-02-91	Wales	Wrexham	Fr.	3-0
44	27-03-91	England	Wembley	Euro.	1-1
45	01-05-91	Poland	Dublin	Euro.	0-0
46	22-05-91	Chile	Dublin	Fr.	1-1
47	01-06-91	USA	Foxboro	Tour.	1-1
48	16-10-91	Poland	Poznan	Euro.	3-3 G1

49	13-11-91	Turkey	Istanbul	Euro.	3-1
50	25-03-92	Switzerland	Dublin	Fr.	2-1 Capt.
51	29-04-92	USA	Dublin	Fr.	4-1 Capt.
52	26-05-92	Albania	Dublin	W. Cup	2-0 Capt. G1
53	30-05-92	USA	Washington	Tour.	1-3 Capt.
54	04-06-92	Italy	Foxboro	Tour.	0-2
55	07-06-92	Portugal	Foxboro	Tour.	2-0
56	09-09-92	Latvia	Dublin	W. Cup	4-0
57	18-11-92	Spain	Seville	W. Cup	0-0
58	31-03-93	N. Ireland	Dublin	W. Cup	3-0
59	28-04-93	Denmark	Dublin	W. Cup	1-1
60	09-06-93	Latvia	Riga	W. Cup	2-0 G1
61	16-06-93	Lithuania	Vilnius	W. Cup	1-0
62	13-10-93	Spain	Dublin	W. Cup	1-3
63	17-11-93	N. Ireland	Belfast	W. Cup	1-1
64	29-05-94	Germany	Hannover	Fr	2-0
65	05-06-94	Czech Rep	Dublin	Fr	1-3
66	18-06-94	Italy	New Jersey	W. Cup	1-0
67	24-06-94	Mexico	Orlando	W. Cup	1-2
68	28-06-94	Norway	New Jersey	W. Cup	0-0
69	04-07-94	Holland	Orlando	W. Cup	0-2
70	07-09-94	Latvia	Riga	Euro.	3-0
71	16-11-94	N. Ireland	Belfast	Euro.	4-0
72	15-02-95	England	Dublin	Fr.	1-0★
73	29-03-95	N. Ireland	Dublin	Euro.	1-1
74	26-04-95	Portugal	Dublin	Euro.	1-0
75	03-06-95	Liechtenstein	Eschen	Euro	0-0
76	11-06-95	Austria	Dublin	Euro.	1-2
77	06-09-95	Austria	Vienna	Euro.	1-3 G1
78	11-10-95	Latvia	Dublin	Euro.	2-1
79	15-11-95	Portugal	Lisbon	Euro.	0-3
80	13-12-95	Holland	Anfield	Euro.	0-2

81	27-03-96	Russia	Dublin	Fr.	0-2
82	24-04-96	Czech Rep.	Prague	Fr.	0-2
83	11-02-97	Wales	Cardiff	Fr.	0-0

★ Match abandoned, caps awarded

Key
Fr. = Friendly
W. Cup = World Cup
Euro. = European Championship
Tour. = Tournament

Caps
1-31 with Manchester United
32-82 with Aston Villa
83 with Derby County

International Managers
Caps
1-7 under Eoin Hand
8-80 under Jack Charlton
81-83 under Mick McCarthy

(Compiled by Sean Creedon)